Outdoor Life®
DEER HUNTER'S YEARBOOK

Outdoor Life Books, New York

Stackpole Books, Harrisburg, Pennsylvania

Cover photo: Leonard Lee Rue III

Copyright © 1987 by Grolier Book Clubs Inc.

Published by
Outdoor Life Books
Grolier Book Clubs Inc.
380 Madison Avenue
New York, NY 10017

Distributed to the trade by
Stackpole Books
Cameron and Kelker Streets
P.O. Box 1831
Harrisburg, PA 17105

Book design: Jeff Fitschen

ISSN 0734-2918
ISBN 1-55654-016-7

Manufactured in the United States of America

Contents

Preface

I shot my first deer with a 12-gauge break-action shotgun loaded with a "punkin" ball—a spherical projectile with the ballistic form of Oliver Hardy and the velocity of a garden slug. Nevertheless, the forkhorn went down at the generous range, I thought, of 35 yards. I accomplished this teen-age feat while sitting in the corner of a fencerow and waiting for a buck, preferably a tender young one, to come down a well-worn game trail to the apple orchard on the Dutchess County, New York, farm where I worked. I had seen them do precisely that many times.

Later on as I began to hunt in other places, I was astonished to find that deer hunting was considered a difficult sport, and I soon found out why. Deer were often scarce, and because hunting pressure was stiff they behaved like Einsteins compared to the carefree, almost suicidal deer of the New York apple orchards. I soon graduated to a sophisticated bolt-action rifle with an excellent scope, and I began to learn about hunting educated deer.

When I joined the staff of *Outdoor Life* magazine as a very junior editor in 1964, I was surprised to find that deer hunting had become a big-time sport. In fact, deer hunters in some areas were attaining new degrees of sophistication and were actually climbing trees at carefully selected locations where deer commonly came by within easy range. The hunters had been educated largely by magazine articles that told them whitetails seldom look up.

Using tree stands has now become an applied science, and hunters employ many other techniques undreamed-of in the middle 1960s. For instance, few hunters even knew what a deer scrape was in those days; now hunters avidly scout for active scrapes so that they can locate a tree stand within easy range. Using any kind of scent was also almost unknown, though some hunters did try to neutralize their own accumulated odors by washing their hunting clothes at least once just before the opener. Now, literally hundreds of masking scents and buck-lure scents are on the market.

This Edition of the *Outdoor Life Deer Hunter's Yearbook* contains 36 chapters—two of them acknowledged *Outdoor Life* hunting classics. For instance,

there is "The Mule Deer" by the late Jack O'Connor—surely the best-known American writer on hunting and firearms.

Two original chapters, published here for the first time and commissioned for this year's new Hunting Gear section, include: "How To Choose a Tree Stand" by Richard C. McGee; and "Choosing a Hunting Boot" by Kathy Etling. Two book excerpts are also included, as is an article reprinted from *Deer & Deer Hunting* magazine. The contents stack up as a varied collection for deer hunters, though most of the material is, as always, from *Outdoor Life*.

You'll find a good cross-section of deer hunting and closely related subjects such as suitable firearms, not only in the mid-1980s but in some of their older, more-traditional forms. In the classic 1960s story "The Buck At The Secret Crossing," Archibald Rutledge—then Poet Laureate of South Carolina—describes hunting whitetail deer with hounds. Today the method is gradually being done away with, even in the South.

At the opposite end of the spectrum are stories that represent the first appearance of entirely new or newly rediscovered methods. For example, in "A Scent for Mule Deer," Clyde Cowan describes how he uses scent glands from a buck's legs to mask his human scent and lure bucks to him. Scents are often used to hunt whitetails, but Cowan is discussing mule deer and he uses *male* glands!

The fascinating thing about Cowan's experience is that he didn't discover the technique in a dusty library. In a comparatively wild part of Canada, he learned about it from a living Indian hunter. That experience has become rare.

You'll also encounter a zany piece of humor by Patrick McManus, as well as several hunting narratives included simply because they are enjoyable, exciting reading (even though you can learn quite a bit by reading them). We hope the *Outdoor Life Deer Hunter's Yearbook* provides you with a lot of useful information and just as much genuine reading pleasure.

George H. Haas
Senior Editor
Outdoor Life Magazine

Hunting The "Least" Factor

By Tim Jones

Whether you're hunting in snowy New England or the arid Western plains, there is a "least" factor that can help you fill your deer tag this season.

All consistently successful deer hunters have a bit of the detective in their nature. Bring your sleuthing faculties to the forefront for a few minutes and play a little detective game with me. I'm going to tell you five stories of successful deer hunts. See if you can deduce what these hunts had in common besides a happy ending. Warning: I'll throw in some extra details to confuse things.

First is a hunt in big-woods country. It could be in the Pacific northwest, Minnesota's arrowhead, Michigan's Upper Peninsula, northern Wisconsin, north-central Pennsylvania, the Adirondacks of New York, or northern New England, but it isn't. In this case, it's the mountain country where Georgia, North Carolina, and Tennessee come together. Our hunter is wearing a backpack, and he carries a lightweight, flat-shooting, scoped rifle. He follows a gated logging road many miles into the back country, where he'll camp out. Every mile or so, like pearls on a string, there's a 10- to 50-acre clearcut, one to five years old and growing up to briers and brush. Between the clearcuts are wide bands of maturing hardwoods that are relatively open except for occasional thick patches of rhododendrons.

Our hunter walks briskly through the woods. He is alert, but not particularly cautious—like a hiker out for a Sunday stroll. When he sees the glint of sunlight in a clearcut ahead, he stops, hides his pack beside the trail, and creeps forward with extreme caution. Staying within the timber, he eases to the highest point he can find on the edge of the clearcut and crawls out into the open, keeping his profile low. He sits, pulls out a good pair of binoculars,

and slowly and methodically glasses the clearcut, looking carefully at each branch and every patch of shadow. In the fourth clearcut, fives miles from the nearest road, one branch, about midway across the opening, shines a little whiter than most. The hunter studies it. It moves. Magically, the profile of a buck takes shape. All the hunter can see is the bedded buck's head and 3 or 4 inches of his neck. At 125 yards, with an accurate rifle and a solid rest, that's good enough.

Next, we're in snows of northern Maine. The deer are feeding in clearcuts at night. They move deep into the featureless timber by day to bed. Our hunter picks up a big, lone track—probably a buck—on the edge of a clearcut at first light. This hunter, like most of us, is a little clumsy in the woods. There's little chance that he can track the buck and kill it in its bed. But he follows the track

Photo by Tim Christie

anyway, moving quickly where the deer has taken a straight, fast line. When the tracks begin to drift and wander, indicating the deer was looking for a bed, the hunter moves 50 yards downwind and slows to the pace of a frozen snail, stopping often to scan the timber with his binoculars. One hour and 100 yards later, he sees what he's looking for—a fallen cedar with some greenery still clinging to it. The partially denuded tree looks like an ear of corn after a raccoon has been feeding on it. The snow around the down tree is pocked by deer tracks. The hunter pulls a heavy wool coat and an insulated pad from his daypack and makes himself comfortable where he has a good view of the fallen cedar. About 11 A.M., just when our hunter is becoming cold and tired of sitting, a gray shape materializes on the far side of the cedar. The shape sports antlers.

It's bow season in farm country, and there are lots of deer. You see them in the fields every evening. They are gorging themselves on alfalfa and clover. But there are plenty of woods here, too, and the deer have steadfastly refused to follow any set pattern in their movements or where they bed. Our hunter has been on stand morning and evening for a week now, but he walks and looks during the middle of the day. Last night brought the first hard freeze of the season. Everything was white and crisp with frost in the morning. Back in the woods, in a little clearing, stands one lone apple tree that is still bearing tiny apples, many of which now lie on the ground slowly turning brown in the warm afternoon sun. Our hunter is in a tree stand 20 yards from the apple tree. The woods are dry, and the hunter is gladdened by the soft crunch of leaves as the deer approach.

Even in the southern Piedmont, it isn't supposed to be this hot in December. The other guys in the club are going to nap in camp after lunch before heading back to their stands in the late afternoon.

Our hunter stows his rifle in his truck and pulls out a 12-gauge pump gun with a short barrel. He stuffs it full of buckshot loads. Clad in soft clothes and wearing tennis shoes, he heads away from all the stands in the hardwoods and the edges of the crop fields, and makes a beeline for a deeply eroded gully that leads down into the river swamp at the edge of the lease. Easing into the gully, he takes a step, looks, then takes another. He is on his knees much of the time to peer under branches and blow-downs for shapes in every shadow. The breeze rising from the swamp is cool, moist, and fragrant—in sharp contrast to the heat in the dry uplands. The hunter's every sense is extended to its maximum, yet he's surprised when a white flag and antlers erupt from a tangle of branches almost at his feet. With a quail-hunter's reflexes, he snaps the shotgun to his shoulder and then swings ahead of his target.

Opening Day—capital O, capital D. It seems like everyone in the world has a rifle in his hands and has headed for this public land. The vehicles parked on the back roads make things look like downtown at rush hour. An aerial view would show a green arrowhead of thick pines thrusting up into the heart of the hardwood hillside. The point of the arrowhead rests on a low saddle in a long ridge. The wide back of the arrowhead is a big swamp that is thick, wet, and almost impenetrable. Our hunter is thinking about that swamp, specifically about an island right in the middle of it. If things don't go right today, he'll don hipboots and quietly take a stand on that island long before first light tomorrow. But this morning, he's at the point of the arrowhead, waiting. At the bottom of the ridge, on the side away from the swamp, is a road. And from that road is marching an army of hunters that is pushing deer like a wave before it. Several deer decide that things might just be safer on the far end of their home range—back in the swamp. To get there, they follow the natural route up to the saddle in the ridge, where the point of softwoods offers hope of concealment all the way to the swamp. One buck never makes it.

Five hunts, all with one thing in common besides success. Do you know what it is? In each case, the hunter virtually ignored a lot of territory that might or might not hold deer, and concentrated entirely on the place or places most likely to produce deer. How did he find those places? First, he did his detective work and gathered all the information he could on terrain, weather, deer movements, food sources, bedding sites, and escape routes. There's no shortcut in scouting. Then, he put together all the information and determined what I call the "least factor."

Simply stated, the "least factor" is whatever the deer want that's in shortest supply. Chances are, if you've scored regularly on deer, you have used the least factor to your advantage.

Sometimes, the least factor is a preferred food. In dry country, it can be a water source. Often, the least factor is shelter from bad weather, heat, or hunting pressure. Sometimes, it's the opposite sex, which is the whole basis of scrape hunting.

For the hunter in our first detective story, the least factor was the food and secure bedding cover of the clearcuts. In the snows of Maine, it was the fallen cedar tree, which deer visited for midday snacks in cold weather, even though they did most of their feeding in clearcuts at night. In the farm-country hunt, it was a change in diet. Deer that have been feeding exclusively on field crops seem to consider frozen apples a special treat. Our Piedmont hunter knew that deer wearing their winter coats take special pains to avoid sun and heat, so he prowled the cool gully and swampland on his lease. Finally, when the woods are full of opening-day hunters in a state like Michigan, Pennsylvania, New York, or Vermont, prime escape routes to thick security cover become the least factor for many deer. It really doesn't matter if it's food, shelter, water, or something else. Whatever the deer want that's in shortest supply, that's your least factor. That's what makes the deer vulnerable.

It's important to remember that the least factor often changes from day to day, sometimes from hour to hour. A change in the weather often brings a change in the least factor. Whatever the deer want *right now* is what will help the hunter most. The smart hunter takes advantage of the deer's immediate needs by considering the options, determining the least factor, and, if possible, getting there before the deer, and letting them come to him.

Unfortunately, there's no shortcut that I know of for finding the least factor in any patch of deer woods on any given day. Intelligent scouting backed up by knowledge of deer habits in the area you hunt is the only sure way to pinpoint the least factor.

The more specific the least factor is, the better it works to the hunter's advantage; but it may be harder to find. Knowing about the single patch of evergreens where deer regularly seek shelter from rain, snow, or wind, or remembering a lonely apple tree that deer regularly visit after the first frost, or finding a perennial spring seep in arid country requires either good luck so that you stumble on it or an intimate knowledge of a small area.

Even hunters who are new to a territory can use the least factor to good advantage. By eliminating large chunks of marginal territory, the hunter can concentrate on the most-productive areas and tilt the odds in favor of success. Topographical maps can sometimes help you find swamps, ridge saddles, or other terrain features. In the case of our mountain hunter, an hour chatting with the local game warden clued him in to the local whitetails' preference for clearcuts as feeding and bedding sites, and this sent him toward the backwoods road with clearcuts strung along it. While the clearcuts encompassed fairly large chunks of territory, they were still small enough to be huntable. And, while the hunter was moving from clearcut to clearcut, he was noting and mentally filing the deer sign he saw to determine patterns of usage that might show deer preferred clearcuts of a specific size or age. Then, he could narrow his hunting territory even more, upping his odds for success. Determining the least factor requires constant attention to detail.

Timing, too, is all-important in locating and capitalizing on the least factor. Escape cover that's so critical on opening day, for example, may not mean so much to deer when a long season is fizzling to its close. A hunter who finds a much-used escape route on a weekday might not be able to capitalize on that knowledge until the weekend influx of hunters forces the deer to seek escape cover above all else. Only when hunting pressure is high does an escape route become the least factor.

Weather can change the least factor to a hunter's advantage as well. The Piedmont deer hunter was taking advantage of unusually hot weather when he deliberately abandoned his regular stand and headed for the cooler shadows of a gully and a swamp. He identified the least factor, and used it. The subsistence and market hunters of the last century often used weather as the least factor with devastating effectiveness. When snow concentrated deer or moose in a winter yard (good winter cover being a prime least factor), the hunters went there. As a result, they virtually exterminated moose and deer over much of the animals' northern range. Today's sport hunter in the North Country can often mimic that success by hunting yarding areas late in the season after a heavy snow. And with today's strict limits, there's no chance of decimating the herd.

There are other times when weather can create a least factor that hunters can utilize. Not far from my home in New England, there's a one-acre patch of incredibly thick hemlocks and pines located on an otherwise open hardwood hillside. You could hunt on that hillside for days at a time and not find sign of a deer. But wait for a day made miserable by a hard rain or high wind, and you can bet your life savings that there will be deer somewhere in that thicket. They rest comfortably and watch the open hardwoods for danger that they cannot hear or smell because of the rain and wind. Such tactics work very well. As many times as I've tried, I've never been able to sneak into the thicket for a shot. Someday, when the weatherman is forecasting rain for the afternoon, I'm going to head into that thicket in the morning, take a stand, and see what happens from there.

Food is something that deer need every day. As the least factor, however, food is definitely an on-again, off-again proposition. There is no harder job for a deer hunter than determining when some specific foods become the least factor. There is also no surer route to success than identifying a limited source of a food that the deer want more than anything else.

It's no secret that deer love to feed on soybeans, alfalfa, clover, corn, winter rye, apples, acorns, mushrooms, honeysuckle, and dozens of other plants, sprouts, seeds, or fruit at different times of the year. But the knowledge that deer are feeding on any of those favorites does the hunter little good if the deer are feeding only at night, or if there are hundreds, or even thousands, of acres of the preferred food available within the deers' territory.

Where I hunt most, there are different species of oaks everywhere from the lowland swamps right up to the ridgetops. When acorns of one kind or another are available, the deer rarely bother to feed on anything else. With thousands of acres of oaks available, however, acorns are rarely the least factor. The deer want the acorns all right, but they can find them anywhere.

Several seasons ago, a gypsy-moth infestation stripped almost all the oaks of their leaves by midsummer. As a result, most oaks didn't bear any acorns. The deer compensated by feeding on forbs in fields, apples in the orchards, and mushrooms and succulents along swamp edges. But because those areas are open and exposed, the deer fed only at night. They were back in the woods before dawn. Hunting was tough that year, and I spent a lot of time walking and looking for travel routes, which I thought would give me the best chance for success. In my wanderings, I found a few oak trees that still had leaves and that were dropping a few acorns. Every one of those trees had deer tracks under it. Like a fool, however, I still concentrated on apple orchards and travel routes. The least factor was right under my nose, and I didn't recognize it. My deer tags went unfilled that season.

Last year was different. The oaks had abundant leaves, and there was a huge crop of acorns. A few started dropping in late summer, but most were still on the trees well into October. The deer had spent the summer feeding in fields and on browse, and they were ready for a change. While bird hunting, I discovered a few precocious oaks that were dropping their nuts earlier than all the rest. The deer were waiting. So was I. On opening day of muzzleloader season, I had a buck down, dressed, and dragged out by 10 A.M. A few days later, acorns were on the ground everywhere, and the deer were no longer concentrated and vulnerable.

There may be times and places where there simply is no least factor to concentrate deer. In 15 years of serious deer hunting, however, I have yet to experience such a time or place—though I have sometimes failed to recognize the least factor when I saw it. Sometimes it's as specific as a single oak or an apple tree with a large crop of fruit or a damp patch of woods with lots of mushrooms. Other times, it's a thousand acres of swamp where hunters never venture. If a large area is involved, you can bet that a secondary least factor such as dry bedding spots in a swamp or browse of the proper height in a clearcut will concentrate deer even more. All you have to do is find out what it is and figure out how to capitalize on it.

The secret then is to emulate a good detective. First, you wear out shoe leather looking for evidence. Then, you sift through the evidence and consider all possible angles. Then, you base your tactics on what you know. One thing is certain: Find out what the deer want most that's in short supply, and you're going to find deer.

PART 1

THE QUARRY

Ten Steps To Trophy Deer

By Kathy Etling

When it comes to trophy deer, Jay Gates could write a book. In fact, he's determined to *rewrite* at least one book—the Boone and Crockett Club's *Records of North American Big Game.* Gates has made an impressive start with a Boone and Crockett Coues deer that scored 110⅝ points and a Columbia blacktail scoring 132⅝ points. But Gates isn't about to rest on these laurels.

Each year for the past seven years, Jay Gates has succeeded in bagging the grand slam of deer. A deer grand slam consists of one buck of each of the following species: mule deer, whitetail, Coues (desert) whitetail, and blacktail. In 1984, when Boone and Crockett split the blacktail division into two categories—Columbia and Sitka—Gates simply added the Sitka to his list.

Each year, Gates also manages to bag excellent specimens of several other major deer subspecies *in addition* to the species listed in the book. Just any head won't do. He tries for and gets the best he possibly can.

What force drives Gates, a family man and beer distributor from Kingman, Arizona, to log close to 30,000 miles each year, locating and taking trophies with such enviable consistency?

"Deer are the most fascinating of all the big-game animals I've hunted," he says. "Trophy deer present a challenge that few other animals do. And only a couple of other guys have *ever* taken a grand slam of deer in one year. I like to think that the record I'm setting will last a long time."

In addition to the Coues and the Columbia blacktail, Gates has taken several muleys scoring close to 180 points and whitetails scoring more than 150 points. Probably no other active deer hunter knows

Illustration by Larry Anderson

as much about the fine points of trophy deer hunting for every species.

To what does Gates owe his success? In a nutshell, he credits the 3 Ps—patience, persistence, and physical fitness. His entire life revolves around the fall hunting season. He lives, thinks, and dreams deer hunting. You can't be as consumed with the desire for trophy deer as Jay Gates is and not have some excellent advice for the rest of us would-be record-breakers.

Gates has deer hunting down to a science. And he calls the method he uses to take excellent heads his "Ten Steps To Trophy Deer." Here they are:

1. HUNT WHERE THE BIG BUCKS ARE

Big bucks have to be *in* an area before it qualifies as a Gates hunting possibility. So he spends hours reading hunting magazines and Boone and Crockett records to find locations where trophy deer were taken.

Gates talks to outfitters, taxidermists, and sporting-goods store owners. He haunts big-buck contests and hunting clubs. And he calls game wardens, biologists, and forest managers to get the latest deer-hunting scoop.

Unlike most hunters, after selecting an area he usually won't lay eyes on it until the first day of his hunt, when he "pre-scouts" the area.

Gates pre-scouts from roads and trails to see whether the area looks worthwhile. If the sign looks good, he'll hunt hard the next day. If not, he moves to a new area. He won't waste his time. If it means covering 5,000 acres in one day to find good sign, that's what he does.

Pre-scouting pays off in other ways, too. Once, a friend picked him up at a California airport and drove him to base camp before blacktail hunting the next day. Jay and his buddy did a little pre-scouting near camp. Sure enough, they located and killed two excellent bucks while searching for fresh sign. "And I nearly broke my neck," Jay explained. "I stalked in those darn slick cowboy boots I travel in and didn't change. But it was worth it, and by far the easiest hunt I've ever had."

2. HAVE THE RIGHT EQUIPMENT

Gates pays great attention to detail when selecting gear. High price alone doesn't mean "the best," he says. Before buying, he evaluates each piece of equipment carefully. And after the season, he decides whether or not it performed according to his expectations. If it didn't, he'll replace it.

3. KNOW YOUR RIFLE

Gates uses two custom-built guns with Remington 700 actions in .270 Winchester caliber. Each is outfitted with a Brown Precision fiberglass stock. Gates calls them his "plastic guns" and wouldn't shoot anything else. The possibility of wood stocks warping in wet weather is a prime consideration.

"When I pull the trigger on a record-class Sitka 6,000 miles from home, a 'flier' because of warpage is the last thing I want," he says.

Both guns have glass-bedded actions and free-floating 20 1/2-inch barrels. They each weigh in right at 6 1/2 pounds, including scope.

Gates has further weatherproofed his guns by outfitting them with Shilen stainless-steel barrels that are nickel-plated and then completely camouflaged. The guns are expensive but worth it, he says.

He reloads for peak performance and, when faced with a problem, consults experts. For example, his old load of 59 grains of H4831 (a very hot load) behind a 130-grain Sierra spitzer boattail bullet resulted in a 1 1/4-inch three-shot group at 100 yards. On his gunsmith's advice, he switched to 57 1/2 grains of H4831 pushing a 130-grain Sierra flat-base and loaded only new or once-fired brass. His groups improved dramatically, to one-half inch.

Gates is a fanatic about sighting-in, too. From May until August, he shoots at least 20 rounds each week. His guns shoot 1 1/2 inches high at 100 yards. This puts the load right on at 200 yards.

4. MENTAL PREPARATION

Physical preparation is easy, in Gates' opinion; mental preparation is tough—especially when faced with a grueling 120-day season.

Mental preparation is what keeps him hunting. "I tell myself that no matter how tough the hunt, or how hard the pack-in, or how miserable the weather, I'm going to stick it out and follow my hunt plan," Gates says. "And then, once I'm in whatever hellhole I've chosen, I hunt every daylight minute of every day I've allotted. Weather means nothing; sometimes, the worst weather makes for the best hunt."

5. PHYSICAL PREPARATION

The words "physical preparation" don't seem entirely accurate when you look at Gates' training regimen. Virtually all of his hunts are walk-ins—by himself. So it's up to him to pack out his bucks alone from some of the roughest country anywhere.

To get in shape, he runs 18 to 20 miles each week from January until May. During that time, he also does aerobics and lifts weights twice each week.

Then, from June until September he runs three times a week in the mountains. Each run is for at least three miles. The other four days, he totes from 40 to 90 pounds on his back through the same mountains for five miles. As September nears, the weight increases. This is in addition to weight lifting and special leg exercises. "If you're not in shape," says Gates, "by the end of a season like mine you're either dead or wish you were."

Photo by Len Rue, Jr.

Gates contends that the biggest bucks, like this whitetail, are usually loners.

6. DESIRE

"Desire is the result of mental preparation," Gates explains. "You must be dedicated to success. Desire is the hand that fans the flame. Any hunter can luck into a good buck once or maybe twice in his life. But to score consistently under the most adverse conditions takes desire."

"Desire is what kept me dogging the tracks of a record muley this year in Nevada," he notes. "I jumped the deer but decided not to shoot at a running animal in heavy brush—I let him go, deciding instead to track him. Another guy and I tracked him for ten hours until his tracks merged with those of another buck. The buck I let go was a monster— between 195 and 200 points—and would have made the book. So I kept on his trail. When the trail split, I went after the bigger tracks. That was a mistake. I had one chance for a shot through some thick cedars and took it. I saw heavy antlers and gray hair, and then I realized that I'd shot the wrong

deer. He was a cactus buck with 17 points on one side and 14 on the other—a trophy, but not when compared with the one that got away."

7. KNOWLEDGE

Each species of deer is different, according to Gates. You can't hunt them all the same way. Each must be studied to learn feeding, bedding, rutting, and living habits.

"To hunt muleys, Sitkas, and Columbia blacktails, climb high early in the morning and glass," Gates says. "Do the same thing late in the afternoon."

"Coues whitetails blend in so well that you need the sun shining on them to pick them out from the landscape. Watch southeastern slopes early and northwestern slopes late, and kick out draws during the middle of the day."

"For all of these species," Gates added, "the biggest bucks are usually loners. I'll often find them on the highest points, often in rimrock or mountain mahogany. Big bucks all seem to prefer the same kind of terrain."

"When whitetail hunting, I glass ridges and coulees to find bedding and feeding grounds or travel lanes. And I try to find a buck's *rutting area*. In the West, where I hunt, nearly every big buck usually has what I call a 'rutting area.' When pressured, either by other bucks or hunters, he'll have a secluded spot to herd receptive does, a spot far from bedding or feeding areas—sometimes five or six miles away.

"To find the rutting area, I glass river bottoms early and late to discover a buck's travel pattern. What I learn determines where I place my stand."

8. DEVELOP GLASSING AND STILLHUNTING SKILLS

Practice makes perfect. And this is where patience and persistence pay off. Stealth is not an inbred trait; it must be attained. And the knowledge of how to use wind, sun, and terrain to your advantage comes from years of practice.

"I like to hunt with the wind in my face and the sun at my back," Gates pointed out. "Deer are at a disadvantage when staring into the sun's glare. I move slowly and quietly and try to use natural cover to camouflage my movements."

Interestingly enough, Gates killed his second-best Coues buck while the wind was blowing on the back of his neck and he was stillhunting. "My scent was blowing right toward him. I jumped him *three* times before I finally killed him. You just never can tell with deer."

Likewise, the skill needed to pinpoint movement and home in on it instantaneously with binoculars isn't acquired overnight. But proficiency will eventually be rewarded.

"Binoculars and a spotting scope are two 'musthaves' that I'm never without," he emphasizes. "I always travel with a walking stick that doubles as a rest for my optics when I'm glassing. And I never skimp on the time I spend glassing. It can take anywhere from 15 minutes to 1 1/2 hours *each time I stop*, depending on the terrain."

9. JUDGMENT

Judgment is important for two reasons: First, you have to know *when* to shoot.

"What I want is a standing shot, or a shot while a deer is in its bed," Gates says. "But when stalking in the middle of the day, I may jump a deer and have to make a split-second decision—to shoot or not. Sometimes, you know the shot is bad and you don't risk it. Other times, you take the chance and it pays off. And then there are those other times you prefer to forget."

Gates' knowledge of deer also helps him decide when to shoot. He knows that he'd better shoot when a buck puts his ears back and flicks his tail. That's a sure sign that the deer will be off and running—pronto.

Judgment includes estimating distances. "Once, I located a dandy nine-point whitetail with a 22-or 23-inch spread," he explained. "I flipped down my bipod and settled it squarely so that it wouldn't wobble. Then I squeezed off a shot, aiming right behind the buck's shoulder. The buck didn't even flinch. I shot three more times. Finally, on the fourth shot the buck looked in my direction when snow flew under his belly. I reloaded and sighted over the buck's back and shot again. Down he went. When I paced it off, what I'd guessed to be a little more than 200 yards was 400 yards. No matter how often you estimate range, you can always make a mistake. Fortunately, I still got the buck."

Judgment is also important for another reason. "Once you pull that trigger, it's all over," Gates says, "and you'd better be happy with what you've decided to shoot. Determine beforehand just what kind of buck you're after and how to identify a buck of that caliber out in the wilds."

Although Gates is looking for record-book deer, he'll take what he considers a trophy regardless of book standards of excellence. A deer with a spread wider than his ears is always a good trophy, in his opinion.

Other criteria Gates uses in judging trophy-quality bucks include muleys that go 4×4 or better with deep forks and long main beams; 4×4 blacktails with heavy beams; 3×3 Coues (excluding brow tines) with long, curving main beams; and whitetails with ten long points.

Gates says that he considers any 4×4 Sitka a trophy because to date he's personally only seen one in the field.

10. INSTINCT

Gates believes that instinct is a skill like any other. It may be born in you or developed over the years. Sometimes, it may be a combination of both. "It's not luck when you take an animal in a remote aspen patch. You're not guessing when you kick out a draw and just *know* that a buck's hiding there. But it *is* a funny feeling when a big old mossyhorn makes a run for it and *you sense where he's going to jump up*. Even if you're born with déjà vu, it takes hard work and good practical experience to make it work for you."

Now, when Jay Gates looks at the Boone and Crockett records, he gets a feeling of déjà vu. He knows he's been there before. And if things work out, he'll be there again—and again and again, until he realizes his dream of having a record-book deer grand slam in all five listed species. When that happens, he'll have literally rewritten the book. And his ten steps to trophy-hunting success will be the reason why.

Diary Of A Stillhunt

By Bud Journey

Tuesday, November 19, 6:30 A.M. My radio alarm comes on. "Continued unseasonably cold temperatures with increasing snow showers throughout the week," says the cheery morning announcer. He adds his own mini-editorial: "Looks like a good week to stay in bed and listen to the radio."

I smile and roll out of bed. I couldn't be happier with the forecast. "One more day of work," I say aloud, "then the rest of the season to hunt. Seven straight days, and the weather couldn't be better!"

My wife squints at me through sleepy eyes. "Do you always have to get yourself psyched up for these hunting trips?" she asks. "You sound like Knute Rockne in the locker room before the Army-Notre Dame game."

I don't respond to her good-natured jibe. We've been through the pre-hunt atmosphere enough times to know that I don't need psyching up. Besides, I have been looking forward to this hunt with more than the usual enthusiasm. A series of unexpected obligations and unavoidable commitments have kept me out of the field for the first four weeks of the season, and I am aching to get out. Now, right on cue, cold weather arrives—just at the time when the whitetail rut is due to begin.

Much to my surprise, I survive the work day, and that night finds me trundling over mountain roads in the dark on the way to my primitive hunting cabin in northwestern Montana.

Wednesday, November 20, 7:30 A.M.

Daylight breaks as I step out of the cabin and onto the front porch. My nostrils pucker as I breathe in the crisp morning air. "Just right," I say with a grin, "about zero. The deer should be on the move."

I am anxious to get going. I will hunt a narrow strip of land that extends along both sides of a creek for about two miles north from the cabin.

If I work it right, the trip will take all day. It's a familiar route, strewn with willows, cottonwoods, firs, and other entanglements—big bucks are there, and that makes it worth the effort. The key to my success is to go slowly, stop often, and rattle antlers whenever I can see reasonably well through the thick foliage.

But first, one last bit of preparation: I smear my boots with doe-in-estrus urine scent. The stuff smells slightly worse than buzzard breath on a hot day, but it's worth it. The wind currents along the creek are unpredictable, and even if the scent doesn't attract a buck, it will help mask my own.

It is cold enough for the snow to squeak under my feet, but I know from experience that the sound doesn't carry far.

I follow an animal trail through a thicket of lodgepole pine, hurrying to an open, old-growth stand of larch just ahead. That's my first mistake of the day. I jump a whitetail in the lodgepole but it scurries off.

"Slow down!" I tell myself.

Paralleling the river, I move along game trails on the hillside, where I can see the creek bottom to my right and the mountain slope to my left. I see lots of sign: scrapes, rubs, and tracks—lots of tracks. But I'm not seeing deer. By noon, I have covered more country than I wanted to cover all day. The result: I've seen one doe and no bucks. The adrenaline of the first day has gotten the best of me. I'm moving too fast.

I sit down for lunch and improvise a plan for the afternoon, which calls for working my way uphill through an old burn. It's an area I've previously avoided because of the morass of deadfalls that litter the ground, but it's rough going and should burn up some of my excess energy.

Two hours later, I'm dragging myself over the ten-millionth (well, at least the nine-millionth) deadfall, wondering where all that excess energy went, when I spot a deer across the gully, about 80 yards away. Wiping the sweat from my brow, I check out the deer with binoculars. It's a doe—a muley doe. I'm not surprised because muleys and whitetails often share the same habitat in northwestern Montana. But I am surprised by her companion—a massive 5×5 buck with high, sweeping antlers that sustain impressive mass all the way to the tips. It takes only a glance to confirm that this big muley is pushing the record book.

Yes, I'm looking for a good whitetail this year, but I'm not elite enough to pass up a trophy muley like this. I set my Redfield Low Profile Widefield variable scope on 9× and start to squeeze off a hasty shot, but I get myself under control just in time and hold the shot. I don't want to take any chances with this beautiful buck, so I risk two steps to the nearest tree, where I lay my Winchester Model 70 .30/06 across a branch and get a dead-solid rest. I inhale, exhale, and squeeze off. The buck gives me one puzzled look before bounding off and disappearing. I follow the buck's trail for more than an hour without seeing him again. There is no sign of a hit.

I'm a disgruntled hunter on the way back to the cabin. A couple of practice shots along the way confirm that my riflescope is grossly out of adjustment. I bitterly decide to retire the .30/06 until I can get a reliable scope for it. Luckily, I have a spare rifle: a Ruger Model 77, .257 Roberts. It's a little light for elk, but ideal for deer.

Thursday, November 21, 8 A.M.

It's 8° F, I am again paralleling a hillside, but this time I'm working some winter range to the east of the cabin. The cold weather is holding, and the skiff of new snow makes hunting conditions ideal. If they're here, I should find them today.

I finally have the adrenaline under control and am able to keep my movements slow and deliberate. I follow a game trail along the contour of the hill, working my way carefully through the cover, stopping often and glassing before moving on. I rattle the whitetail antlers often from areas of concealment. I suspect, however, that it is past the best time for rattling because I'm getting no interest in areas where I've rattled successfully before.

I put the antlers in my pack and move on around the hillside. I slowly work my way through a thicket of fir and stop before moving into the semi-open ponderosa pine stand ahead. I catch a movement to my right. It's a whitetail doe, about 50 yards uphill from me. She stops and looks back, then moves on into the fir thicket ahead.

"OK, Bud," I say to myself, "this is what you've been waiting for. Don't blow it." I kneel beside a pine tree and ready my rifle. A surprisingly long time later, perhaps two minutes, a buck emerges through the lightly falling snow. He stops where the doe had stopped and sniffs the air, curling his upper lip back toward his nostrils. I slowly raise the rifle and bring the crosshairs to a stop at the white

I jump a whitetail along the trail, but it scurries off. "Slow down!" I tell myself.

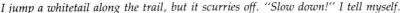

Stillhunting for trophy-size bucks requires great stealth and plenty of patience.

Photo by Bill McRae

spot on the buck's neck while I look him over. He is a perfectly symmetrical 4×4 with a spread of about 16 inches—too small to shoot, but he may still teach me something. I carefully remove the antlers from my daypack, slip behind the tree, and give my sincerest rattle. The buck whirls and disappears into the mist, convincing me that it's too late in the rut for effective rattling.

I spend the rest of the day working my way through the winter range area without seeing another deer.

Friday, November 22, 8 A.M.

It's colder this morning, −3°. There is a cutting wind. I can find no deer and very few tracks in the burn where I missed the big muley. I'm bundled up in all of my extra clothing, but my ears and nose are cold and my hands are numb. My eyeballs sting from blowing ice crystals. It's time to leave this open country behind and do what the deer do when it gets very cold: head for the protection of the old-growth timber canopy.

I move down through the south and westfacing canopies. The conditions are less severe here, but when I stop for lunch, the apple I brought along for a snack is frozen solid, and each time I want a drink I have to chip ice from the neck of the canteen with a hunting knife. I get back to the cabin after dark without seeing an animal.

Saturday, November 23, 6 A.M.

At 17° the temperature is not moderating much. I have slight frostbite on my nose and little finger. Today is another good day to hunt the winter-range canopies.

I hunt all day and see only three does—all solitary animals. There are, however, some fresh tracks. The animals are moving around some to eat, but the frenzy of the rut seems to be absent. This might be one of those times when too much of a good thing isn't so good. The cold appears to have put the rut on hold.

Sunday, November 24, 7:30 A.M.

It's −3° today, but I think I'll stick to the canopies anyway. It's a good day to hunt the area north of the cabin again.

I work my way carefully through the lodgepole

thicket this time, but I move out into the open area of the old-growth larch stand too abruptly. An outstanding whitetail buck spots me. He is already up, out of his bed and alert. He is a fully mature buck with multiple points and at least a 20-inch spread. We stare at each other as though paralyzed. I remain stoic as the breeze bounces ice crystals off my eyeballs. The buck is alert, his half-raised tail gently oscillating in the wind.

It's a game.

We both know that he is in no danger—a brushy bench lies comfortably just behind him. Nevertheless, I won't concede him safety.

"Now, be a good boy," I murmur as I slowly begin to raise my rifle. "Stand still for just five seconds." Of course, he doesn't. One bound, and the buck is gone.

I am disappointed at my costly lapse in hunting astuteness, but my spirits are buoyed by the confrontation with the big buck. I consider the meeting a privilege. However, I resolve to pay closer attention. The lack of game during this cold snap is making me careless.

I hunt carefully for the rest of the day, but I see no more game. The extreme cold is keeping the rut out of synch.

On the way back to the cabin, I note that something is missing. My nose is not stinging, and my fingers are not numb. The weather is warming up.

Monday, November 25, 7:30 A.M.

I smear my boots with estrus scent, unzip my vest halfway, and head northward from the cabin. It's 3° and it seems almost balmy this morning. I'm feeling good about the hunting prospects. I control my exuberance and go slowly. Today, I take a different route.

The cold weather of the past few days has frozen the creek solid, and the ice is thick enough for me to walk on. I can skulk along next to the bank and break up my outline with the streamside vegetation while walking in absolute silence. The conditions are perfect. Now, if it's just warm enough for the rut to resume . . .

I go only about one-half mile when I spot a small 4×4 whitetail browsing on the hillside above me. I watch him for five minutes without his knowledge, then continue upstream. I reach an area where the creek runs through an old-growth stand of larch. Visibility is very good here.

I see a spike whitetail hurrying along a scent trail, stopping occasionally to sniff the air. He is definitely in the rut. I watch him until he disappears, then continue upstream.

About one mile later, I turn east toward another south-facing larch stand. I am just topping the first rise above the riverbank when I meet a whitetail buck face-to-face. He is a symmetrical 5×5 with a 22-inch spread. He takes one quick glance at me and scampers into the streamside vegetation, taking two does with him. Another missed opportunity!

I follow the buck's tracks for a few minutes before losing them in a maze of other fresh deer and elk tracks. Sign is everywhere.

"Well, this is what you've been waiting for," I tell myself. "The deer are in the rut. Now, take advantage of it."

I quickly cut another set of nice whitetail tracks and follow them to the top of a rise, where I stop to look and listen. Then, I hear a sound that makes me freeze in my tracks. The sound doesn't come again, but once is enough. I recognize it as the sound of an elk's stomach rumbling. I remain immobile and intently peer through the foliage just ahead. A nervous elk calf moves into view and stops only 30 feet away. The calf senses my presence but is unable to locate me. I search through the trees for another elk and spot a larger-bodied animal partially hidden by the vegetation, slightly ahead of the calf. A quick appraisal of the second animal with binoculars reveals that it is a spike. Although I was hunting deer, I'm not one to pass up an elk—even in the midst of a revived whitetail rut. One shot to the lungs with a 117-grain bullet from the .257 Roberts puts the elk down to stay.

I spend the rest of the day getting the elk ready to take out.

Tuesday, November 26

The weather remains relatively mild; I spend the whole day getting the elk out.

The deer sign is plentiful.

Wednesday, November 27, 7:30 A.M.

No doubt remains about where to hunt whitetails. I am heading north from the cabin once again. It's 6° today and I am sure that the rut is still in full swing. Hunting should be good, but regardless of what happens on this last day of the season, I can only count this hunt as a success. The three big bucks I've seen, as well as the several smaller ones, and the elk all add up to a good outing.

Moving down to the frozen stream, I comfortably settle into the same route I took on Monday. I have no trouble keeping a slow pace. I want to prolong this last day as much as I can. When I get to the old-growth larch stand, I sit on a log and glass patiently through the trees.

After about five minutes, I'm satisfied that there are no animals in the immediate vicinity, so I put away the binoculars and resume my trek northward. I take only two steps when I'm surprised by a whitetail doe running straight at me. She swerves slightly and skirts past me at about 40 yards.

Almost immediately, two nice whitetail bucks come galloping along her trail. Suddenly, the doe and the bucks stop—broadside at 40 yards. The bucks are almost equal in size, so I take the closest one. A single shot does it, and another buck falls victim to sexual fervor. He's a nice animal—not Boone and Crockett class, mind you, but he has five points on one side and six on the other with a 19-inch spread. All in all, he's a respectable and fitting capper to an overall decent hunt. 🦌

Secrets Of
The Licking Branch

By Kathy Etling

Silently, the hunter slipped through the woods, slowing his pace as he neared the scrape. When he finally saw the scrape's bare outline, he also saw something else—a buck moving onto the trampled earth. The hunter paused. He was very close, but the deer had no idea he was there. As the hunter watched, the buck pawed at the sodden ground and then reached up to nip and nuzzle the branch hanging over the scrape. Easing forward, the hunter carefully took aim.

Bob McGuire was the hunter stalking in the woods that day in 1984. And though it would have made an interesting story if he had killed a record-book buck, he wasn't even carrying his bow. It was springtime, and hunting season had been over for five months. Instead, he carried a camera. The images on that roll of film excited him more than anything he'd ever seen or done, for this was the first time he'd been able to document the phenomenon he calls "the licking branch."

Licking branches aren't new. They've undoubtedly been around as long as the whitetail deer has. But it took a non-scientist like Bob McGuire to recognize them for what they are—a year-round way for deer to communicate, and another tool for the deer hunter to use when out to tag a buck. Once McGuire did that, he set about putting that knowledge to work for him.

"I wasn't looking for anything earthshattering," he said. "It was May, and I was looking for remnant activity in old scrapes. This is a great way to keep tabs on the local bucks and pre-scout my hunting area. Instead, I wound up watching a display unlike anything I'd ever seen before.

"There before me was a buck with stub velvet antlers, standing in what appeared to be an old scrape. But he was pawing and scraping just as bucks do in the fall. While he did that, he also nuzzled and licked the branch hanging over the scrape. I automatically thought of the term 'licking branch' before I really knew what I was seeing.

"I didn't know whether I was watching latent activity from the last rut or early behavior for the next rut. I was totally confused. And, in a way, I'm still confused because I saw pawing and scraping going on in May, and I haven't seen it at a licking branch since outside of the rut."

McGuire, a 43-year-old mining and mechanical engineer, lives in Johnson City, Tennessee. He currently makes his living by writing books and producing videos on hunting. Strictly a bowhunter for the past 20 years, McGuire has taken many large whitetail bucks. He knew that what he saw meant something, at least to the deer, and he was determined to find out what.

McGuire lectures on hunting at outdoor shows and seminars all over the country. But after this fateful day in May, he did something of an about-face. He began asking his audiences the questions. And he listened and learned from their answers.

McGuire had no set or preconceived ideas about what a deer should or shouldn't do. And as he delved into other hunters' experiences, he found out that the all-season licking behavior he had observed wasn't an isolated occurrence. Many others had seen deer do the very same thing.

That started him thinking. "I'd had a lot of success during the previous three or four years with

Field edges such as this are prime places to look for licking-branch activity—and wall-hanger bucks!

my mock scrapes," he said. "And the more I thought about it, the more I realized that I was taking good bucks every year not because I was so clever with mock scrapes but because I was working with licking branches before I knew what they were. I'd thought I was starting early scraping activity by using doe-in-heat urines in likely spots when all I was really doing was monitoring normal licking branch behavior.

"I was selecting the place to make my mock scrape on the basis of live, overhanging limbs that may already have been licking branches. I, like many others, had made the connection between a scrape's appeal and the limb above it. But I'd unwittingly decided that a live limb was very important.

"Licking branches may be as valuable to the whitetail hunters of the late 1980s as scrapes were to hunters in the 1960s. They're nothing short of revolutionary, in terms of all-season whitetail behavior and ways to scout such activities all year."

Just what is a licking branch? According to McGuire, a licking branch is a gathering place for highly social deer. Contrary to past beliefs, McGuire thinks that deer aren't nearly as territorial as was once thought. The licking branch serves as a focal point for all-season chemical communication.

Everyone has heard of pheromones, those mysterious olfactory agents present in a deer's body fluids and secretions. For the theory of licking branches to be valid, however, there must be yet another source of pheromones that hasn't been suspected before—pheromones that work when the deer aren't scraping and rubbing. McGuire believes that these pheromones are present in the deer's saliva. They act as a deer's signature card to tell other deer that he visited the licking branch.

This "signature" is very important to the deer. It helps them establish and maintain status within the hierarchy. When breeding depends on it, rank becomes very important.

"There is a lot of body language at the licking branch," McGuire maintains. "The hierarchy is obvious. You can watch the dominant buck threaten a subordinate or give him a hard look, but they tolerate the lesser buck's presence as long as it's not the rut. The lesser-ranking animals respond to such threats with a submissive, swaybacked posture. But because of the whitetail's social tendency, bucks tend to hang out together during the spring and summer. Where? At the licking branch.

"Remember, the important thing about licking branches is that you can look for and find activity during hunting's off-season," McGuire continued. "Best of all, the highest concentration of activity is before scraping begins, which is something completely new.

"Now, hunters can take matters into their own hands," McGuire explained, "by careful all-season scouting for licking branch locations. Some of the really good hunters have already incorporated licking branch knowledge into their hunting techniques, much as I did, without knowing what they were doing but acting on instinct."

Alan Altizer, a neighbor and good friend of McGuire's, is a good example. Although Altizer hadn't yet heard of licking branches, he found a summertime location in 1984 where deer seemed to congregate. He saw several bucks but concentrated on one in particular whose tracks were as round and broad as a small cow's.

Although Altizer was hunting in a national forest, he managed to get away from the crowds. When he found a torn-up spot under a small, live limb, he just assumed that it was an old scrape. But now, he's not so sure.

"I got my Tennessee state record buck right near a branch that showed signs of heavy use," he said. "And when I heard Bob talking about licking branches, it all clicked. I knew that this was what I'd stumbled upon. So in 1985, I intentionally looked for any branches that showed signs of nibbling and licking with bare spots beneath that weren't necessarily scrapes—just beaten ground where lots of hooves had kept anything from growing."

Altizer must have known exactly what to look for. After killing the state-record buck, which scored 173 Pope and Young Club typical points, with his bow in 1984, he got a good eight-pointer by hunting an area with licking branch activity. The following year in Tennessee, he used his bow to take a broken-horned eight-pointer as the buck came in to a licking branch after the rut.

"Hierarchy is important all year," McGuire commented, "but it's most important during the rut. Once the velvet is rubbed off, the nature of licking branch activity changes drastically. I think that the dominant buck exerts his authority more seriously at the licking branch than anywhere else. He is intent on controlling the other bucks' activities. And because the licking branch is where they usually hang out, he's going to be there to see what goes on—whether or not a scrape is under the licking branch.

"I'd like to report that I've used this knowledge to take record-book deer, but unfortunately that isn't so," McGuire said. "I've been so busy that the only time I've gotten to test licking branches while actually hunting was during November 1984 in Ohio.

"There were four of us hunting: Larry D. Jones and his wife, Miriam, from Springfield, Oregon; Jack Lape from Grove City, Ohio; and myself. We had three weeks to bowhunt, and we'd decided to concentrate our efforts on a licking branch that we had found.

"This branch was located on a southfacing edge of a soybean field," he explained. "Sunlight seems to be a factor in licking-branch location. Soybeans

that should have been growing under the branch had been destroyed and replaced by worn grass. That's how we discovered it in the first place. Field edges, especially southfacing ones, are good places to scout for licking activity. And it's interesting to note that though there were many big, bold, beautiful scrapes in the vicinity, we saw absolutely no deer visiting them.

"This was the peak of the rut. And during the time we watched the licking branch, no less than eight different Pope and Young Club-class bucks visited it. Two deer would have made Boone and Crockett Club records for sure—a typical that would have scored more than 170 points and a nontypical in the 195-plus range. Another would have scored in the upper 160s, but none of us had a chance at these three bruisers.

"The deer that we got a crack at were in the 130- to 150-point class," McGuire continued. "Though none of us got a buck, we had good, consistent action for the entire three weeks by centering our activity around a licking branch that a few weeks earlier everyone would have ignored."

For hunters to capitalize on licking branches, they first must know how to find them. And though he hasn't had much time to hunt them, McGuire does know how to find them. "The easiest way is to get out into the woods during the spring and summer to look at the previous year's active scrapes," says McGuire. "Look for one that appears freshly 'worked over.' The apparent scrape marks are from the bucks' feet as they dance while licking the branch. And once you find such a spot, observe from a distance without disturbing the summertime marking."

Another secret is to get topographic maps and concentrate on east-west features such as ridges, rivers, ditches, and fencelines. "I look for geographic features where bucks can travel unobserved while encountering little human scent," he explains.

"Then I start at the western end of these features. I especially like the western end of a ridge that overlooks a favorite crop field. Choose a spot and work out from there 100 yards in all directions. Focus on old rubs and scrapes while looking for any likely branches. Check the branches for signs of licking or nibbling, but be sure that the limb is still alive. And wear clean rubber gloves while you investigate.

"Then I 'thread' the branches—tie a light indicator line to the branch so that the line will break if a deer starts nibbling on the limb or dancing beneath it. And, I may also carefully expose moist ground beneath the suspected licking branch to thereby monitor any activity.

"Remember," McGuire warns, "that there are many branch-marking locations, especially over scrapes. Branches are marked during the rut by the bucks as they rub their forehead sudoriferous glands on them. These glands are most active during the rut. But although these branches may look like licking branches, there is a difference.

Pheremones, present in a deer's saliva, may act as a buck's calling card when deposited on the licking branch. Big-buck activity will center here before long.

Photo by Wyman Meinzer

"There are very few all-season licking branches. And although the area beneath usually develops into a scrape, it's not always the biggest or most obvious scrape in the woods. It may actually be quite small and inconspicuous. But bucks will focus their activity in this location—at least until they start tending estrous does. If a branch above a scrape is a licking branch, subordinates approach covertly when the rut begins. They also take pains to avoid stepping in the dominant buck's scrape, something that's apparently not tolerated."

One way to decide whether you've found a licking branch is the manner in which the deer behave there.

"If it's not the rut, all deer approach the same way," McGuire said. "Bucks walk up, look at the branches, and pull their front feet together. Sometimes, they'll squat in the normal urination posture rather than the rub-urination posture that's common at active scrapes. Then they will lick, nibble, and nuzzle the branch. If it's higher than the buck's head, he'll raise up off the ground to dance on his hind legs.

"Deer also seem to mark licking branches with their foreheads, noses, and chins," McGuire continued. "And trophy hunters should note that dominant mature bucks seem to mark licking branches more often during the summer than do subordinates."

McGuire has several techniques for hunting at licking branches. He approaches from the side that is opposite where he expects the buck to appear. And he likes being high enough in a tree, or downwind enough, so that his scent is diluted. By the time the buck gets edgy or suspicious, McGuire

wants him in his sights.

But perhaps the best method of hunting at licking branches, especially when there is doubt as to whether they *are* licking branches, is to create your own.

"You can make a 'licker set' at any time, but they're most effective in the spring and summer," McGuire says. "A licker set simply provides an ideal licking branch where you want to hunt. Be sure that the branch angles down and is alive. This works well in big timber where there's little understory to provide branches within a buck's reach.

"I bend a small sapling over and tie it off with heavy, dark nylon line so that it hangs over in an inverted U, like a giant bow. Tie the line about 4 feet from the base of the trunk while keeping the top of the tree 3 to 4 feet off the ground. If the potential licking branch is too close to the ground, break off the branches at the proper height.

"Another aid in starting a licker set could come from your next buck. Swab the dead deer's gums and tongue with Q-Tips carried in a sealed plastic bag. Only handle the Q-Tips while wearing rubber gloves, and don't get blood on them," McGuire added. "Both natural and new licker sets are enhanced when I treat them later with these Q-Tips. Wet them a bit to freshen the scent, swab the limb gently, and you're in business."

Licking branches are big whitetail news. Knowing how to locate and and identify them can shorten your scouting time. And knowing how to use them will make deer hunting even more exciting. Knowledge about what makes the whitetail tick can be used to outwit him. Knowing about the licking branch may tip the scales in your favor.

Weather And Whitetails

By John H. Williams

In Michigan's Upper Peninsula, late November often brings some of the meanest storms of the year. Just the day before, wind gusts of up to 70 mph had forced the closure of the "Big Mac" bridge for some 12 hours and, in addition, had driven every deer in the entire region into hiding. Such conditions rarely bode well for hunting (especially for the lone hunter), but today was different—much different.

As I drove down the two-track long before dawn, I figured that we had less than one-half inch of snow on the ground; the previous day's winds had died entirely. Visibility was bad as the beams from my truck's headlights reflected off the steadily falling snow.

Donning my heavy parka and boots, I slung my daypack over my shoulder and headed toward the cedars, one mile distant. Despite the late-breaking daylight, I had no problem seeing, for even in the cedars, the freshly fallen snow had filtered through enough to increase visibility greatly. Several days before, I had located three cedars growing in a tight clump. There was just enough room at the center to provide me with a natural blind, and it was there that I took up my vigil.

As the moments passed, my ears adjusted to the stillness, and except for the sound of the falling snow, it was a silent world: No woodpecker's tap-tap-tap greeted this morn; no raucous crows swooped and screamed; no wind stirred the tree-tops. Silently, I waited.

Shortly after 8 A.M., I watched as a deer drifted through distant trees, much too concealed for me to identify its sex and in any case much too protected to offer a shot. Time passed; the snow fell; and the silence continued unbroken. By 9 A.M., I noticed that the snow had completely covered the gun cradled in my arms. Involuntarily, I shivered; the snow and the silence seemed, somehow, to make it colder than it really was.

At 9:30, and without prior warning, I heard brush crackling and the sounds of a large animal running among the twisted windfalls behind me. The big buck broke into the cedars just as I turned in that direction. He ran several yards and stopped, head held high and very alert. As the crosshairs settled on his chest, I squeezed off my shot. He bolted through the trees. I shot twice more, and as suddenly as it had been broken, the silence returned.

Not wanting to track the buck immediately, I was nonetheless fearful that I'd lose the trail in the falling snow. After reloading, I quickly headed to where the buck had stood when I first shot. There, spilled across 6 inches of newly fallen snow, were several spots of bright arterial blood. Knowing then that I'd gotten my hoped-for lung shot, I took off on the buck's track at once. He'd turned after only 30 yards, and after leaving the cedars he had headed into an open field beyond. Fifty yards past where I had first shot, I almost stepped on him; the falling snow had already begun to cover him up.

Hanging my orange parka in a nearby tree, I headed toward the truck to gather my camera equipment. On the way, I cut six sets of deer tracks

but, in the excitement, didn't think much of it at the time. Arriving at the truck, I poured a cup of coffee from my Thermos and fiddled with my gear. After finishing the coffee, I headed out again. Almost at once, it dawned on me that my own tracks were obliterated, yet I continued to cut fresh deer tracks in the snow.

A quirk? Unusual that so many deer just happened to be moving on such a day? I can only point to other days under very similar conditions, during which I've either scored on deer or at least witnessed their increased level of activity, to counter such a guess. I believe, based upon numerous such incidents spanning at least 20 years, that one of the very best times to be afield during the deer season is in, and/or immediately following, a major snowstorm.

For some reason, whitetails react to the first few big snowfalls of the year like children on a playground. It seems to exhilarate them. They romp, they run, and they cover a lot of territory in a short time. As a hunter, I want to be in the woods and fields when they do this. Under these circumstances, I have all of the odds stacked heavily in my favor. Because it's the deer that are increasing their activity, all I need to do is pick an area that I feel routinely supports a lot of deer traffic, and wait.

I first noticed this phenomenon many years ago while hunting a thicket adjacent to some agricultural lands in southern Michigan. It had begun snowing sometime late the night before; by dawn, we'd had well over an inch, and it was still coming down heavily. By late morning we had 5 inches on the ground when the only deer I'd seen—a buck—broke through the brush in front of me. While dragging him the one-half mile to my Jeep a few minutes later, I was amazed at the number of tracks I kept cutting.

Up to that point in the season I had hunted for five or six days and had seen only a handful of deer. There simply weren't that many deer per square mile in that particular area. Yet coming out that morning, despite the snow still falling, I cut fresh tracks everywhere. The reason I'm stressing this point is because many hunters fervently believe that deer lie low during major snowfalls, and hence the hunters do, too. Perhaps that's true later in the year, but early winter snowstorms have just the opposite effect, and for the hunter who's nestled next to a fire in camp, it's a wasted day.

RAIN AND WIND

Rain is another major weather pattern that dramatically affects deer behavior. Precisely what that effect will be depends on several other related factors, including concurrent winds, duration and intensity of rainfall, accompanying fog, whether it's an isolated rain or a rain in a continuing pattern of wet weather, and the temperature. (There may well be other associated factors, but I have found these to be the major ones.)

There's probably nothing that can completely ruin a hunter's day afield more than rain accompanied by high winds. We're not talking about light breezes here or occasional gusts, but unrelenting, tree-bending gales. Such weather strikes fear deep into the very soul of deer. Under these conditions, their senses are totally befuddled. They can no longer rely on their noses, their ears, or their eyes. All of their senses have been quite effectively blocked.

From every direction at once, there is noise and movement. If there's a sudden influx of alarming odor, it's there one instant and completely gone the next, much too suddenly to identify, let alone pinpoint. Without meaningful exception, this dictates that the deer lie low. Storms of such magnitude never last long, and the deer will simply ride them out while locked up in very dense cover.

However, given the right circumstances—proper cover and fellow hunters—all is not lost on such days. Years ago, I learned quite by accident a valuable lesson about hunting in such weather. If you hunt as a member of a party, you may someday be able to use this insight to your advantage.

It was the kind of day no one in his right mind would have been out in, but for one thing: Three of us had left home at about 3 A.M. and driven more than 200 miles, and we weren't about to just sit around. We hunted despite the weather. The area we were in was cultivated and interspersed with pockets of dense lowlands. Our initial idea was to take up stands in these smaller pockets, hopefully allowing hunters in the surrounding larger thickets to push deer our way.

Shortly after daybreak, when it became obvious that we were quite alone, we changed our minds, deciding that our only realistic hope of scoring was to drive. Despite (and actually because of) the driving rain and the wind gusts that threatened to blow us away, we did push deer. In fact, in our third swale that morning, one of my companions nailed a fine eight-pointer as the buck attempted to escape with a couple of does. We saw plenty of other deer that day as well, including other bucks, but somehow we never quite managed to hook up. Nonetheless, it was one of those days that I'd have never thought worthy of our efforts. But by driving the deer from small, well-defined cover, I was proved wrong.

In a rainfall that's been going on for some time, the deer eventually get to a point where they'll pretty much ignore it and get on with their routines. Food must be obtained, and if a threatening or rainy night precedes a day-long rain I want to be in the field, rain or not, the following evening. In fact, I want to be nestled over a known feeding area by midafternoon. The only exceptions I'd make to that would be in the event of a torrential rainfall, rapidly falling temperatures (in which case I'd have been there earlier), and/or high winds. Even then, small openings in dense protective cover could prove to be a good bet.

For the hunter working alone, stillhunting

through dense bedding areas during midday periods is a good tactic. The deer under such circumstances are hungry much of the time, and though they may not venture out into the open, they will feed frequently for short periods of time within the cover. Thus, an excellent approach is actually a combination of stillhunting and stand hunting; work thoroughly every area capable of sheltering deer, and remember that these areas need not be large. In heavily hunted zones, be alert to out-of-the-way plots of cover or any cover that for one reason or another has been consistently overlooked by other hunters.

For group hunters, these days are custom-made for driving. Groups large enough to completely cover the available area should block all exits and drive as usual. Small parties, even if there are just two hunters, should post blockers on major runways within the cover being driven. Drive silently and slowly, and in all probability the deer will simply try to slip around you rather than exit the area.

An approach I've seen succeed under such circumstances is for two or three hunting partners to drive smaller pockets of cover by actually alternating their activities. The drive starts, for example, at 10 A.M. with two hunters taking stands within the cover being driven, while the third partner does the driving. At 11 A.M., and by prior planning and agreement, one of the two standing hunters begins his drive while the first driver assumes a stand. This alternating of drivers continues until the drive is completed or until someone connects. There must

Areas near water that offer plenty of cool shade are your best bet when the weather turns hot.   *Photo by John Weiss*

Photo by Tim Christie

When the mercury descends, so should you—down to the sheltered lowlands.

be no yelling or talking among the hunters. Everyone knows exactly what his functions and responsibilities are before the drive begins, and he must then carry them out precisely.

The hunter who is moving should do so slowly (but faster than he would if stillhunting) and quietly, and he should do so without regard to wind direction. Research has shown that whitetails seldom forsake their home territories unless there are more than 20 hunters per square mile. Otherwise, they choose simply to slip around the hunters or to lie low and let the hunters pass by. This is precisely why the technique works so well.

On occasion, you'll have a storm that starts out slowly—with fairly light rains, for example, that persist for a day or so—and then intensifies. The period immediately preceding such a change is an excellent time to be afield. Deer are very alert to an impending change of this nature, and they will begin feeding heavily just prior to its arrival. Post-up either overlooking feeding areas or on runways leading to heavy cover at such times. Do so regardless of the time of day.

Following such a storm, concentrate your efforts on known feeding grounds, and again do so without regard for time of day. Deer that have been forced to lie low, even if only for ten or 12 hours, are hungry, and they'll feed voraciously as soon as there's a break in the weather. In areas with intense hunting pressure, hunt the very edges of cover, as well as those areas within the cover that have plenty

of browse. In less-pressured zones, look to more-open spots. Following prolonged periods of inactivity, deer actually seem to enjoy getting out of thick cover, provided they feel they can do so safely.

Periods of moderate temperatures with slow-to-steady rains are other times that are uncomfortable for the hunter, but productive nonetheless. Four or five years ago, I was hunting in southern Michigan's farm country. It was Thanksgiving Day, about 45°, and it had been raining steadily since daybreak. Actually, up to that point it had been a very wet and rainy deer season. This had greatly reduced hunting pressure in the area I was in, and any deer movement was quite natural. At about 11 A.M., a little spike came picking his way through the hardwoods. To me, he looked about as miserable as I felt. We looked at each other for a long, lingering moment, I bid him good day, and he slowly walked away.

By dawn on the next morning, the rains had slowed but drizzle persisted. Almost 24 hours to the minute after I had let the spike go, the buck of my dreams suddenly materialized before me. From a hunter's point of view the story has a sad ending, as my execution left something to be desired. But the point is to see the bucks you seek. An excellent time to do just that is during a slow, steady rain, particularly one that has persisted for several days.

For the hunter who chooses to stand under such conditions, the dark, generally colder nights mean little feeding activity for the deer. Daylight then finds them more active than usual and for longer periods of time, and the diminished hunter activity ensures more predictability. Do your best to select stands overlooking known feeding areas and along well-used runways.

For the stillhunter, such days of moderate temperatures with slow to steady rains are tailor-made. Areas frequently off-limits to the stillhunter can now be hunted much more effectively with the combined effect of dripping water and damp earth muffling any sounds.

Winds are generally more predictable on such days, allowing you to be more certain of just where your scent is drifting and how best to approach cover.

Such weather accompanied by near-freezing temperatures is quite a different matter. Not only is it extremely uncomfortable for you, but it is miserable for the deer as well. If you hunt during such days, get nestled amid thick cover and stay put. Whatever feeding the deer will do will occur completely within the cover they're in, and it will be done in frequent but short periods of time. Two or more hunters working together can execute simple drives designed to move the deer slowly about within the cover they have selected.

FOG

Fog is yet another weather-related element often associated with rain and with excellent deer-hunting opportunity. November 28, 1982, found me standing in a clump of partridgeberry bushes in Michigan's southern Thumb region. It had been wet and dreary for days on end. Late in the season, with temperatures hovering around 40°, I was virtually the only one left hunting on the farm.

My stand overlooked a mosaic of broken cover in a 60-acre parcel sandwiched between crop fields to the east and a pasture to the west. A slight, intermittent breeze had been wafting the fog forming over the low-lying cattails that stood in front of me. At times, I couldn't see the cedars just 20 yards to my right. Most of the time, I couldn't see the cattails 50 yards ahead or the poplars 50 yards to my left. Except for the incessant dripping of the woods, everything was silent. Even the deer (all does) I had seen that day seemed to drift past in a surreal, almost ghostly manner.

At precisely 1 P.M., a light gust cleared a path between me and another clump of bushes to the left. There, suddenly, jutting above the cover, was a wide, heavily beamed rack. Slowly I raised my slug gun and slipped off the safety. As the buck's shoulder cleared the thicket, I touched the trigger and claimed my prize. Admiring my trophy moments later, I couldn't help but smile when I thought of how many times that day I'd consciously reminded myself to continue the hunt despite my numb feet and cold fingers.

Fog seems to lend an air of confidence to deer. Perhaps its accompanying chill also permeates their coats. I don't know. But I do know that they move a lot on foggy days. Enveloped in its cloak, deer will even move brazenly far out into open feeding areas during midday periods. Therefore, when fog is widespread, I'll hunt over feeding areas. Stillhunting is highly effective at such times and allows me to work several different areas. I particularly like to overlook runways that weave their way through low fog-forming areas during these times.

EXTREME COLD

Cold—bone-chilling, teeth-chattering cold—has a way of quickly sapping a deer hunter's enthusiasm. It also causes deer to do their disappearing acts. It's as though they said, "Beam us up, Scotty," and then vaporized. They do disappear, but they always materialize again in the thermal cover, and it's there that they stay. Several years ago, I was hunting in northern Wisconsin's forested region. For days, I'd been looking over a number of deer in the uplands while temperatures ranged in the 30s and 40s. Then, overnight, the weather changed. Temperatures plummeted, the mercury disappeared, and along with it went the deer.

An inch of new snow preceded the falling temperatures, and the next morning, with moderate winds and below-zero temperatures, not a track could be found where I'd seen deer just the evening before. For two days, my suffering from cold hands and feet was exaggerated by my inability to find deer. In an attempt designed more to keep warm than to locate deer, I headed down off the hillsides. There in the hemlocks and swamps below were the deer. A maze of tracks and well-trod trails awaited me; tagging a buck became a simple question of biding my time.

Just this past fall, Joe Frankum, a friend from Union Lake, Michigan, got tied up with business obligations and missed the first week of our season. When he finally arrived in the Upper Peninsula, the temperatures hovered in the low teens or below. For the eight hunters in his camp that week, it was an ominous beginning. But with six bucks on the meat pole by week's end, their spirits, if not the temperatures, warmed considerably. They had beaten the odds, and beaten them soundly, by heading for thick cover. Lowlands and sheltered areas out of the winds are your ticket to success in cold weather. Areas with cedars, hemlocks, and immature, densely planted pines are where you'll find the deer under these conditions.

In areas where such cover does not exist, look to thickets of any kind, particularly to those in low-lying areas. The deer under such conditions are *always* going to head for insulating cover. The critical question to ask yourself is: "Where, given this particular environment, can I find cover that gives deer the most protection from the wind and cold?" Answer that correctly, and you will have successfully located the deer every time.

Your best hunting strategy under such circumstances is to take a stand and wait the deer out. Most feeding is going to take place during daylight hours, and a lot of it takes place during the warmer periods of the day. By using such knowledge, a friend of mine finally tagged an old buck that had previously been giving us the slip.

We knew this old boy was holing up in one particular thicket routinely, yet despite Jim's being on stand every morning long before daylight, the buck beat him to the cover every day for more than a week. Finally the weather turned bitterly cold with a stinging northerly wind. The next morning, Jim slipped into a blind south of the thicket and tagged the buck as it was sneaking home late.

I'm certain that the deer was feeding later than normal that morning as a direct result of the lower temperatures. Deer under such conditions won't normally begin feeding until later in the morning and therefore can often be caught later than usual out in the open. In heavily hunted regions, such feeding will occur within the cover itself. In more remote, less-pressured sections, look for openings near the cover and for areas protected from the wind.

HOT, ARID CONDITIONS

Very much the same approach is required to succeed under unusually hot conditions. Look for cover offering plenty of shade, as well as for areas that are low, particularly those adjacent to water. Early-morning periods are the best times to waylay deer under these conditions. Be posted-up overlooking feeding areas early or on runways leading from feeding areas to cover. Hunt water sources during midday periods and again just before dark.

The effects of days with clear skies and bright sunlight are dependent on the kind of weather before and after them. Days such as these that either precede or follow foul weather are particularly productive, as the deer attempt to satiate their hunger. On clear-breaking mornings that follow a day or more of inclement weather, position yourself—whether standing or stillhunting—to overlook known feeding areas, and hunt these until later in the day than you normally would. In heavily pressured areas, hunt bedding sites having southerly exposures, and be alert to heightened daytime feeding activities in these spots.

Under such circumstances, the deer literally try to make up for lost time, and they'll feed for much longer than normal. This is especially true when such weather coincides with the end of the rutting period. Big bucks—those most-heavily taxed by the rigors of breeding—will often feed for at least twice as long as normal, and they will very often do so even during daylight periods. It is for this reason that we find so many of the very best bucks taken each season (especially in the Northern states) during the last few days each year.

Orchards, mast-bearing hardwoods, and crop fields in less-pressured areas will often be visited by bucks even during midday. In more-heavily hunted regions, such feeding binges are much more likely to occur within the cover. But make no mistake about it: Those bucks are feeding somewhere, even during daylight hours—and it's your job to discover where.

Many years ago, I had the opportunity to watch a big buck that lived near my home. For weeks prior to the season, I'd seen him here and there as the summer's bounty fattened his body and nourished his headgear. As the fall progressed, he gradually became more and more reclusive, and his space dwindled. He finally took up residence in a dense tangle bordered by planted pines on the east, cornfields on the north and west, and a cover field and thick-set fencerow on the south.

As so often happens, deer season brought with it the fall's worst weather. Even when it didn't rain, skies were sullen and overcast for days at a time. Each morning found me patiently waiting and watching my buck's thicket, hoping to catch him sneaking in late or exiting early. I never did.

In mid-season, a cold front moved in quickly and temperatures dropped. The next morning, the winds were out of the east and the skies crystal-clear when I took up a stand on the very edge of the thicket, just west of the fencerow. Early on, I saw two does feed slowly from the fencerow out into the cover field and then slowly work away from me. Later, a lone doe stole into the thicket itself. Then, for a long time nothing moved. At midday, while I was enjoying the sun's warmth and my eyes were growing heavy, I detected movement in the fencerow just south of the thicket. Though immediately alerted, I couldn't identify what I'd seen.

After an hour passed and nothing stirred, suddenly there he was, right where I'd noticed the earlier movement. The lure of the first sunlight in days had been his undoing. Just a few short yards from complete sanctuary in his thicket, he'd bedded in the fencerow. Such behavior is quite common.

Being able to plan your hunting strategy based upon the weather depends on your ability to predict the weather. For this very reason, I always try to catch the latest weather forecasts. The particulars aren't nearly as important as the trends. A few degrees one way or the other is insignificant; a shower or isolated thunderstorm means little or nothing; but major changes should be noticed and capitalized on. Deer, just like most other animals, seem to have a built-in ability to foresee weather changes, and deer react to the potential changes long before they're obvious to you and me.

To be sure, an awful lot of information and insight must guide us in our hunting efforts, but weather is one of the key criteria that many hunters either seem to little understand or simply overlook. When employed properly, it's the one element that may decide the outcome of your whole season.

Whitetails And Elk: The Same Game

By Roland Cheek

You are an experienced whitetail deer hunter from an Eastern state. You have dreamed of making a hunt out West for the wily elk. But you're reluctant because you know nothing about hunting elk. Right?

You may know more than you think. Let your mind run for a moment. Suppose that your Eastern whitetail has undergone just two major physical changes: First of all, it has grown four to five times its normal body size; second, it is no longer a solitary creature, but a herd animal instead. What comes to mind when you think of an 800 to 1,000-pound herd animal with whitetail instincts?

I think elk. I'm an outfitter with some credentials. I have spent nearly two decades guiding Eastern whitetail hunters after elk in northwestern Montana's Bob Marshall Wilderness. I've hunted elk myself for more than 30 years, both in Montana for Rocky Mountain elk and for Roosevelt elk in Oregon, where I grew up. In addition, Montana's Flathead County—where I've made my home for the past 20 years—is noted for record-class whitetail deer. And over the years, I've come to realize that there are marked similarities in characteristics between the two species. Enough so that an experienced whitetail hunter has an edge if he uses his acquired knowledge.

Yet, all too often, I've actually had Eastern hunters apologize for their lack of elk-hunting experience when inquiring about our hunting trips. One such inquiry reads:

. . . You should know we are inexperienced big-game hunters, having the opportunity only to hunt deer in our part of the country. We also have never before been on a guided hunt, and very much want it to be a success.

Another:

. . . I have hunted deer all my life, here in Michigan. But an elk-hunting trip by horseback is something I have always wanted to do. Is an elk hunt possible for a novice like me?

When a man stops by our sports-show booth and tells me he's hunted deer in Wisconsin or Minnesota or Pennsylvania all his life, but he'd like to try for elk out in Montana, I smile inwardly and get serious in telling him about our outfit. Few elk hunters come complete with an understanding of our wilderness mountains. But I know automatically that the guy is likely woods-wise, with an inordinate amount of patience—two important criteria that all good elk hunters must someday acquire.

I also know how that man will probably react under a given set of hunting conditions. Much of the time, his reactions will be correct for elk as well as for his Eastern whitetail deer. Above all, I know that I can, with a minimum of training, modify some of his reactions to make them more applicable to 800-pound herd animals dwelling in the rugged Montana mountains. There's little doubt in my mind that the whitetail hunters we've guided become competent elk hunters more easily than do broadly traveled hunters without whitetail or elk experience.

Why is previous hunter training necessary if I'm an outfitter/guide with credentials and broad experience of my own?

I know the country where we hunt America's

greatest big-game animal in its natural environment, and I know that there is only so much any guide can do for his hunters. I know that sometime during the course of a ten-day hunt, we'll likely exhaust our knowledge. We'll bugle our guts out during the rutting period. But sometimes bull elk won't come to the call. If conditions are right, we can track the big critters. But sometimes there just isn't a skiff of fresh snow, or the ground is not soft from a soaking rain. Above all, we know our country well. We know where tiny meadows or natural mineral licks or wallows or well-used game trails exist. We know where we've seen elk and where our hunters have taken elk in the past. But sometimes those areas aren't productive during a particular hunt, or with a particular hunter. When that inevitable time comes and the elk are sticking tight to the thick stuff, then I know that my hunter's best chance for success may well lie in his going into the brush after them alone.

At that time, I know I'm a millstone around his neck. Two of us simply cannot slip as silently as can one through a forest. But the critter we're after is every bit as elusive as an old mossyhorn whitetail. Because of the foregoing, I know that the best way I may be able to help my hunter is to explain the lay of the land to him; maybe take him by horseback to the head of a drainage, then move his horse around to pick him up at another spot some distance away. When that time comes, it's imperative that a sneak-hunting elk hunter know his animal. That's the time when an experienced whitetail hunter, with habits slightly modified for elk, has an advantage.

Any outfitter worth his salt will spend as much time as possible discussing with his guests the country, the animal, and what he believes to be the best hunting methods—at least as much as they seem inclined to grasp. It's vital to success.

When I explain to an experienced whitetail hunter the similarities between elk and deer, I first call attention to the horns. Each horn point stems from the main beam for both species. Branched antler points are a non-typical rarity for either.

If it's during the rut, I tell my hunters that bull elk, like whitetail bucks, sometimes do inexplicably stupid things during the peak time. Aside from them coming to an imitation call, I've seen them crash wildly through the brush, drawn to the sounds of a packstring moving through the mountains (horses snapping twigs and clicking rocks with their steel-shod hoofs). Is that much different from a whitetail buck drawn to a hunter who is clicking horns together with his hands? The buck thinks that he's coming to the sounds of two cohorts sparring. The bull is drawn to what he believes are the sounds of an elk herd on the move.

Both whitetail deer and elk make scrapes and rubs to mark their territory. With both species, aggressive territorial defense is the mark of a dominant individual and serves to markedly lessen actual combat during the all-important rut.

Of course, a bull elk's scrape may be 8 or 10 feet in diameter. And it may appear to be tilled up like a garden spot where he's ripped the soil with his massive horns and churning feet in mock or real anger. His whitetail counterpart's scrape is seldom more than 3 feet across—a 4-foot one is big for a deer. Likewise, whitetail bucks rub small trees, and they usually rub 2 to 4 feet off the ground, while bull elk always set their goals upward, sometimes rubbing higher than a tall man can reach. Yet, with both species, rubs and scrapes serve a biological, territorial purpose. With both species, fresh scrapes or rubs indicate the presence of rutting males. It's an indicator to which a hunter should pay attention. He should get serious with his stalk.

Many times over the years, I've watched a big bull stand or lay motionless behind a scant screen of brush or small trees, apparently thinking himself adequately hidden and willing to let a hunter wander past. Doesn't that trick sound like a favorite whitetail ploy? And doesn't it make you wonder about the many big bucks and bulls who've used it successfully while a hunter trudged wearily by, convinced that the area chosen for the day's hunt was stripped clean of critters the week before?

Both species, I believe, depend much more readily on sound and smell than on eyes. An elk's nose is particularly keen, and if the wind is gusting at your back, you'd be better off going on back to camp for a cribbage game. So it is for whitetail deer.

Whitetails have an edge when it comes to keenness of hearing. But their edge is more a result of solitary habits than of their Maker-crafted, more sensitive ears. Place a bull elk off by himself, and you'll find that his ears are effective, too. Because big bulls are more inclined toward solitude than is even the oldest cow, it's safe to say that a noisy sneak-hunting elk stalker may also do better at the cribbage board.

It's true, however, that any elk will pay less attention to common forest noises than will whitetail deer. Elk simply cannot move through a forest as quietly as deer can. It's their size and their herd instinct. An elk will break an occasional dead limb, kick over an occasional stone, swish an occasional branch. But make that sound an alien one—swish a branch with your vinyl rain pants, unzip your raincoat, curse in a low voice—and you can kiss that bull goodbye.

What about their eyes? Why no respect there? Well, the mountain elk and valley whitetail can't match their eyes against mine. Or, likely, yours. They're color blind, just as is commonly believed. I think it's true. I've stood quietly too many times, dressed with an orange vest or a red hat, and had either elk or whitetail deer graze around me. I do believe that their eyes are light-sensitive, though. Blaze Orange will stand out as a light-colored object against a deep-green forest, and it attracts attention when on the move. And red will stand out as dark against snow.

Both whitetail deer and elk sometimes tend to

Every whitetail hunter knows that the presence of rubs indicates a buck—preferably a big one—is close at hand.

Photo by Len Rue, Jr.

disbelieve one sense alone. Often, they'll hear your noise but wait until they can see you before leaving for parts unknown. Or they'll circle to get your wind. Sometimes, they've spotted your movement but wait to hear or smell, distrusting their eyes. It's a weakness that's likely academic, anyway. Most times, the first glimpse you have of the critter is some seconds after the bull or buck has claimed you with his second sense and is well on the move.

Track a bull elk in snow. Let him know you're back there. It's likely that an Eastern whitetail hunter will be surprised to find a bull trying every wily whitetail trick in the book to keep his edge on a hunter. He'll circle; he'll climb, only to drop back again to a creek bottom. He'll lie screened, watching his backtrail. He'll hook, switch back, lose his tracks in a maze of others, follow his own backtrail. And your guts will be twisted up before it's all over.

Bull elk bed in whitetail-likely spots: on a brush-screened knoll, near the point of a ridge, on a small bench. Two steps, and they're gone in any of several directions.

Occasionally, the unusual will work with whitetails or elk. I once jumped a whitetail buck, then whistled sharply when I realized that I didn't have a shot. The buck stopped momentarily—long enough for me to sight in—then bounded away. When I quit laughing, I filed that trick away in the memory bank. Since then, I've talked to many whitetail hunters who've used a whistle to pause a big buck.

Similarly, I've jumped bull elk and many times used a bugle or a grunt to stop them for a few seconds, despite the fact that they were in full flight. A huge bull elk bursting wildly through a thick stand of timber at one moment, then stopping on a dime at the next, can be a sight to see. I've several times imagined what's going on in his mind: "What the heck? Did I make a mistake?" Then, he'll almost shake his head as the wheels grind on: "No . . . no, by gosh. That *was* a human!"

Which brings up another point: When elk—any elk—decide to go somewhere, they'll go. It doesn't seem to make any difference how many or what kind of deterrents are in the way: over a pass, up an open hillside, through a narrow canyon.

Though I've never participated in drives for whitetail deer, many friends have told me that whitetails have this same characteristic, sometimes determined to exit the woods at a most unhealthy spot and seeming not to care in the least.

I once received another interesting letter: . . . *Here in Pennsylvania, we hunt deer in bowhunting season by sitting on game trails. Most of our stands are in the trees. I don't have any experience stalking. . . .*

Will the stand-hunting method work on elk? Well, yes, I think so, though it's underutilized out West even for whitetail deer. I certainly have not given stand-hunting for elk a fair shake because I'm a born-and-reared Western elk hunter. Oh, we've now and again left a selected hunter sitting at a good elk trail, and a few have connected. Enough so that it's caused me to reconsider our hunting methods.

I said "reconsider"—we haven't adopted stand-hunting with any seriousness as yet. Before anyone adopts elk hunting via the stand method wholesale, they'd best consider two very important qualifiers:

• Not every hunter is psychologically equipped to handle sitting all day. Heck, I'm one of 'em. My friends call me a nervous hunter—a deserved axiom. Ask me to sit all day while hunting, and fellow, you've just received my notice to quit. Yet, there are hunters who are excellent at the method. Many

Elk, too, make rubs. It is believed that rubs and scrapes are territorial markers.   *Photo by Ed Wolf*

are experienced Eastern whitetail hunters.

But just because I like to travel at a high lope when I'm elk hunting doesn't mean that everyone should. The key is one that a good outfitter learned long ago: Find out the method your hunter is best at, and use that method as much as possible in his hunt. That's a method a hunter would and should use on his own, too.

There's little doubt, though, that we've underutilized the stand, particularly for some of our people with Eastern whitetail experience. And in my estimation, a tree stand would be even more effective, for precisely the same reasons why they're effective in the East.

• Another key is to stand-hunt only in areas elk are using. For productive growing land, the Bob Marshall Wilderness is not Lancaster County, Pennsylvania. Growing seasons are short, and winters are particularly harsh. In good whitetail habitat, a hunter can justifiably assume that there are deer around. It's simply a matter of seeing them.

Prime Eastern farmland will produce, say, three times more foodstuff per acre than our best Montana farmland. So will the woodlands. Are there three times more deer per acre in the East? Probably. Divide a typical Eastern deer population by three, and you have a more realistic estimate of ours.

But wait a minute! The high mountain country inhabited by elk cannot match our productive Western lowlands. Say, one-fifth? And what about elk? They're four times larger and require four times more feed. It's safe to say that you could divide the Potter County, Pennsylvania, deer herd by 30 and have a more realistic idea of mountain elk populations. Are you willing to sit perched atop a tree stand and hunt a critter only 1/30 as plentiful as the Eastern whitetail? Compound those fewer numbers with the realization that whitetail deer are spread throughout their habitat but elk are herd animals, tending often to concentrate their numbers in a relatively small area. Even solitary elk are generally found in a herd's vicinity.

However, that's precisely the reason why a tree stand may work—*if* a hunter can first find an area where the elk are, then locate a stand. Certainly, elk have favorite areas they use, depending on seasons. Most often, the rut goes on in deep timber and sometimes lasts for days. It takes tremendous pressure to move elk from that type of secluded refuge. They may move temporarily, but only to drift back at the first opportunity—this is a good place for your stand.

Likewise, maturing food sources are important. Perhaps a meadow sedge turns succulent after a first frost, or a browse plant becomes palatable after a soaking rain. Identify those areas, check for sign, then locate a stand.

Staging areas for migration can be important, too, but they're generally more briefly utilized. They can certainly be productive for the hunter who finds them, though.

I've tried to make the point that there are lots of similarities between elk and whitetail deer. Now let's talk of the differences and how a whitetail hunter must modify his approach for elk hunting.

Well, a big one was just listed above. Unlike whitetail deer, elk simply are *not* everywhere. Some Eastern deer hunters never learn that it does precious little good to pussyfoot for elk if there are no elk on the mountain. That's why most Western elk hunters learned to hunt at a high lope, and why we sometimes tend to overrun 'em when we do locate the critters.

The ideal elk hunter would be one mobile enough to cover ground until he located elk-using areas, then patient enough to hunt as though he were after a trophy whitetail buck back East.

Perhaps the greatest difference is in habitat. Due to their size and herd instincts, elk, unlike whitetail deer, have never learned to adapt to civilization. No farm lots for them. Today, the best elk ranges lie in the most rugged and remote mountains of the West.

Many Eastern hunters simply cannot comprehend the monumental difference our rugged mountains and tremendous distances make to Western hunting. It may be an overworked piece of advice, but good physical conditioning is much more important for elk-hunting success than for hunting deer. Without reasonably good physical conditioning, you may not be mobile enough to find where the elk are in the first place.

Whitetail bucks, unlike bull elk, never collect a harem of females. At first, one would think it a comparative weakness for the harem-collecting bull, but the contrary is true. A whitetail buck in the rut, like a bull elk, has his mind elsewhere. But unlike the buck, the bull has several sets of eyes and ears and several noses at work for him. A hunter stalking a herd bull is far more likely to first spook a cow, who'll then spook the herd, than to get a shot at the herd bull.

Far more vulnerable than the herd bull are smaller bulls working around the herd's fringes. They haven't any assistants helping them out, and their minds are more likely figuring how to steal a cow from the herd bull than how to avoid an approaching hunter.

Which brings us to another point: Suppose you are slipping quietly along through a forest rich with recent elk sign. Suddenly, a crashing erupts just out of sight before you. What will you do? Unless you are an experienced elk hunter, you'll stop in surprise. Then, when you overcome your initial surprise, you'll continue your stalk, perhaps doubling your caution.

Wrong! The elk have just left the area.

If you are an Eastern whitetail hunter, you're unprepared. Though the same thing has no doubt happened to you many times before, you've seldom heard the wily buck, as that nimble-footed, delicate animal slips away at your approach. Not so with elk. Because they are four times the size of whitetails and have herd instincts, they really don't care a whit how much noise they make in hasty retreat.

The best thing you could've done when the noise erupted before you—in fact, the *only* thing you could've done—was to dash forward quickly. I've used this method to run into a herd of feeding elk that were staring in wonder after their fleeing counterparts who'd just spotted me. A wasted moment or two, and the herd would've identified me and been gone.

The flagging tail of a whitetail deer is an eye catcher, but so is the buckskin-colored rump of a retreating elk.

A cow elk's gestation period is a couple of months longer than a whitehead's—hence, the bull's earlier rut. At any rate, September is a more pleasant time than November to hunt in our Montana mountains.

Whitetail bucks and bull elk are canny critters with many of the same habits and instincts. Both represent the ultimate in American hunting challenge, trophy, and tradition. Learn to hunt one, and you've learned to hunt the other.

The Buck At The Secret Crossing

By Archibald Rutledge

The author of this classic tale of old-fashioned deer hunting with hounds was then South Carolina's Poet Laureate. It originally appeared in *Outdoor Life* in March 1965.

There are many standard deer crossings on my South Carolina plantation. These do not differ from those in any other state, regardless of the differences in the topography of the land. Once I asked an old backwoodsman why deer persist in running these same crossings year after year. "That's easy," he answered. "They want to get from here to yon, and they knows the best way."

Wherever a man hunts whitetail deer, I believe he will find that this splendid animal's crossings are of two kinds: crossings used by all deer, and those preferred by bucks. These latter stands are usually secret and in unexpected places, though at one of them a buck may just fool a hunter by coming straight at him. This always makes for a difficult and disconcerting shot. I believe that the two hardest shots at any deer are the head-on shot and the straightaway one.

As a rule, however, a buck circles in a drive, and if he comes out at all, he sidles out. I once had a grand old stag pass me in a wide arc and then skulk around in a dense cornfield. Beyond the field was a road, and beyond that a huge stretch of wildwoods. The buck's natural run would have been straight over the road and then into that dense forest. But he didn't do that. He kept circling back

toward me. I thought I knew what that wise old boy had in mind. He was doubling back in order to cross a river nearby. I intercepted him on a typical buck stand. A stander on the road would have been at an obvious crossing, but no wary buck would have done anything so lacking in craft as to have run that way.

Before I tell about the buck that is really the subject of this story, let me say a word about deer and roads. In the shadowy hours of twilight and early dawn, as well as in the dark of night, deer love to loaf along old roads. It has been my experience that deer, and bucks especially, prefer to roam in open places in the darkness. In the case of the buck, perhaps this is because of his horns. Incidentally, I once knew a man who ran down a buck that had been only slightly wounded. The buck carried a tremendous rack, though he had only a

Photo by Kathy Etling

At any secret crossing anywhere, the hunter should be slightly elevated so he can see what's coming his way. A buck is all too likely to slip by a man who stands in a depression.

medium-size body. The man seemed to think that the weight of the antlers wore the buck down. Such a supposition is by no means unreasonable.

It was in that very same drive that another thing happened. I knew of a secret buck crossing in a wild stretch of country. I doubt if anyone else knew of it, though years ago it was a favorite of one of my sons—a boy I lost in World War II. For reasons you will understand, I had not cared to go there for a long time.

But shortly before Christmas in 1956, I stationed my eldest son on this crossing. He hadn't killed a buck in two years, and I was eager to have him get one. He's an experienced deer hunter, and when I placed him on the crossing, he was skeptical.

"Has a deer ever run here since the Revolution?" he asked.

"Wait and see," I told him.

In my county, which is only about seven miles from the ocean, we have no real hills, but we do have elevations of considerable height. It was at the top of one of these that I posted my son. He looked so dubious about the place that I wasn't sure he would stay there. There were a lot of other crossings covering the head of that drive. He knew them, and I realized he might decide to change his stand.

"Hold this place, son," I said as I turned to leave him. "Try it this once, and see what happens."

Then I went to cover another crossing down in a swamp 300 yards away.

The place where I left my son was at the juncture of an old road and an old dirt bank—both permanent features of the landscape. Every deer hunter should remember that, though deer know the forest better than he does, they usually steer their course by big trees, tar kilns, charcoal hearths, ancient animal trails, and even by huge rocks that have marked certain locations from time immemorial.

I know a famous crossing called Saddle Oak. It's an ancient post oak with a deep crook near the base which resembles the seat of a saddle. To this tree, not to thousands of others around it, countless generations of deer have run. It is on one side of the famous Turkey Roost Drive, and it's one of my favorite buck stands. Over the years, I have killed seven bucks at that crossing. In my long and misspent life I have killed 283 bucks; but it must be remembered that in my early life there were no bag limits, and also that, to this day, my state of South Carolina has no bag limit on deer in some of its counties, and a high five-bucks-a-season limit in its county where I live.

Before my son's stand was a rather steep declivity overgrown with dense bushes that grew taller at the bottom than at the top. In the low thicket, a deer could hardly be seen before he was within gunshot range, but as he mounted the hill toward the old road, he would have to break cover.

This crossing might seem a difficult one to handle, but then, any crossing is if you don't know

how. I had advised my son to stand on top of the old bank and to the right of the deer's run. That would give him a left-hand shot, but he shoots equally well from either shoulder. The advantage lay in the rise, since at any crossing anywhere the hunter should be slightly elevated so he can see what's coming his way. A buck is likely to slip by a man who stands in a depression.

It was warm that morning and, fortunately, very still. I say fortunately because stillness is perhaps the greatest advantage a deer hunter can have. On a windy day, game is skittish and hunters are skittish. There are so many noises that deer sounds cannot be detected or distinguished. But if the day is still, the hunter can use his ears as well as his eyes. So far as I'm concerned, I can take cold, rain, and snow while hunting, but wind drives me crazy. I'd rather stay at home.

This particular morning was made for deer hunting. In addition to my eldest son and namesake, I had with me my youngest son, now a lawyer in Maryland, and one of my grandsons, aged 12. As a rule, I have many friends hunting with me, but for some reason, this particular hunt was a family affair.

The drivers went back almost a mile to the Santee River, faced about, and then came toward us, whooping, yelling, and beating clubs against trees. For half an hour there was nothing in their approach to indicate they had started after a deer. Yet they were driving a long-deserted plantation, little hunted, and in perfect deer country.

For some reason, deer hunters who do not live in the South often regard with some scorn our use of the shotgun and the hound. Yet our way of hunting is akin to the ancient English and European custom. It is both safer and more exciting than ordinary stalking.

I have hunted deer with a rifle in the snowy mountains of West Virginia, Maryland, Virginia, and Pennsylvania. Frankly, I didn't like it. Aside from the bitter cold, I didn't care for the multitude of hunters, the constant whine of high-powered rifles, and the way in which everyone—men, women, and children—took to the woods. Nor did I like the way four hunters tried to take from me a buck I had killed. There is an ancient fraternity among woodsmen—almost a kind of sacred bond between brothers—that should forever prevent disgraceful performances of this kind.

Earlier I mentioned an old buck that circled me on a wide arc. Though that buck was far out of sight and hearing, I could tell approximately where he was by the position of my two hounds, Jeff and Southwind. The exact position of a fleeing deer, however, can't be told with certainty since a deer usually runs several hundred yards ahead of the hounds, and sometimes as much as half a mile. For example, the dogs may be heading away from you at full speed, and before they make the turn that will tell you what is happening, the buck, having doubled back, may be right beside you. When I hunt deer with inexperienced hunters, I have the hardest time convincing them that, while it is well to listen to the hounds, the deer is not where the dogs are.

Whether you hunt with hounds or without them, it is astonishing how many bucks slip past watchers on crossings. All of us must pay tribute to a buck for being able to leave his bed, steal along within easy range of a stander, and get by without being seen or heard. On the other hand, I have had a doe or a yearling nearly scare me to death by exploding out of a thicket. Delicacy of maneuver is supposed to be feminine trait, but when it comes to the white-tail deer, the buck has this quality to a supreme degree.

An hour after my son and I had stationed ourselves at our crossings, I heard Jeff trailing about half a mile away. I may be wrong, but I've always felt that, given the option of trailing a buck or a doe, the hound would always choose the buck. I once had a hound that would never run anything but a buck. The scents of buck and doe, of course, are different. In fact, I believe that every individual deer has its own aura. How else does one particular deer find another particular deer?

If old Jeff should come on the tracks of a brontosaurus, imbedded in mud that turned to rock about 2,000,000 years ago, he will not take the trail. But if an old buck has walked anywhere in the vicinity during the previous eight or ten hours, especially if trailing conditions are good, he'll take notice at once and advance. And as the trail gets warmer, he'll tell the world, and especially me, that an old stag is wandering, nearby.

Few things in nature are so amazing and mysterious as the sorcery of the trailing hound. My long observation leads me to believe that no dog of any kind pays any attention to any track. The scent is the whole thing. A whitetail, of course, leaves two scents. One is laid on the ground by the glands between the hoofs, and the other is deposited on bushes by glands inside the back knees. These glands are surrounded by heavy projecting tufts of hair. I have long thought that the purpose of these tufts is to transfer the scent from the glands to bushes which the deer brushes in passing.

It might be thought that a hound will run directly after a deer, literally following his track. But since a deer is often a long way ahead, the hound may run wide of the exact direction the deer has taken. The dog picks up the scent in the wind, and by the time he reaches a certain spot, such as a road, the scent will have drifted far to the right or left. I have known a good hound, in full cry, to cross a road 100 yards from where the deer had crossed.

It has always seemed to me that the glands inside a deer's back knees give off a stronger scent than those between his hoofs. A really good hound works on the bushes, as if he knew where the strong scent was to be found.

In the country before my son and me, the brush was so dense we couldn't see the hounds. But they were coming fast for us—Jeff and Thunderbird, Music and Southwind. As I've said before, you can rarely tell the exact location of a deer by listening to the hounds. They may be half a mile back and off to your right, while the buck is passing you on your left within easy range. A stander has to be silent and alert.

I was standing in a swampy area, and my son was on the elevated bank above me, and to my left.

Suddenly, in the thicket of water oaks in front of me, I heard a deer crack the brush. The foliage was so thick I couldn't tell just where he was. Almost immediately, though, I heard my son shoot twice.

The hounds swept by me on the trail, passed my son, and kept on going. I didn't like that, since they were headed for the broad reaches of the river a mile away. My driver came up running; so did my youngest son and my grandson. For a dismayed moment, all we could do was listen to the retreating hounds.

"He's turned," I told the boys, as the hounds began to make a wide circle. "I don't believe he can make it to the river."

All of us broke into a run. My driver, with unerring instinct, seemed to anticipate where the buck and the hounds were headed. He vanished into the thicket ahead of us. Then there was silence as the hounds stopped running.

We found the buck near a little pond, dead where he had fallen. He had run about half a mile from where he'd been shot.

His body was only medium-size, his coat was very dark, and he had a rugged, wildwood look. But his antlers amazed me.

Ever since early boyhood I have been a nut about deer horns. I used to collect them, and I would travel miles to examine a reputedly fine pair. I have seen thousands, but none like these.

In conformation, they are normal. They have eight points, and they spread only 18 inches. But in color they are almost black. The circumference of the beams at the bases is eight inches (an American record, I believe). The beading is the heaviest I have ever seen, extending almost to the tips of all the tines. This great rack has an indefinable ruggedness and majesty, taking one back in imagination to pioneer days. Old deer hunters out of the swamps and backwoods have traveled far to see these remarkable horns.

When I first got a good look at this buck, I thought he must be a stranger (a few bucks were imported here from Michigan). But the fact that he ran to that secret crossing convinces me that he was born right here. His horns make the kind of trophy few men ever have the good fortune to bring home, even in a lifetime of hunting.

PART 2

HUNTING WHITETAIL DEER

Wilderness Whitetails

By John H. Williams

Back in the early 1970s, I was chasing whitetails in Michigan's Ontonagon County. As I pulled into a restaurant late one evening, a car pulled in beside me. I got out and stared in disbelief at the two bucks draped across the hood. They were huge by anyone's standards. Two of the most beautiful ten-point racks I'd ever seen. What struck me as utterly amazing was the fact that, as I later found out, they had both been taken from the same stand, with the hunters standing in essentially the same spot; one in the morning, the other that afternoon!

Having dropped his deer first, the gentleman whose car it was had suggested to his wife that she sit on his stand. Because she'd had no activity on hers and he had seen several other deer, she agreed. As though repeating the previous scene in every detail, an almost-identical buck had wandered down the same runway within minutes of her arrival on the stand.

After congratulating the happy couple, I passed off the whole affair as nothing more than mere chance and put it out of my mind, or at least I tried to. But it just kept nagging at me. How was it that in all that wide expanse of country, those two bucks were found in such close proximity? It was only several years later, after I had gained much more insight into wilderness whitetails, that I realized this event represented a lot more than mere happenstance. Those bucks were tagged in precisely that manner for some very basic reasons, and if I could figure out why, I'd undoubtedly be much more successful in my own hunting efforts.

36

Ontonagon County, in Michigan's Upper Penin-sula, is about as wild and remote as any piece of real estate you'll find in whitetail country. Some-what less than one-half of its more than 750,000 acres lie in a state park and a national forest. By far, the majority of the county is a tractless expanse. There are a great many square miles where no mo-torized vehicles (ATVs included) can penetrate its denseness. There are a good many miles of its in-terior that never see a hunter year in and year out. The few local hunters there fare pretty well, but success rates among non-locals are quite low.

The terrain in Ontonagon County varies from the ruggedness of the Porcupine Mountains in the ex-treme north, along the Lake Superior shoreline, to a flat or gently rolling landscape in the south. The habitat varies from solid stands of mature mast-bearing hardwoods that tower to 80 feet, to hemlock swamps so dense that even sunlight has difficulty working its way through. There are tag alder swales that defy hunter penetration, and clearcuts that once sported poplar and birch and will again in just a few years' time.

There's one other thing about Ontonagon County (and remote wilderness areas like it)—it is big-buck country. Deer densities are invariably low, about seven to nine per square mile over most of the range. But there are also very few hunters. Those who do hunt here do so because of the aura of the countryside, as well as a very realistic hope of tag-ging the buck of a lifetime.

How do you narrow down a wilderness area to huntable proportions? Unless you're quite familiar with wilderness regions, understand the habitat, and are knowledgeable regarding the biological needs of whitetails, that's a might difficult but cru-cial question to answer. We'll certainly be off to a very solid beginning, however, by first realizing that all that vastness in any wilderness area is not cre-ated equally.

I remember well the frustration that I experienced the first several years I hunted Michigan's remote Upper Peninsula. I wandered for miles, seeing little sign and even fewer deer. I was overwhelmed by the immensity of the land and the habitat. Not hav-ing an experienced wilderness hunter to give me directions, I was forced to slowly learn the ways of these whitetails on my own. It took me five years to tag my first U.P. buck, but I learned a lot about them during that time, and now the sightings are much more common and the opportunities more frequent. Here are a few of the things I've learned over the years.

First, take a good hard look at any wilderness area and you will soon see that, both in the small scale and over large spaces, the habitat is rarely uniform. The cover along a creek bed, for example, is much different from that along a ridge. The mixed woods are vastly different from the cedars down in the bottoms. The oak thicket varies greatly from the midgrasses.

In addition, within each area the habitat is vastly

Photo by Mark Wilson

The key to hunting wilderness whitetails is understanding the ways of the deer relative to their environment at the time you are hunting.

different at various times of the year. When they drop their mast crop, mature hardwoods serve as strong whitetail magnets. At times, as much as 50 percent of a whitetail's diet will consist of acorns if and when they're available. But these same hardwoods offer precious little at any other time of the year. Due to the total absence of any understory growth, there's neither food nor shelter there for the greater part of the year. Therefore, very few whitetails will frequent the area.

The cedar/balsam, hemlock, and spruce/balsam swamps of the North are what allow whitetails to survive the extreme harshness of winter. The cedar is the only known tree in these areas that can completely fulfill the whitetail's winter needs, both nutritionally and as protection from the elements. Yet the cedar, though critical to winter survival, is practically ignored throughout the rest of the year.

More than anything else, it's the understanding of factors such as these and their effects upon deer that separates successful from unsuccessful nimrods afield in wilderness areas. Though it's vital to know where the deer are most likely to be, the chief benefit to this type of thinking is in how much area it can eliminate from consideration. The vast, sprawling wilderness effectively becomes much smaller. The real key to wilderness whitetails is, then, an understanding of their ways relative to their environment at that point in time. Literally, what you must force yourself to do is see the trees rather than the forest. You must mentally dissect the habitat and then work the most productive areas.

That was precisely what I did to tag a nice buck a few years ago. It was the latter part of the season and the snows were already beginning to pile up, and though I knew it was too soon for the deer to be yarded up, I also knew they'd be moving into close proximity of the cedars in the area. While bird hunting a month earlier, I had seen a lot of sign in and around the hardwood ridges in the area.

The mast was gone, and because there was no browse whatsoever in the hardwoods, I knew that the deer had moved on. Their yarding area was an immense concentration of bogs and cedars four miles or so to the east. In between and along the western fringe of the swamps were thickets of lowland willows. This is a favorite whitetail food, so it was there that I headed.

Almost at first light, I knew I'd hit paydirt. Fresh tracks crisscrossed the willows everywhere, and late that morning my hunt ended when I connected with a nice six-pointer. You must learn to read the habitat.

Monocultural areas never sustain large whitetail populations, whether we're discussing a large Southern pine plantation, a mature climax forest in West Virginia, or a rolling prairie in South Dakota. Such uniformity cannot meet a whitetail's basic survival needs.

I've never hunted whitetails anywhere—nor have I ever heard of an area—where habitat variation didn't produce a great many more deer. I eagerly

seek out areas with a lot of edge. Avoid unbroken forested regions, whether they're mixed or not. A great many of the more desirable foods of the whitetail are intolerant of shade and grow only in open or semi-open areas. It is precisely this that makes clearcuts and natural meadows strong attractants.

Ontonagon County provides a good case in point. The data compiled by the Michigan Department of Natural Resources can be misleading (not intentionally so; it's simply a question of the DNR's needs as compared with a hunter's). The information compiled is given on a county-wide or even region-wide basis. According to the data, the average deer density is seven to nine deer per square mile. In point of fact, there are huge areas of Ontonagon that probably don't support two deer per square mile. There are other, much smaller areas that may support 30 or 40 deer per square mile at certain times of the year. In fact, throughout the winter months there are areas within the hemlocks where you'll have several hundred deer per square mile!

The areas with the highest deer densities will be those areas with plenty of brush, a good age mix to the timber, sufficient hemlocks to winter the herd, and plenty of openings. They'll also have a water source nearby, and they'll be in the more southerly portion of the county, away from the deep snows and high, brutal winter winds that typically come off Lake Superior.

A key is also to know the whitetails' favorite foods. Biologists rank the whitetails' food sources according to primary and secondary foods. Primary foods are those most preferred, sought after, and nutritious. Secondary foods are sought out only when primary sources are depleted, and they are generally nutritionally inadequate as well. For example, in the Midwest these are preferred foods in the northern forest regions: white cedar, white pine, jack pine, red osier (dogwood), birch, hemlock, and various maples, willows, viburnums, poplars, and sumacs. Areas deficient in these vegetation types will support fewer deer.

In addition, besides the essential browse plants, there should be an adequate amount of summer grazing and forage foodstuffs. This category includes various fruits, forbs, mushrooms, and grasses, as well as the greenery grown by shrubs and saplings. These foods are important—both in quality and quantity—to fatten the deer so that they enter the harsh snow period in optimal condition.

Can you go out, right now, into the areas where you hunt and identify what the deer are feeding on? Can you list four or five of the whitetails' preferred foods in your hunting area? A great many, perhaps most, hunters cannot. If you can't, then you're fighting against the deer-hunting odds all the way. Turn things around. As a deer hunter, your biggest challenge is to make every facet of the whitetails' life cycle work for you. Learn the deer's food preferences and how to identify each one, and stack the deer-hunting odds in your favor.

Photo by John Weiss

Can you go out into the areas you hunt and identify what the deer are feeding on? If you cannot, you're fighting against the deer-hunting odds all the way.

Practically every DNR agency in the country publishes lists and brochures describing, in some detail, the deer's preferred foods in that area. Take advantage of this information. Even if no such lists are published by your state agency, the area biologist is a ready source of such information and will eagerly assist you.

Knowing the limiting factor in the immediate environment in which you are hunting will also help you narrow down a huntable area. A limiting factor is whatever parameter in that environment most effectively controls the size of the deer herd. What we're most interested in identifying are those factors over which we have some sort of control. Once identified, they can then either be sought out or avoided, depending on their influence.

For example, throughout the extreme northern portion of the whitetails' range—wherever deer must yard up to survive the winters—cedar, hemlock, spruce, and balsam are crucial. Snow depths, on the level outside these swamps and lowlands, may reach six to eight feet or more. When this occurs, there can be unlimited browse just 100 yards outside the swamps, and it won't do the deer one

bit of good. It might just as well be on the moon. With snows of such depths, the deer cannot reach outside their swamps, and if the food supply inside falls short, they'll perish.

Whenever snow depths are this great, these retreats become the limiting factor in the environment. There's no other habitat type where the deer can successfully winter. Therefore, large expanses of the extreme north that lack such cover, or areas in which such cover is too mature to offer adequate browse, should be avoided (although hunting within the swamps themselves is normally not very productive in a true wilderness area). This is true no matter how perfect the rest of the habitat is in that area.

You can have an area perfect in every way but for the one critical element that will determine the upper limit of the deer population; know what that element is in your hunting area, and you will be way ahead of the game. It may be free-standing water or prickly pear cactus, as in the Southwest; it may be the number of free-grazing cattle and, consequently, the amount of brush along the creek beds, as in the Northern plains. But whatever it is, you should be aware of it and should plan your hunt accordingly.

The maturation and succession of habitat—whether helped by man's hand or not—is an insidious thing. It never stops, and it's generally so slow and subtle that we're not even aware of it. But change it does, and when that change is maturation, it's almost never good for deer. Those hardwoods that were 20 years old when you took your first buck may now be 60 years old. The poplar thicket is now a poplar forest with its canopy 40 feet above the open ground below. The planted pines that had provided both food and cover to those deer all those many years ago are now completely open to a height of 20 feet.

With changes such as these occurring in the habitat, the DNR generally pushes for the thinning of the herd, in order to ease it into the increasing constraints of the environment and to prevent the needless starvation of the herd that surely would otherwise follow. Regardless of whether or not doe permits are issued, herds in maturing habitats are going to decline, and that's a fact we cannot change.

It's much easier to target a specific entity for our frustrations—the DNR and the culling of does, for example—than to deal with, or even be aware of, the nebulous, changing complexity of the habitat. But it doesn't do the deer any good, and the rift caused between hunters and the DNR doesn't do any of us any good, either. The rule is simple enough: For improved deer hunting, avoid maturity in any habitat. A corollary to this thought is that it's highly unlikely that one area, over a prolonged period of time, is going to offer the best hunting you can find.

As habitat in one area matures and deer-hunting quality declines, other areas can be timbered, burned, or grazed. Too many of us become complacent and hunt the same places year after year, without regard to the changes that surround us. The most successful hunters are going to be those who adjust to a maturing environment. If, for whatever reason, you do need to hunt in an area that is too mature to be optimal, then search out the naturally occurring edge areas: natural glades, openings around swamps, lake shores, and creek and river beds. You'll find improved food sources in such areas and hence increased deer usage.

One of the most productive counties in all of Michigan is Dickinson County, again in the Upper Peninsula. Dickinson is remote, with a very low human population. It has few roads and is covered with a good mix of habitat types and ages. There's a very active timber-pulp industry, which assures an excellent supply of browse as well as lush forest openings for a wide array of soft plant types. Deer populations, as a result, are very high. To increase your deer-hunting odds, such areas should be sought out, no matter where you hunt. Remember, the critical height for deer browse is less than 6 feet; deer simply cannot reach anything higher than that.

In snowbound areas, the browse ideally should be between 2 and 6 feet high.

After you've narrowed down your hunting area and you feel confident that deer are working that area, how do you best hunt it? Depending on the area itself, the number of deer working it, and your own preferences and abilities, any of the traditional approaches can and will work, provided you employ them in the proper manner and at the proper times.

Before delving into actual hunting strategies, I think it's important to discuss a couple of other points worth mentioning.

Some runways, from a hunter's point of view, are surefire winners and should be hunted heavily, but others are meaningless and should seldom, if ever, be hunted—it's important to know which is which. Runways in cedar swamps, in wilderness areas where there are few hunters per square mile, are the result of massive winter use. There are few deer in these areas until after the snows pile up, so hunting there is futile. (This is not true in rural areas where there is heavy hunting pressure. In these areas, the cedars are often very productive as the deer seek shelter and isolation.) Deer feeding in open areas—hardwoods with no understory, for example, or in abandoned orchards—wander at will, so runways traversing these areas are not of importance when the deer are feeding there.

Other runways may be your only chance to score. I've hunted brush-choked areas in northern Michigan and southern Texas that were so dense that there was no way through them except on runways. When the deer are in these areas, the runways are heavily used, and they should be hunted. Runways around boggy-ground areas are sure bets as well. Whenever traveling around watercourses or marshy areas, the deer use runways, and you should be watching them.

By far, the majority of wilderness areas are managed as multiple-use lands. Frequently in the western states, they're used as open rangelands, and generally throughout forested regions they are managed primarily for their timber products. As a result of this approach, the habitat is rarely ideal for whitetails; deer populations, though healthy, are seldom high. (The nice thing about such circumstances is that buck/doe ratios are invariably high, and although you won't see a lot of deer, your chances of seeing a buck are excellent.) Persistence thus becomes a cornerstone to deer-hunting success.

The most successful wilderness deer hunter I've ever known was a gentleman who hunted in my father's hunting group for many years. Every year, Tracy got his buck—every year, that is, for more than 30 years! The secret to Tracy's success? He made arrangements to hunt the entire season every year (if that's what it took), and he never left the woods from daylight to dark, day after day.

Very often in farmland and rural hunting situations, the buck kill is extremely high, and most are claimed relatively early in the season. In my home state of Michigan, for example, more than 80 percent of the legal bucks in southern Michigan are taken each year, and fully one-third of these fall on opening day. Clearly, if you don't score early, the odds are increasingly stacked against you. This is not the case in wilderness areas, where only a low percentage of the herd's bucks are taken; your odds at the tag end of the season are essentially the same as they were in the beginning. The bottom line, then, is to hunt deer whenever and for as long as you can.

If your time afield is limited and you must pick and choose when to hunt, then at least try to have it coincide with changing weather patterns. In the event of rain and/or high winds, try hunting immediately before and after such fronts. In the event of snow, particularly the first heavy snow of the year, hunt both during and immediately following the storm itself. A lot of hunters leave the field during major snowstorms, but it has been my experience that the height of the storm is when I'm most likely to connect.

Contrary to popular opinion, deer drives can be very successful in wilderness areas, but the key lies in hand-picking those areas to be driven. Generally, these drives work best with just two or three hunters. Once harassed, hounded, or stirred up, whitetails are quite likely to vacate an area, but if this has not occurred, they're far more likely to simply skulk about within the cover in which they're found. With as few as two hunters, you can then post one and have the other move about slowly and quietly.

For the moving hunter, this should be nothing more than a stillhunting exercise. Beginning deep within the cover, the hunter should start stillhunting in ever-increasing circles. If he begins on one edge, the hunter should start casting back and forth slowly as he advances through the cover. In either case, the posted hunter should be overlooking a well-used runway or runways.

A technique I've employed on many occasions is excellent whenever the cover is in the form of bands or strips, such as along creek beds or hillsides. The hunter who is going to post-up goes on ahead for 300 to 400 yards. While advancing, he stays well back from the cover to be hunted, and he moves quietly downwind or crosswind. When he reaches a predetermined location, he settles into the cover itself, overlooking a run and at least on one of the edges. Once a certain amount of time has elapsed, the other hunter or hunters advance, again quietly and slowly. The hunters can take turns, switch roles, and move forward again. Very often, it's the moving hunter in this type of drive who sees the game. Drives such as these can be effective at any time of the day, but they frequently work best early and late, when the deer are more prone to be moving on their own. When executing middle-of-the-day drives, be sure to do so through known or likely bedding areas.

For those having the skill and patience, stillhunting is highly productive in wilderness areas. It allows the hunter to continue important observations of his area while actually hunting at the same time. Any shifts in deer activity or any areas of deer concentration missed in pre-season scouting are far more likely to be picked up by a stillhunter than by a hunter on stand.

Whitetails in wilderness areas are generally far less spooky initially than whitetails closer to human populations. A good stillhunter will often be able to stalk within easy range of these animals without spooking them. Concentrate your efforts more on known feeding areas or areas between feeding and bedding sites early and late in the day. During midday, hunt resting areas in the hope of catching the deer feeding within the cover. It's unlikely that you'll successfully roust deer from their beds and get a decent shot.

Wilderness areas are rarely hunted hard, and for this reason, these deer do not normally head for the really heavy cover as other whitetails do. It's best to hunt the edges of dense cover and avoid the jungles themselves. If you have reason to believe that a big buck is sticking to the heavy cover, then hunt the runways in these areas.

Provided that the hunter selects his stand in those areas we've already discussed as having the greatest potential, stand-hunting is probably the most successful approach to pursuing wilderness whitetails. Because these deer encounter so little human intrusion, they are far less nocturnal than a lot of their non-wilderness brethren. They are, therefore, more active during daylight hours, browsing later and beginning routine evening activities earlier in the day. It is not uncommon for them to move freely to watering areas and feed quite placidly even in the middle of the day.

Good stand selections are those overlooking feeding areas and along runways on the edges of bedding areas. Several stand sites should be selected. And never hunt the same stand on consecutive days. This helps avoid the buildup of human odor in the area (nothing spooks wilderness whitetails quicker). If you hunt in a state where the season coincides with the rut, stands on runways near feeding areas can be expected to produce at any time of the day.

I'm a great believer in hunting all day, every day, no matter where I hunt. But when hunting wilderness whitetails, I simply refuse to leave the woods. Research has shown whitetails to be far more diurnal than previously thought, and this is particularly true in remote areas.

Dress comfortably for your area, narrow the vast expanse of your immediate area down to manageable size, and place yourself in the most advantageous spot you can. Carry a snack or lunch and hunt the whole day through, and you'll find that solving the riddle of wilderness whitetails is really not that difficult.

Track A Buck— Step-By-Step

By Jeff Murray

The two of us were fast onto a big buck's track, and the drama should have been mounting like the last page of a suspense novel. It wasn't, at least for me.

To be perfectly honest, I was pretty darn nonchalant about tracking down a buck. I mean, who really depends on this method to get a deer? Sure, it's nice to follow a fresh set of tracks in the woods after a new snowfall, see what the deer have been doing, and snoop around where they used to be. But by the time you get close enough for a glimpse, much less a decent shot, they'll be long gone. Big bucks, as the overworked cliché goes, didn't get that way by being dumb. Right?

"Shh!"

Noble Carlson, my tracking mentor, stopped dead in his tracks to emphasize his warning that it was a good time to be quiet and alert. His blue, Scandinavian eyes glowered beneath bristling, bleached-orange eyebrows.

"Murray, how am I ever going to make a tracker out of you?"

I did not respond. What could I say? Moments earlier, we had been half-trotting right on top of a deer trail. Why, Noble himself had snapped three twigs. I'd heard them easily (and I was counting). Now, he was yapping at me to be totally silent. Tracking deer, Noble Carlson-style, is weird.

This buck is a keeper in anyone's book. Noble Carson's ten-pointer weighed 240—dressed!

Wait a minute—what was I thinking? This was no silly safari I was on with some crazy bush-pilot guide. This was Noble Carlson, a man who had already shot four bucks that fall—all by tracking—and more than 100 from seasons past. (This is legal in Minnesota, where party hunting is permitted.) This was a guy who never made outlandish statements about anything in the outdoors unless he could back it up. If anyone could "track a buck," it would be Noble Carlson.

Still, the gnawing feeling that it might not happen with me around kept tugging at me. After all, I was two steps behind him, not a two-hour drive away.

"That buzzard," he said. "I'm starting to get mad."

"What . . . why?" I questioned.

He flicked the barrel of his Model 722 Remington through the snow in disgust. Next to the little depression he made was a fresh deer bed. We'd just spooked it out ahead of us. Just as I thought it would go.

"He must have heard me shush you, Murray. How am I going to make a tracker out of you?"

Under normal circumstances, Noble would leave the buck alone and try to cut another fresh buck track. From nearly 30 years of tracking whitetails, he has learned that it is usually futile to try to stay on top of a spooked buck; it'll just outrun you. But this time, circumstances were a bit different. Instead, he knelt down and sized up the bed. As he looked northward, he asked me how badly I wanted the buck.

As a devout stand hunter, I've seen many a day when the deer weren't moving. If I could track bucks on those off days, I could be a lot more effective . . . .

"Look," he said, reading my mind, "I know you aren't even sure whether this was a buck or a doe. But I know. Get a sniff of this."

He tossed me chunks of snow that were stained yellow from the hock gland where the buck had lain. It was rancid. It was musky—all male. I was convinced.

"He's a trophy buck . . . by your standards," Noble teased, referring to a comment I had made earlier. I had said that any deer with ten points and thick beams would make "my" record book. "Look at the width of the track. See how deeply it penetrates the snow? And the tips are rounded off pretty good. No young buck has round tips like these.

"If you want to go for it, I can guarantee at least a 50/50 shot at him, but you have to do exactly what I say."

Guarantee? Gads, there he goes again.

"Whatever you say, Nobes."

The previous night, on his kitchen table, he had scratched out his basic strategy on the back of a Hershey-bar wrapper. He had told me how important it was to read the tracks and make the correct reaction to what the buck was doing. It sounded so simple. When the buck ran, we were going to run.

When it slowed down, we were to do the same. Finally, when the buck left signs that it was about to bed down or, better yet, was feeding between bedding stints, we would be in a good position to sneak up on it from an inconspicuous angle.

I remember the anxiety I had about the prospects of having to take a good shot at a running animal, something with which I hadn't had a great deal of experience or success. But Noble said that it was nothing to be concerned about.

"Of all the bucks I've tracked down," he told me, "I'd bet that more than 90 percent never saw me or knew what hit them."

Another fear I had was the one that must plague all hunters who give tracking even a feeble try: How do you know whether the deer is a mile away or just over the next hill? Again, Noble had a reassuring explanation with plenty of experience from which to draw.

"You can boil it all down to two things," he began. "First, when that buck is on a runway, he's moving, looking for company—you know, a hot doe. Otherwise, he'd be off on his own, looking for a safe place to feed or bed down. So, when he's on a trail, you've got to work to keep up with him. And you can't keep up if you're worrying about being quiet. Besides, it doesn't matter a lick because he's going to be way up ahead and will probably associate any noise on the trail, at this point, with that of another deer.

"And second, when his tracks start meandering—splitting off to the side here, straying over there—you know that he's slowed way down. When you get to tracks like these, you can't make a sound, and you can't be on the trail, either. If you are, you're dead, because he'll be spending more time watching his backtrail than watching where he's going."

Suddenly, this all began to click for me. We had jogged across the runway and slowed down when we saw the buck's track splinter off the main trail. We were just about to pull the final maneuver of getting off the tracks when we spooked the buck up ahead. Many hunters are proficient at getting on a fresh track, and some are even pretty good at distinguishing a buck's print from a doe's. But the reason why most of us fail, from Noble's point of view, is that we don't know how to handle what he calls the "end-around."

"When I told you that I'd teach you how to track up a buck, you probably had it in your head that we were going to sneak up on a deer in its track. That's how everyone thinks it's done. But I hardly ever walk up to a buck from his trail; he's too busy watching it for timber wolves and guys like you. No way.

"The trick is to dodge around and up ahead when you see him monkeying around, feeding, or looking for a place to bed down. While he's looking behind him, you'll be sneaking in from the side at an angle he won't be expecting. But you've got to be quiet and see him first."

As Noble points out, a buck's track will be wider and more blunt at the tip than a doe's.

From his bed, the buck had literally jumped the span of a mid-sized river. I marked it off at 20 paces between the prints in the snow. The bucks Nobel hunts are perhaps the biggest in the nation, averaging 225 to 240 pounds field-dressed. Northern Minnesota deer have to be big and tough or they won't survive the harsh winters and the relentless pursuit of wolf packs year-round.

We stayed on the trail for 100 yards before the tracks started to tighten up again.

"See here, Murray," Carlson said to me. "This is a good sign. Notice how he is already starting to slow down to a more normal pace? He couldn't have winded us."

That much I could understand. Countless times, deer I had jumped continued on with those loping, Olympic strides. Those are the deer to leave behind. But not this one. And he seemed intent on going in one direction, slicing northeastward across a northwest wind. Had he decided to circle around to wind us, we would have given up on this guy, too. No sense trailing an edgy buck when there are plenty of others much more vulnerable to Noble's system even in the area he hunts—in and along the edge of the Boundary Waters Canoe Area Wilderness, where the head count is often less than five deer to the square mile.

The buck carved a trail along a creek bed, pretty much in a straight line—no meandering, feeding, or bedding yet. Then we found a fresh rub at the edge of a clearing; thin wood shavings powdered the base of a 5-inch-thick cedar. A rush of adrenaline pumped through me. Only a heavy buck would take on a tree that thick.

It was time for another major lesson in tracking. After the buck had made that rub, he had waltzed right down the middle of the clearing, not along the edges as one would expect from a smart animal. It was time to make a decision. The right one would allow us to continue the game; a wrong one would end it then and there.

"What are we going to do now?" Noble asked. He was setting me up.

"Well, we have to keep up, don't we? The buck isn't showing any signs of letting up or anything."

"Not necessarily. This is one of their tricks that most guys blow it on." Noble bent down and drew a diagram in the snow, showing me how bucks like to pause on the opposite end of an opening so that they can watch their backtrack. "They do it all the time, especially when they're heading into the wind."

"So what do we do?" I asked.

"Every time a buck pulls this on you, there's only one thing to do: circle around the opening. Sometimes he'll be there, sometimes he'll continue on. Let's go see."

It took what seemed to me an awfully long time to skirt the edge. And, sure enough, the buck was nowhere to be found. But Noble was dead on. Tracks left behind told the story of a buck pausing in two places on the inside edge of the opening. I could easily imagine him looking over his shoulder, waiting for some dummy to walk through the clearing. Then he'd snort the wits out of his pursuer and dash off.

The trail continued on in a relatively straight path, coursing through open aspens and balsam thickets. Each time, we circled around the open stuff and snuck through the thickets. It was rough country with no roads, and I shuddered to think that Noble never wears a compass. He has such an uncanny sense of direction in the woods, with his built-in radar, that he has never been lost. But he would

never recommend that anyone go without a compass. Still, he gets a kick out of my insistence on carrying two of them when I hunt in that area.

Now the trail was joined by another set, and within 50 yards there were three different sets to unravel—another of my fears when attempting to track down a specific animal. This is a time for utmost caution, requiring attention to every detail. However, confusion sets in if the tracker doesn't keep sight of "the big picture," looking ahead to where the tracks are going. Of course, this is second nature to Noble because he surveys the country ahead more than he dotes over tracks.

By examining each set made over old beds and under some balsams, where the snow was shallower and the points more distinguishable, it was evident that a fawn and a doe had become part of the drama; an interesting footnote had emerged for another valuable lesson in tracking.

"Ah, the plot thickens," Noble whispered while bending over some droppings, and squishing one of them between his fingers. "They're still soft. And that little one is a fawn buck. He'll show us what's going on."

It made so sense at the moment, but it soon did. Over the next quarter mile, the three traveled together, with the smallest track occasionally darting off to one side. Each time that happened, Noble pointed it out as though it were something significant that I should know. Finally, I had to ask what it meant.

"The buck is chasing him off," he whispered. "But he keeps coming back to the doe. That tells me that the buck wants to jump the doe, but she isn't quite ready yet. The next time we circle around, we can get right on top of the buck. He's distracted. But we can't forget about the other two."

Our next end-around taught me another lesson. The fawn and the doe disappeared from the scene, and the buck started circling back toward our direction. Quickly, Noble changed his course, with me on his heels. We made a wide arc in the opposite direction of the buck's. Without any warning, the buck attempted to check his backtrail, and he almost caught us off guard. We were able to cover a lot of ground in a hurry without tipping him off. It's another "buck trick" that Noble has caught on to from years of tracking, and a counter-maneuver was needed to keep the chess game going.

Noble wears felt liners inside zippered rubber overshoes so that he can feel the landscape underfoot and avoid setting his weight in the wrong places. With these, he can nimbly roll forward as he walks. He made me promise to equip my feet likewise or he would refuse to enter the woods with me. "Otherwise, we'd just be wasting our time," he said.

We picked up the track again at the edge of a small meadow. We had crossed some older tracks on the way that would have sidetracked me if I were on my own. Fortunately, Noble has not only learned how to distinguish a buck's track from a doe's, but also how to differentiate one buck track from another. At first, to me, they all looked alike. Sure, there were big, medium, and small ones. But soon I was sure that his method of looking at the tips, the width (or thickness), and the arch of the spoor was indeed foolproof. But graduating to the point of telling individual bucks apart was a big step. The only confidence I had that we might be on the right track came from Noble's confidence. He took the time to reassure me.

"Your buck here isn't real old, but he's got pretty old, rounded hoofs. Maybe a five or six-year-old. Those others were only about three or four years old. They looked big, but their tips were much sharper and pointed. Besides, yours is missing a small chip out of his left front hoof. I'm surprised you haven't noticed it.

"How am I going to make a tracker out of you?"

By now it was snowing, with leaden skies to the west portending little relief. The tracks were beginning to fill in almost as fast as they were made. This is a time of both perfect and impossible tracking conditions. It's perfect for the tracker who has cut a fresh track and can stay on it because he can silently move in for the kill. It can be impossible at those times when your track gets intermingled with others; a two-day-old track and a brand-new one will both fill up and appear identical. When this happens, all you can do is wait for an hour or so and look for tracks again. The ones you'll be able to see will obviously be fresh because all of the others will be covered up.

Noble's all-time favorite situation for tracking down a big buck is during the season's first or second snowfall. He can "just about ride their backs" under these conditions. He's got four solid reasons. First, the deer haven't been pushed by wolves for seven or eight months. Second, hunters haven't pushed them by their tracks. Third, they won't go very far once it starts snowing heavily, so he doesn't have to cover much ground. And fourth, the deer think that they still blend in with their surroundings and are apt to stand around in fairly open patches when, in reality, they stick out in the snow.

"If a guy isn't tracking then," Noble said, "he's missing the closest thing he'll ever get to a sure bet on a buck."

Luckily, we didn't run any other tracks that afternoon. But the snow was getting so deep that it was hard to tell which way the buck was heading. At one point, he headed over a hill and veered around a beaver pond, making a little loop. Which way was he going? In a muffled voice, with his chopper over his lips, Noble explained an easy way to tell:

"I'll show you a little trick, Murray. See these little tufts of snow? They're kicked up by the buck's paws after he lifts them up and out of the snow. In deep snow, they always point in the direction the buck

is heading because they are pushed out in front of the track."

When we reached a small stream, I noticed how the skim ice was broken by the buck's fresh track while the rest of the stream remained frozen over. I pointed proudly to my observant discovery, and Noble immediately wrenched my head with his left paw, his eyes glowering again. He growled in his throat.

But it was too late.

The fresh bed, 60 yards away, meant only one thing: We had spooked the buck again. Ordinarily, the buck will give you a warning when he is about to bed down. He'll skip from one balsam or cedar or spruce to another, turning around while scenting and gazing over his backtrack. This time, he didn't.

"Damn, I saw it coming," Noble said in disgust. "When it snows heavily like this, sometimes they just go to a bed right away. He must've seen your movement."

The sun was less than one hour from setting, so it was too late to look for another track. From tracking in the area for many years, Noble knew where the buck might be headed—a knoll at the tip of a large tag alder swamp. It was the perfect place for a buck under hot pursuit to hide out, because any predator would announce its presence when it broke through the swamp and the buck could lay near the edge, winding the other side. If we could get there first . . . .

We took the side of the swamp opposite the one the buck took, and were squeezing around the outer edge when it happened. Like magic, we picked up the buck's trail, and I thought I saw where another deer had joined it from the west. Instead of continuing ahead or making a circle, Noble whirled around to the west with his gun up.

"Are you going to take him, or do I have to shoot your deer for you?"

I looked to the west and saw the buck standing with its nose up and ears back. He was looking over the trail he had just made. I don't remember pulling the trigger, much less taking aim. But somehow, the gun went off. And the deer bolted.

"You hit him!" Noble yelled.

He didn't go very far, probably less than 200 yards. The bullet had grazed the heart and punctured both lungs. His massive neck was swollen with the rut, and the base of his rack was as thick as my wrist, ten points strong. Noble flipped him over and brushed the snow off his front paws.

"Here's your buck, all right," he said with a bit of pride. "See the chip in the hoof?"

I glowed. But how did he do it? How did he know to look over to the west, where that tracked appeared to join in?

"That was another buck trick," Noble declared. "He doubled back down his track and stood off to the side of the trail. He was expecting us to be trailing behind."

It was one "buck trick" I'll never forget, along with all of the others.

Hunting The Dominant Buck

By John Weiss

Many deaf-mutes communicate by using sign language, and though whitetail deer are far from deaf, they frequently communicate by making rubs on trees and exhibiting certain body postures. To interpret these signs, however, a hunter must know their meanings in advance.

These thoughts flashed through my mind last year while I was on a tree stand. A handsome six-point buck was moving quietly toward me. As he drew closer, I sensed the deer was actually fleeing from some bully. The first tipoff was that his tail was clamped tightly against the backs of his legs, and confirmation came when I noticed recent scrapes and scratches on his flanks and shoulders. At that, I lowered by slug-loaded shotgun and allowed the frightened animal to continue to escape from what, to him, obviously had not been a very pleasant experience.

My hunch paid off. An hour later, the bully himself showed up, and it was clear why the first buck had chosen to make off. Judging by the size of his rack, this buck was at least a year older. He was also heavier, and he appeared to swagger in an arrogant manner.

As I began field-dressing the buck, one of my largest to date, I thought about the complex social lives deer live and how they silently communicate their rankings in the pecking order.

Antler rubs on saplings are among the commonly recognized signs of deer activity. Although easily identified for what they are, antler rubs are also, unquestionably, the least understood. For genera-

tions, many hunters have maintained that rubs indicate places where bucks have removed the velvet from their antlers and polished and sharpened the tines. Other hunters claim antler rubs are the first signs that the bucks are going into the rut. They say the animals spar with trees to strengthen their neck muscles in preparation for the inevitable fights with other male deer. Both ideas are dead wrong.

When a whitetail's maximum annual antler growth has been attained, the velvet dies, dries, and begins falling away in shreds largely of its own accord. On occasion, particularly when stringy remnants of the velvet obscure the deer's vision, a buck may hasten its removal by randomly thrashing his rack against a small bush. It's a brief happenstance with little or no significance to hunters. Once the velvet is gone, the main beams are already smooth and the tips of the tines are pointed. There is no need or instinctual desire whatsoever to hone or polish them.

Instead, rubs serve the very specific purpose of enabling each buck in the local deer population to establish a breeding territory. Whitetail bucks are not territorial, however. They don't make efforts to defend their home ranges and chase away other bucks. Because their ranges sometimes encompass several square miles and must necessarily be shared

Photo by Len Rue, Jr.

A whitetail buck anoints a branch with forehead-gland scent before making a rub. Rubs warn off other bucks.

by many other individuals, territorial defense would be virtually impossible.

Still, individuals of most animal species must indeed acquire a *space* in which they feel secure before any attempt at mating can occur. Additionally, the individual buck must reach a social status that prevents restrictions being placed on him by other members of the same species. When one individual is clearly dominant, subordinates in the same area may leave to find their own breeding places. If the buck ranks so low that there is no available place not already occupied by a superior animal, the low-ranking buck may become so psychologically castrated that he may refuse to attempt to breed, even if the opportunity presents itself. In many places where deer populations are at the maximum carrying capacity, this explains why button and spike bucks seldom impregnate does, even though they are capable of doing so.

Breeding success among whitetail bucks depends mostly on finding a place where the animal feels confident. It is only after the requirements of space and social status are met that a buck becomes mentally fit to reproduce. Paradoxically, therefore, breeding areas among whitetail bucks are usually well established as much as two months before scraping and doe-chasing actually gets under way.

There are several ways in which whitetail bucks sort out the matter of who's who. These include antler rubs and, during the rut, mutilated branches hanging over scrapes. Aside from serving as visual cues, both are also anointed with saliva and forehead-gland scent to reinforce each animal's attempt to delineate his breeding area. If these signs fail and there is an encounter, the bucks then display various other signals that include bluffing and posturing. Finally, if these don't resolve the issue, head-to-head combat follows. Contrary to what romanticists would have us believe, these "combats" are no more than brief pushing matches.

Biologists refer to tree rubbing as "signpost-marking," and there is a definite correlation between the size (diameter) of the trees the buck rubs and the ranking of the animal that makes them. Generally, thumbsize willows, tag alders, and small evergreens that have been rubbed are the work of juveniles—1½-year-old spike bucks and forkhorns.

Larger rubbed trees up to about 2½ inches in diameter usually indicate a 2½ to 3½-year-old buck. These are usually six- and eight-pointers with rather low, tight racks and slender beams and tines.

Rubbed cedars, pines, or smooth-barked hardwood saplings that are 3 to 4½ inches in diameter, and sometimes much larger, are favored by the largest deer with the best headgear. These bucks are usually at least 3½ years old and carry eight, ten, or 12-point racks. Of course, as the age of the deer increases, the width, height, and overall massiveness of the rack increases until the time later in life when the deer begins to decline in health and can no longer grow a bigger rack.

None of this, however, is so universal that it has been carved in stone. I once watched angrily while a huge buck tore up tiny Scotch pines on my Christmas-tree farm in southern Ohio. Once, I also saw a forkhorn working over the 20-inch girth of an old beech. Despite occasional exceptions to the rule, however, the diameter of rubbed trees is a very reliable indication of the age of the deer.

Although whitetails seem to examine a rubbed tree and equate its diameter with the social rank of the deer that made the rub, the important factor is recognizing and interpreting the forehead-gland scent worked into the exposed, moist cambium of the tree trunk itself. At the University of Georgia, prominent deer biologist Larry Marchington performed microscopic examinations of the forehead glands of whitetail bucks and came to the conclusion that there is a direct relationship between a buck's age and social status, and forehead-gland activity. As Marchington explained it: "The position of an adult male in the hierarchy is reflected in the level of activity of his forehead glands."

Whether the oldest and most dominant bucks instinctively rub larger trees to deposit greater quantities of forehead-gland scent is unknown, but it seems logical. In any event, the glandular secretions serve to contribute the buck's own individual scent to the rub.

There are numerous ways hunters can use this information. Because tree rubbing and the establishment of hierarchical rankings takes place well before scrapes begin dotting the landscape, the early-season hunter should focus his scouting on finding the largest-diameter rubbed trees. Be sure to investigate places where there are aromatic trees such as cedar, pine, spruce, shining sumac, wild cherry, and sassafras. In the absence of these, bucks will rub virtually any tree, but they prefer these aromatic varieties. This is probably because the bucks sense that the oily, resinous cambium of these species will retain their forehead-gland scent longer. With non-aromatic species, deposited scent may conceivably wash off during the next rainstorm. This makes the rub less effective as a signpost.

I make an effort to mark the location of each rub I find on a topographic map. If this isn't done, each find may seem totally random. If you can study large numbers of rub locations on a map, the perspective broadens and a pattern can often be discerned that may indicate a dominant buck's habitual pattern of movement.

Although some experts like to find a well-defined line of rubs in the belief that it indicates the regular route a buck follows to get from A to B, I feel that this is too chancy. A buck may not be using that particular route until after full dark. Instead, I boost my odds by searching for concentrates—places where exceptionally large numbers of rubs seem to be concentrated in a rather small area. This indicates that the buck is spending quite a lot of time in that place, and this increases the likelihood of getting a shot there.

When sitting on a stand in such a place, however,

Photo by Tim Christie

A dominant buck will often stand pawing the ground in frustration at the scent of a mock rub, waiting for his "challenger" to return.

keep in mind that you may see many different bucks that happen to be sharing the same turf. If you want a big deer, you must still determine which of the animals is the dominant buck.

When a subordinate deer passes through the area, he is well aware of his social status and shows respect for superior bucks by displaying his inferiority. The most common subordinate posture is a slinking gait that reminds me of a retreating dog that had been swatted on the rump for wetting on the floor. It's a cowering posture with the tail held tightly against the hindquarters, a somewhat sunken back, and the head held low. If two bucks see each other, the subordinate one will make a concerted effort to avoid direct eye contact with the higher-ranking deer. The dominant buck generally allows the inferior deer to continue on his way without incident.

The best way to describe the demeanor of a dominant buck is "proud and unafraid." With head held high, a dominant buck may seem to prance. The tail is high and extends straight back. Threatening postures include facing another deer perceived to be subordinate and staring fixedly at him. If a dominant buck is fairly close, you may also see that the dark hair tufts covering his tarsal (lower leg) glands have been erected and are rhythmically moving to dispense the buck's unique glandular scent. This may be followed by rub-urinating, in which the back legs are squeezed together and the back hunched up to allow urine to dribble down the legs and over the leg glands to carry additional tarsal scent to the ground.

The difficult thing about hunting dominant bucks is determining which is *the* most dominant animal in a given place. While bowhunting in Virginia's Shenandoah Mountains, I watched from a distance as two bucks sorted out their hierarchical ranking. In a short time, the submissive deer, a six-pointer, showed respect and quickly withdrew. The other deer also had a six-point rack, but as he drew closer I could see that the beams and tines were heavier, indicating that the animal probably was a year older.

As I patiently waited for this "dominant" buck to come within range, I caught a slight flicker of movement far to my left. Suddenly, the buck I was watching dropped his head and turned away. I knew what that meant. The deer had a higher social rank than the smaller six-pointer, but he was lower on the totem pole than a third deer, a real bruiser, that was now coming onto the scene.

As slowly as possible, I turned my head to the left and saw a magnificent ten-pointer glaring at the six-pointer. For a moment I came unwound, and I must have moved suddenly because in an instant both deer vanished.

I have always wondered whether the ten-pointer was *the* dominant buck in that area. He certainly ranked higher than the big six-pointer, but could there have been a still-larger buck? I'll never know, but the wishful dreams of deer hunters are made of such things.

In addition to rubbing, or signpost-marking, and body language to establish the pecking order, there are two other related matters that any enterprising hunter should consider. One may seem laughable, but I am convinced it works. It is a technique I've been developing over the last few seasons that I call "mock rubbing."

Most serious hunters are familiar with the advanced deer-hunting method known as "mock scraping," developed by expert Tennessee bowhunter Bob McGuire. I described this technique in detail in the October 1984 issue of *Outdoor Life*. Very briefly, the hunter creates an artificial scrape to attract buck deer to a place where it is easy to get a shot, usually from a stand.

To illustrate, let's say there is a deeply gouged trail leading to a known feeding area, such as a standing cornfield. Throughout the adjacent woods, you have discovered numerous rubs of various sizes, indicating that several bucks of different age classes are nearby. After thoroughly reconnoitering the terrain, you determine that the trail leading to the corn is the best possible place to install a portable tree stand, but this gives birth to a perplexing question. What if a six-point buck materializes? Should you try to take him? He may well be that area's dominant buck, but he may have a relatively low social ranking and be subordinate to others that have more impressive antlers.

Mock rubbing is the way to find out. Swab your knife blade free of all odor with an alcohol prep pad. These pads come in little sterile, hermetically sealed packets available in any drugstore. Next, make phony rubs in four to six saplings which are at least 2 1/2 inches in diameter but no larger than 3 1/2 inches by stripping off the bark. Don't entirely girdle the saplings because that would kill the trees, and don't touch the mock rubs with your hands or your human scent will be left behind. The trees you use should be within easy shooting distance (gun or bow) of your stand.

Climb into your stand to begin your vigil, and carefully observe the reactions of any of the bucks that come down the trail. When a buck spots one or more of the new artificial rubs and, more specifically, the diameter of the trees that were rubbed, the animal will instantly display its hierarchical ranking. You can then decide whether the deer fulfills your expectations and shoot or refrain from doing so in hopes of seeing a better animal later.

I haven't done this, but if a ten-pointer spotted one of my bogus rubs on a 3 1/2-inch-diameter sapling and cowered, I just might let him pass in the hope that he was using silent body language to tell of something still larger in the neighborhood. To date, that type of opportunity hasn't yet presented itself, although I can credit this method for three eight-pointers I did shoot.

Another method that can be employed alone or in conjunction with mock rubs is to use a "territorial infringement scent." Officially labeled as Dr. O's Buck Lure (Box 111, Niverville, NY 12130), the product is the brainchild of brothers Ed, John, and Jody Boll and chemist Brian Beberwyck, who, over a six-year period, developed the unique scent.

This deer scent is unlike any other in that it doesn't smell like deer food, mask human odor, or simulate a doe in estrus. Made with 13 natural ingredients, Dr. O's Buck Lure essentially duplicates the smell of a buck. As John Boll explained to me, the best time to use the lure is well before the rut begins, during the period when bucks are in the process of establishing their intended breeding grounds and pecking orders.

Because each whitetail buck is well aware of all others inhabiting the same general area and the characteristics of their individual odors, the scent simulates, so to speak, a new kid on the block. This engenders hierarchical investigation.

As Boll said: "When a buck gets a whiff of the lure carried by either the wind or thermal air currents, the deer becomes intent on identifying the source so that the buck that supposedly produced it may be appropriately ranked."

Equally as revolutionary as the lure is the unique application process. Using a golf tee with a small ball of foam sponge affixed to its top (both supplied with the bottle of scent), the hunter places the tee and pad anywhere he chooses within shooting range of his stand. Then he applies several drops of the lure to the sponge. Because the tee elevates the scent pad, the scent is more easily carried through the air than if it were merely dribbled on the ground. In addition to placing the scent on the pad, the hunter squeezes a few drops onto the fresh cambium of nearby mock rubs.

Whenever a buck comes within range of the airborne scent molecules, the animal has an ingrained desire to investigate. Depending on the deer's own social status, the buck will display either subordinate or dominant behavior. This tells the hunter whether he should try for the deer or allow him to go about his business in the hope that something better will come along.

"Subordinate bucks will approach the scented tee pad in a very submissive posture," John Boll told me. "They are attracted to the scent and want to check it out, but they'll do so with evident caution because they know their ranking and fear that the other "buck" they smell may be much bigger.

"It's another matter entirely, however, when a dominant buck smells the lure," Boll continued. "The spectacle that follows is something few hunters have ever witnessed firsthand, and it can be an unnerving experience especially if the hunter is not safe in a tree stand but right on the ground close to the deer. Typically, a dominant buck goes into a rage at having his breeding territory encroached upon by another deer he's not familiar with. The deer seems to literally go berserk, almost in the same way a dominant buck responds to the sound of rattling antlers. His eyes bulge, the hairs on his back stand up, his nostrils dilate, and he makes a beeline for the source of the scent. When he reaches the source, which in this case is the lure, the buck often becomes frustrated because he cannot make visual contact. He will often stand there and paw the ground, trying to understand the source of the scent and even rub-urinating in an attempt to cover the strange scent with his own. I've seen bucks try to bury the tee-pad by scuffing leaves and dirt over it and then urinating on it. Others pace around the lure, 15 to 30 yards away. I observed one buck that periodically rushed the scent on the dead run with his antlers lowered and then circled and jumped around the tee-pad. Finally, that animal bedded down right next to the tee-pad, apparently waiting for the interloping deer to return."

Knowing a little about the physical signs and silent body language deer use to communicate their social rankings can greatly increase a hunter's chances of taking the biggest buck in the woods. And a mock-male buck lure is the newest way to exploit that knowledge.

Hunt The Buck's Bedroom

By Harry Vanderweide

Wayne Hockmeyer can show you whitetail buck tracks. Lots of big ones. Tracks big enough to hold an apple. The sort of tracks trophy hunters dream about.

On any given day of guiding hunting parties in the rugged mountains of northwestern Maine, he may come across a track made by a whitetail buck with a live weight of 300 pounds or more and, on rare occasions, one that will actually field-dress at more than 300 pounds. The vast woodlands north of Moosehead Lake are home to hundreds of genetic giants of the whitetail clan, robust eight to 12-pointers that field-dress at 200 to 250 pounds.

It wouldn't be correct to say that Hockmeyer is not excited when he finds the tracks of one of these oversize deer. But, given a choice, he would much rather locate the dainty-toed hoofprint of a doe. After 27 years of hunting and guiding in the big woods, Hockmeyer has developed an unusual philosophy of deer hunting that focuses not on the tracks of the 200-pound-plus bucks his clients routinely bag, but rather on the comings and goings of does, around which all fall deer activity is centered.

Hockmeyer calls his system "hunting the buck's bedroom." He believes that his methods will produce big deer anywhere in the North Country, where deer are not numerous but do grow big. Certainly, Hockmeyer's hunting methods have been proved by the test of time. Year after year, his hunting camps hang up an array of bucks few other deer-hunting operations can match.

"When hunters come this far north for deer, what they've got in mind is something massive," Hockmeyer said. "Up here, there just aren't lots of deer, so it certainly isn't numbers. When you read about deer hunting in states like Texas, Alabama, or even Pennsylvania, it sounds as though there is a buck behind every tree. Well, up here, deer are few and far between. What we do have are big-bodied deer. It takes a big deer just to survive our winters. One of our bucks will weigh as much as two from the Deep South."

There's another major difference between deer found in the immense commercial forests of the North and their smaller brethren of the South.

"You'll hear about deer having a home territory of less than one square mile," Hockmeyer said. "That's just not the case with our Northern deer, especially during the hunting season, which coincides with the rutting season. In this country, it's routine for a buck to walk four or five miles in a morning. If the buck doesn't find what he's looking for, he can easily go another few miles before dark."

What these wide-ranging bucks are looking for, according to Hockmeyer, is a doe that's ready, or nearly ready, to mate.

"It's amazing how everything focuses on the does," Hockmeyer said. "When a doe is ready to breed, she'll attract every other deer on an entire mountain, including other does, fawns, and every buck around. The bucks are constantly searching for receptive does. They just keep moving all the time. They hardly stop to feed, and they never seem to bed down except for a matter of minutes. I know a lot has been written about hunting over scrapes as an effective method to take big bucks. You can forget about that method in the North Woods. It's true that these deer make scrapes, but they don't hang around them. Here, it will take several days or even as long as a week before a buck comes back around on his circuit to the spot where he made a scrape."

Does Hockmeyer really pass up large, fresh buck tracks to go looking for a doe track? The answer is, it all depends; but many times he will pass up a buck track in hopes of finding a new doe footprint.

"There is no question that tracking on new, soft snow is the most effective way to take a big buck in the North Woods. Tracking is my personal favorite hunting method, and no other method is as effective when conditions are right. But the truth is that weather conditions on most mornings make it impossible to use this method. A large percentage of the time, bare ground, crusted snow, or noisy conditions make it impossible to sneak up and shoot a buck."

But that's only part of the reason why Hockmeyer doesn't rely on the tracking of large bucks in his guiding operations.

"Most hunters do not have the physical stamina required to follow a giant buck mile after mile," he pointed out. "These are deer that think nothing of walking up one side of a mountain, down the other, across an almost impenetrable cedar swamp, and finishing off the jaunt by swimming across a white-water river. Even experienced deer chasers get discouraged when they try to walk up on one of these ridge-running bucks when it decides to take a serious hike."

All of which left Hockmeyer with the problem of finding free-roaming bucks when tracking conditions weren't favorable, or when his clients were not up for a multi-mile chase into uncharted territory. His problem was made more difficult because of the general scarcity of deer in the North Country. Most of the woods do not contain any deer most of the time. The deer are constantly on the move, and their patterns are erratic.

"What I found out early in my career of chasing these Northern bucks is that finding a fresh buck track is no guarantee that there is a deer in the immediate area," he explained. "The bucks move all the time, going from area to area and looking for does. There is little point in taking a stand in a piece of woods just because you find fresh buck sign. Chances are the buck is only passing through and is long gone. So I began to work on a system that helps find where the bucks will turn up. Gradually, I discovered a way to hunt in the buck's bedroom."

Hockmeyer's methods are somewhat novel, but it's not hard to see the logic behind the system. He tries to beat the bucks at their own game. Instead of hunting the buck, he looks for what the buck is hunting. That means does or, more specifically, the area that does are using to feed, rest, and wait for bucks to come calling.

"Find the does, and the bucks will be around," he said. "If not right away, then pretty soon, and usually there will be more than one. It's a fact that I have been able to rely on again and again over the years. What makes this really important is that unlike bucks, does don't normally travel great distances. Sometimes, a group of does will move a mile or so, but they tend to stay put for much longer periods than do bucks. I've checked areas where does were staying and found that they sometimes will go only a few hundred yards in an entire day. As a general rule, does will hide in a particular cover as long as similar weather conditions exist. They just feed back and forth and rest. I guess they know that the bucks will come looking for them sooner or later. A doe feeding along the side of a creek will usually be in the same general area two hours later, and because she is there, there will be bucks. If a buck isn't there at 8 A.M., he will be at 9 A.M."

Hockmeyer's careful study of deer during the fall months has shown him just how powerful a magnet does can be.

"There is a constant procession of bucks coming to visit the doe," he continued. "So long as she has not been bred, each buck in the area will try to spend time with her. The closer the doe gets to coming into heat, the more powerful her attraction and the more bucks she will hold around her. It's my experience that a doe coming into heat attracts other does and even non-breeding bucks. The scent she gives off seems to be appealing to all deer. For me, to find a doe in heat, or one about to come into heat, is the ultimate situation. The entire area will contain deer. The rest of the woods will be devoid of deer, as they all congregate around the doe. When I manage to sneak into such an area, that's what I call hunting in the buck's bedroom. There seem to be deer everywhere. They feed and circle and don't move far at all."

Until you walk into one of these buck bedrooms, it is hard to believe how concentrated deer sign can be in the wilds. It happened to Hockmeyer just last fall:

"I happened onto a small valley that had been cut over about a dozen years ago. A doe in heat had fed in the new growth along the side of the valley. Behind her came three different bucks and, to the sides, other bucks and does. It gave the impression that I had stumbled onto the greatest concentration of big-woods deer I had ever seen. There were at least a dozen deer in that half-mile valley, and they had fed there all morning. The next morning, I had four hunters posted carefully around the valley—but no one saw a deer. The

Photo by Wyman Meinzer

To tag a trophy buck during the rut, follow the does. That's where the action is.

receptive doe had left and taken all of the other deer with her. During the next few days, the deer spread out and I could find no similar concentration until the next time a doe went into heat."

Which just goes to show that there are never any sure things in deer hunting, even when you find a buck's bedroom. Still, hunting under such conditions is the best chance to get near large, dominant bucks. There is, says Hockmeyer, a practical, biologically sound reason for this concentration of deer during the breeding season.

"When a doe comes into heat, nature desires that she be bred and that the biggest, strongest buck do the job," he said. "By having all of the deer attracted to her, the doe increases the chance that a buck, most likely the biggest buck around, will find her during the relatively brief period when she is able to breed. There is much less of a chance that a big buck will fail to find her because he was pursuing another doe a distance away. Because even the does are attracted to her, they drag the bucks along with them."

Sounds pretty good, doesn't it? Find a receptive doe and just hang around until a giant buck wanders into your crosshairs. If you've guessed it's not that simple, you're right. As usual, there are complications. Finding a doe in heat in the North can be a challenge, especially because only a few deer are scattered over large distances in the first place. How difficult is finding a doe in heat? "It's extremely tough," conceded Hockmeyer, "and most of the time you won't. But there are methods you can use to find does, and from time to time you will also come across one ready to breed.

"If you have a new snow or even an old snow, look for a doe track, not a buck track. Chances are there will be does around. Remember, finding a buck track only means that a buck has passed through the area. Find a doe track, and you can be reasonably certain that there will be bucks around. The other method is to follow a buck track until he meets up with a feeding doe, and then take a stand in that area. But if you choose to follow the buck, it's best to be prepared for some serious walking."

Once you've located the area a doe is using, the first part of the problem is solved, but it will take some doing to tie your tag onto a jumbo buck.

"What you do not want to do if you get close to a feeding doe is chase her or let her know that you are there. If she runs away, your bedroom has just moved and you are no longer in it. Though it is okay to move rapidly—not even hunting—until you catch up with the doe, once you see signs that she is feeding, you must move extremely slowly. Ideally, you don't want to actually catch up with her; you just want to almost catch up. Bucks in the area will be all around and can come from any direction. Movement must be slow and deliberate. One false move will send all of the deer running.

"You've got to be conscious of wind direction and choose the paths you travel with care. Keep to the high ground or other areas of high visibility. The object is to get a buck to walk to you, not the other way around. The odds that his dark shape will materialize out of nowhere are as high as they get. Patience is everything.

"When a buck comes, it will usually be with head held low, seeking the scent of a doe. He walks deliberately, making low grunting sounds. If he is a breeding buck, he will be consumed with passion, stretching his neck, pursing his lips, and rolling his eyes. He is out of control—but let him see you or get a whiff of you, or let another deer spook, and he will regain his composure instantly and be gone in a few jumps."

Though Hockmeyer advises to look for a doe track rather than a buck's, he doesn't always follow his own advice. Perhaps you won't want to either, if you are in good enough shape to go ridge-running and have faith in your ability to find your way out of the woods with a compass.

"Sometimes, I follow a buck track, either backward or forward. The buck has either come from a doe or is going to one. When using this method, you travel as fast as possible, and do not hunt while following the buck. Only when the buck finds a doe do you slow down, and then not until you see that the doe has started to feed in a wandering manner. Then you know you are in the bedroom, and it's time to get slow and cautious."

Even in the North, there's not always enough snow on the ground to make tracking possible. That's when woodsmanship and knowledge of deer habits pay off. The objective remains the same: Find an area being frequented by a doe.

"Without snow, locating a doe is difficult," Hockmeyer said. "A hunter familiar with a region usually can make a guess about which areas does prefer. The edges of streams are particularly good, as are softwood or hardwood edges. Use your eyes and other senses to notice signs of feeding deer. Spotting fresh droppings and small, fresh tracks are your clues. When you spot them, you must assume that deer are feeding in the general area. If you are wrong and the doe has moved on, you probably won't see any deer that day, but that's par for the course when you hunt in the big woods."

Hockmeyer doesn't belittle the results of those who make a specialty of finding the fresh track of a large buck and then doggedly sticking with it. He acknowledges that when conditions are perfect, tracking is the ultimate method. But he does point out that this rugged hunting method is not for everyone and that conditions are not always perfect. His system of hunting the buck's bedroom is offered as a productive alternative.

"Tracking requires speed and stamina," he said. "Hunting the buck's bedroom requires patience and stealth. To be successful, I think that it's best never to confuse the two."

Hot-Weather Whitetails

By John Weiss

Throughout the Northeast and upper Midwest, generations of whitetail hunters have come to rely upon "good tracking snow" as the most accurate barometer of their anticipated success.

Sometimes, however, Mother Nature throws them a curve in the form of sultry air temperatures that seem more in keeping with August weather than that of late November. Hunters are confused as to where the animals are and which tactics might work best. As it often happens, many of them simply elect to watch a water hole in the hope that they will ambush something that wanders by.

For many years, I was a member of the wait-by-the-water-hole fraternity. Then one fall day, I was invited to hunt deer on an old plantation in Butler County, deep in southern Alabama. The temperature was a blistering 102°, quite a bit warmer than the usual 85° deer-hunting weather. Yet every member of our party collected a nice deer.

These hunters, it suddenly dawned on me, almost never had the opportunity to pursue their quarry with snowflakes sifting down. Some of them didn't even own insulated boots or longjohns, and to them, numb fingers were something you momentarily experienced while adding still more ice cubes to your favorite elixir at day's end. Yet these Southern pals consistently enjoyed just as high a rate of success as did my cronies north of the Mason-Dixon Line. Clearly, the old adage about "good tracking snow" being a requisite to success was pure nonsense.

Through the help of sound game management programs, whitetails now range over a vast expanse of our continent and have colonized an infinite variety of terrain. Therefore, few concrete axioms can be laid down that will apply to every hot weather deer hunt. But by taking a page from a Southern deer hunter's notebook, then filling in the local conditions, hunters anywhere can make the odds more favorable.

First, consider a whitetail's need for water. Deer have a daily requirement of 1 1/2 to three quarts of water per 100 pounds of body weight. The reason why this rate is so variable is because other factors such as energy expended, evaporation rates, and percentage of mineral salts in the diet play a major role in the frequency with which body fluids must be replaced.

The type of forage may also influence water requirements. Curiously enough, warm temperatures during the fall and winter prompt especially high water intake because succulent vegetation is rapidly disappearing and the animals must drink more water to compensate for this omission in their diet. After early October, deer are also wrapped in their insulating heavy coats to retain body heat. In hot weather, the deer must increase their fluid intake to help regulate their body temperatures.

Many hunters presume that deer satisfy their water needs by regularly visiting obvious sources such as lakes and streams, but this may hold true only in certain parts of the country. From the arid Plains states down through Texas and into the deserts of the Southwest, hiding in cover and watch-

ing a *resata* (stock pond) may indeed be the secret to collecting many venison dinners, as may watching a bubbling creek where pre-scouting has revealed the convergence of several deer trails. In such regions, whitetails are intimately aware of the locations of major, widely separated water sources and regularly home in on them.

The opposite situation exists, however, in many other whitetail states where water is found in many forms. My farm in southern Ohio is a ready example. I've seen deer drinking at conspicuous water sources such as the small lake behind our house, from the three streams that meander through the acreage, and from several springs that pockmark the landscape. Just as often, though, I've seen them drink from many inconspicuous places such as roadside culverts, drainage ditches, rain puddles, and sheet-metal stock tanks.

In hot weather, therefore, a hunter who takes a stand near an obvious water source in country where there is an abundance of water may be doomed to disappointment. Deer are opportunists when it comes to water, and there is no assurance that they will only visit a specific source. Conversely, in arid regions or during severe droughts, a lone source of water can attract deer from afar like a magnet.

At the 21st annual conference of the Southeastern Association of Game and Fish Commissioners, biologist E. D. Michael shed more insight on the drinking habits of deer. His findings should benefit hunters who have studied local conditions and decided that water-watching might pay off. Michael learned of three peak times of drinking activity: 7 A.M., 11 A.M., and from 4 P.M. to 6 P.M. If deer could talk, we could ask them to explain why they prefer to drink at these seemingly arbitrary times— perhaps their cud-chewing periods and related body metabolisms are determining influences—but in any event, a hunter will want to keep these periods in mind.

During the remaining hours of the day, whitetails may pursue any number of other activities, provided that weather conditions and air temperatures are normal for the particular time of year. If unseasonably warm weather begins baking the countryside, though, there are some specific behaviors they're most likely to exhibit. Again, the topography of the real estate pipes the tune as to where they'll be and what they'll be doing.

I remember one October day when my pal Jerry Bartlett and I were hunting in Sumter County, South Carolina. The temperature had pushed well into the 90s. Our conclusion was to sneak-hunt the ridgelines, where we figured slight breezes

In hot weather, think leafy canopies and shade—it's where you'll find the deer are headed.

would offer deer some respite from the heat. We were dead wrong; the sun was pounding the ridges relentlessly. So, we plodded downhill into a winding, narrow bottomland bordered by sheer hillsides. It was shady there, but because of the close confinement not a wisp of air could move; it was like being in a sauna with the lights turned off. No deer there either.

Finally, we decided to hike back to our trucks for lunch. As we made our way out of the bottom and came to an adjoining ten-acre soybean field, Jerry spotted a six-point buck standing in the middle of the beans. Just as suddenly, the buck dropped down and out of sight, as though he had fallen through a trapdoor.

"This is going to be the easiest deer we've ever taken," I whispered with a wide smile.

Crouching low, we began slinking across the bean field, confident that when we got within 25 yards of the buck, he would stand up and we'd have fleeting seconds to drop him at point-blank range before he could run away. We never really decided which one of us would take the shot, but it didn't make any difference because neither of us got the chance. Before we had covered one-half of the distance to the buck's location, four does—which we had no idea were anywhere nearby—rocketed out of the beans several yards in front of us. Seconds later, the buck unceremoniously followed on their heels, leaving us flushed with embarrassment.

Nevertheless, we'd made an intriguing discovery by pure chance. We forgot about eating lunch and hunted every soybean field we could find, first by hiking the perimeters and then by walking between the bean rows. We jumped more than 12 does and five bucks that afternoon, and we attached our tags to three of the latter.

In retrospect, it's now obvious why the deer had elected to bed in the bean fields. The waist-high canopy of overhead cover offered concealment and shade from the sun, irrigation furrows between the rows of beans provided a ready source of water, and they had instant access to one of their all-time favorite foods.

For the same reasons, cornfields can also be havens for whitetails during heat spells. Even in northern climates, where it has become increasingly common to leave corn unharvested late into the winter or until it is sold or needed for stock forage, you can find the main ingredient for many a venison dinner.

When considering how deer react to hot weather, it's worth reemphasizing that the terrain and cover native to an area have an undeniable influence on deer location and behavior patterns. Perhaps the only rule that applies to all regions is that hot weather prompts whitetails to be far more active during the nighttime hours than usual. It stands to reason that when the deer are wearing their heavy coats, they are far more comfortable moving around in the cool darkness than in the blazing sunlight. By the time the morning sun has lifted off the ho-

Photo by John Weiss

rizon, you can count on the vast majority of the animals to be in their selected hiding places for the remainder of the day.

As a result, the best time to sit in a tree stand or a ground-level blind is during the first hour or two of morning light. After that, you might as well abandon your post and go searching for the animals, as they are not likely to come to you. This is true even at dusk, because in hot weather it generally takes a while for the evening air to cool, and the deer may not begin to stir until two or three hours after full dark.

We've already seen that grainfields are premier deer areas during the midday hours. In nonagricultural regions, think "shade." In many parts of the upper Midwest, throughout the Plains states, in scattered portions of the South, or wherever the terrain is relatively flat, mature woodlands are automatically eliminated from consideration. Hardwoods have long since lost the leafy canopies that at other times provide shade.

In the hilly or mountainous regions, however, that predominate in the Northeast, down the Atlantic coast to the Carolinas, then westward to the Ozarks, the story is entirely different. The ideal place to poke along gingerly is a forested east-facing slope where a mixture of thick, dead brush and successively aged hardwoods are bathed in shade for all but the early morning hours. The next best bet is a very steep north-facing slope.

In any region inhabited by whitetails, whether flat or hilly, stands of evergreens and cedar remain green and "leafy" throughout the year, and if the stand is surrounded by wide expanses of territory exposed to the sun, virtually every deer in the immediate vicinity will be secreted deep within its shaded confines.

The trick is locating middle-aged conifer plantations. Tall, mature trees won't hold deer because their lower branches have long since died from lack of sunlight; in a self-pruning manner, this has left the understory void of the necessary cover. Immature trees, which conversely have dense whorls of branches close to the ground, are not yet tall enough to provide understory shade. Those that are middle-aged, however, range from 20 to 30 feet in height and afford both shade and concealment.

Close-range shots become the rule in this thick cover. In fact, because the predictably present carpet of pine needles offers such silent footing, its's sometimes possible to walk right up on sleeping deer. Soft wool clothing aids the effort by not signaling your approach when pine boughs brush against your sleeves and pant legs.

On the most sultry days, when high air temperatures are combined with oppressive humidity levels, whitetails also seem to gravitate toward those shaded areas bordered by cool, moving water. Find a stream tumbling down from higher elevations, such as one capable of supporting trout or a smallmouth bass river rushing through a rocky gorge, and the swath of terrain bordering its northern and/or eastern sides will seem almost air conditioned because of the shade and the misting effect of the bubbling water.

How close deer will be to the actual edge of the water, where it's coolest, depends on how much noise the water is making: the animals don't want their sense of hearing impaired so that they are vulnerable to anything that may not have their best interests in mind.

If the water is slapping rocks and boiling through shallow rapids—which is typical in the canyon-like band of real estate stretching eastward from Missouri and Arkansas, through Kentucky and West Virginia, and down into North Carolina and northern Alabama—look for the deer to bed singly in pockets and recesses high above the water; or in small groups of two or three in the shade of boulders, outcroppings, or small clumps of cedar or hawthorn. In this situation, approaching a deer's suspected location from above by skulking along the rim of the gorge and peering down into the jumbled cover formations can be quite effective.

If the water is only serenely gliding along, however—common in the flatlands of Michigan up through Minnesota and into the Dakotas—deer may bed in large groups at the water's edge wherever it is shaded. The density of the cover, however, offers you little choice but to drive the animals out to hunting partners stationed at downstream or upstream vantage points. This can be a tricky proposition, as we once learned while staging such a drive along the banks of the Kettle River near Hinckley, Minnesota. We found ourselves reminded that whitetail bucks don't always play fair.

The drive ran like a well-oiled machine, and every hunter placed on stand saw deer. Unfortunately, they were all does. The one buck, we later learned, refused to follow the does as they attempted to escape in a northerly direction. Instead, he ran west, dove into the river, and began swimming toward the opposite shore. We spotted him—a nice eight-pointer—just as he climbed out of the water and up the muddy bank. He then proceeded to stand there for long moments and gawk at us. The buck must have sensed the predicament we'd have been in if one of us had dropped him with an easy 75-yard shot because it would have taken two days of backbreaking labor to drag him from that side of the river to the nearest access road; that state of affairs bought his ticket to freedom.

I mentioned earlier that contrary to the beliefs of most hunters, forested ridges are not always comfortable for deer in hot weather. Yet there are several exceptions worth noting.

If you can find an exceptionally large tree, such as a beech, sycamore, or maple, that has recently been uprooted by a tornado or knocked down by lightning, it may well be a spot to check. For approximately two years after the tree has fallen, the latticework of branches and limbs offers a dark catacomb of hiding places, and a crafty deer may belly-crawl right into the middle and not budge unless an equally crafty hunter kicks the limbs as though he were trying to flush a rabbit from a brush pile. As one might guess, this type of deer hunting definitely is not for the weakhearted because nothing is more unnerving than a whitetail buck crashing up and out of such cover only yards away.

Near my home in southeastern Ohio, honeysuckle commonly is head-high and nightmarishly dense. Whitetails that bull their way through the stuff will, in time, create an endless network of passageways and tunnels. Because honeysuckle prefers south-facing slopes and may even blanket entire hillsides in an almost impenetrable, jungle-like fashion, this is an ideal place for a buck to escape both hunting pressure and the unrelenting heat of the midday sun.

Understandably, when deer are in honeysuckle, the hunting that follows ranks as possibly the toughest done anywhere, except perhaps when deer are hiding in the vast seas of thornbush and cactus of southern Texas. In both cases, even the hunter who is quick with a rifle is destined to have a discouragingly low success rate if he chooses to hunt alone. About the only tactic that merits consideration is a well planned pincer movement, with large numbers of drivers stationed close together to prevent the animals from dodging the hunters and sneaking back through the drive line. Or, find one of the main trails deer use to enter and leave such cover and be there at least one hour before morning's first light.

Hunting deer during unseasonably warm weather doesn't have to mean that the balance is tipped decidedly in the animals' favor. It only means that their habits will have temporarily changed to adapt to the prevailing conditions. If you keep the words water, shade, and cover in mind, you'll find the spot that the deer themselves have decided is the best place to be.

Doing The Apple Mash

By Gerald Bethge

It had been another fruitless day of hunting. The Massachusetts bowhunting season was a week old, and outside of a couple of brazen does that had marched past my tree stand on opening day, there wasn't much doing in the woods. Frank Falconi, my longtime hunting partner, had fared no better. We glumly ate dinner, threw a couple of quartered wild cherry logs on the still-glowing wood stove, and retired to the living room to discuss the next morning's strategy over a tall glass of apple mash.

It didn't seem to make much sense at the time. We knew the deer had to be around, but where? Tactics for the next day sounded valid, as they always do on the night before a hunt. Yet, deep down, we both knew that our chances of scoring weren't getting any better.

Outside, a full moon—a "Hunter's Moon" I think it said in the Farmer's Almanac—shone off a light blanket of powdery snow. Although the clock read midnight, the scene looked more like midday. Snow crystals twinkled in the moonlight on the fallen apples that lay half-rotted in the field around the house. And, like clockwork, right on time came the deer. There were six of them in all sizes—sniffing, nuzzling, and finally munching on the apples beneath the trees.

I didn't bother to wake Frank. We had seen the same show for three consecutive nights, and there was no need to get more frustrated.

From the condition of the snow the next morning, it was obvious that more deer had joined the group long after I had gone to bed. However, they were long gone by first light, and they never showed up near our stands that entire day.

Apples, like acorns, are deer magnets. But just as standing under any old oak tree won't produce many deer, merely standing near an apple orchard won't yield a lot of venison. There are specific times of day and year that will yield deer in and around apple trees and orchards. If you can figure out exactly what time that is, hunting deer can be as close to a sure thing as any other strategy.

Two years ago was the wrong time. By July, our two dozen or so apple trees drooped heavy with fruit. Golden Delicious, Red Delicious, McIntosh, and crab apple trees were all heavily laden, and all I could think of at the time was the great deer hunting opportunities that lay ahead in the fall. We had several tree stands in place near our field along entry and escape routes and had already spotted several does feeding on the lush summer grasses.

However, long after Christmas, the apples that we hadn't picked for our own use still lay frozen beneath more than five inches of snow. The deer never bothered with them until mid-January. Even then, they would dig through the crusted snow, eat one or two apples, and take off. Surprisingly, many

Photo by Richard P. Smith

Orchards aren't always the sure things they're cracked up to be, especially when the mast crop is good; but the apples are usually appealing. Time of day is also a deciding factor.

rotten apples remained even after the snow melted in the spring.

Luckily, we had realized just before the season that focusing all of our hunting efforts on the field would have been a waste of time. We did in fact see deer in the very same field during the course of several fall evenings; however, they continually turned up their noses at the apples, each time preferring to browse on grass. I watched them walk to within a few inches of fallen apples numerous times while never so much as mouthing one. Why?

Acorns. It may have been an excellent year for apples, but the mast crop was equally good. There is nothing that deer love more than acorns. Both bucks and does will pound oak ridges again and

again, scooping up all of the acorns in sight, before moving on to other foods. Luckily for me and other hunters who prefer to hunt near apple orchards, mast crops aren't good every year. And when the mast crop is poor, apples become much more appealing to the resident deer herd.

Uncle Joe's hunting techniques are a good case in point. Preferring to hunt from the same apple-tree stand each deer season, no matter what the mast or apple crop situation, he still manages to be pretty successful. However, his success typically fluctuates according to deer food abundance. When acorns are plentiful, he'll grumble about the lack of deer sightings. When mast is limited and apples are abundant, he'll usually score on a good buck. His lack

Photo by Jeff Murray

Come November when other foods become scarce, apples become the drawing card. Cold nights and warm days speed up the fermentation process, making the fruit irresistible to deer.

will refuse to come into an apple orchard until dark. The key, then, is to meet them on the trail that leads to the apple orchard. Often, they will use several trails, and it will be up to you to decide which one is receiving the most traffic. If there is snow on the ground or if you've hunted a particular orchard in the past, narrowing down the most-used trails should be quite easy. Patterns on trail use should present themselves clearly, because once the deer know that there are apples to be found, you can bet that they'll come in night after night. If there's snow, backtrack the deer to better find out where they are coming from.

In an area that I hunt, the deer typically bed down during the day in the thicket south of a particular field. The nearly impenetrable cover offers them protection, and the apple trees in the field offer them food. Getting between the thicket and the field helped me arrow my first buck.

It was obvious from the half-eaten pieces of apple scattered about the field that deer were feeding in the area consistently. Tracks along the deer trails seemed to indicate that the majority of the deer that were feeding in the field refused to make a beeline from their bedding area into the orchard, preferring instead to circle the oblong-shaped field from the southwest, probably to wind it before approaching. My stand was in the thicket of tall pine trees about one-quarter mile from the apple-tree field, along the approach trail. As dusk neared, I heard a deer making its way from the bedding thicket. It didn't waste any time, no doubt wanting to get to the apples as quickly as its legs would carry it. When the deer got to within 25 yards, I drew my 55-pound recurve and fired. The deer then spun, headed back for the safety of the thicket, and dropped in a heap.

I ran back to the house, more to calm down than to let the deer stiffen up, and returned about two hours later. The heavy blood trail was easy to follow, even with a flashlight. Not 25 yards from the spot where I had shot it, the deer lay on the ground. It was then that I noticed the antlers—a fine six-point rack. (Both bucks and does were legal targets, and for some reason, I never thought to look at the headgear.) Choosing the most heavily used deer trail leading to the field of apple trees, and then getting back far enough on the trail so that I could get off a shot with enough shooting light remaining, was the key.

What if finding the best trail leading to an apple orchard isn't all that easy? The answer is simple: Make your own. Unless forced to do otherwise because of intense hunting pressure or because they are being chased by predators, deer prefer to travel along the route of least resistance. This is especially true of bucks. If you've ever followed a buck track

of success last season (when, as mentioned before, there were plenty of acorns) bolsters my theory.

So, then, it stands to reason that posting near an apple orchard when apples are abundant and mast is not will get you a deer—right? Wrong. It's just not that easy. Deer that have been hunted will rarely show themselves near apple trees and orchards during the daytime. Instinct tells them that standing out in the open, no matter how luscious the feed, can be dangerous once hunting season nears. You may catch an occasional doe or young buck out in the field during hunting hours, but more often than not you'll have to amuse yourself by watching field mice. So what's a hunter to do?

Deer—and, as a general rule, the bigger deer—

through the woods, you have noticed that it tends to go around heavy brush rather than right through it. Quite simply, buck's antlers get hung up. The field near my home is ringed with thick alders. The most-used deer trails leading to the field are distinguishable because they are relatively uncluttered with brush. Using a chain saw to clear away these alders and wild blueberry bushes has helped us funnel the deer onto these paths of least resistance.

As mentioned previously, deer seem to prefer to dine on apples at dusk and on through the night. Although I'm sure that many hunters have had success by posting near apple orchards in the morning, I often scare the deer out of these fields on my way to the stand. I've tried varying my approaches and using numerous other little tricks, but I have had little success. Getting into my stand by 2:30 P.M. and then waiting it out until the end of legal shooting hours has worked best for me.

Figuring out the best time of year to hunt near apples can also be difficult. If the bow season opens in October in your state, it's best not to concentrate your hunting efforts on apple orchards. Unless you are hunting in a commercial apple orchard where deer are used to feeding all year long—munching on trees in the winter and spring and on apples in the fall—you will likely find that deer rely most heavily on other browse early in the fall. Instinct may tell them that the lush browse won't be around much longer and to get it while it lasts. Deer may occasionally feed in the orchard, but not with any predictable pattern.

Come November, when other foods become scarce, apples are *the* drawing card. I've found that deer prefer to wait until the first few hard freezes before targeting apples. The cold nights and warm days speed up the fermentation process in the fruit and make it impossible for the deer to resist.

In late November and December, apples seem to become the number-one deer food. The deer can smell them under several inches of snow, and they feed on them constantly. When the weather is about to turn miserable, deer will often try to get a quick fix of the easily located fruit before holing up.

In upstate New York three years ago, a bone-chilling downpour greeted us on the morning after Thanksgiving. While the smarter hunters stayed in camp, my buddy Bill and I threw on some raingear and headed out. By the time we hit the front door, the rain had turned into a blizzard. Thinking that the deer would head for the relatively warm and dry hemlock thicket, I stillhunted down the edge of a field and slipped quietly past a couple of apple trees and into the hemlocks. Although the storm gained in intensity, it was a great day to be out in the woods. By noon, I was soaked to the bone, so I trudged back to camp. My heart sank when I got back to those apple trees and noticed that at least a half-dozen deer had ripped up the snow around the trees and grabbed a quick meal. By the rate of the falling snow, I guessed that the tracks were no more than 10 to 15 minutes old. So close, and yet so far.

Crab apple trees in the woods can sometimes be hunted as effectively as orchards. Although, in the Northeast, the trees appear sporadically and are rarely found in groups, they have been around for decades, and you can bet that all of the deer in the area know where to find a quick meal.

Perhaps the best part about crab apple trees is that they grow in the thick woods. Therefore, the biggest bucks, which are more hesitant about being caught out in the open, can feed on the crab apples in safety. However, because there aren't as many of the trees in a single area, crab apples won't draw deer with the consistency that orchards will. You can increase your chances by finding an area that has one or two large crab apple trees that normally yield lots of fruit. If these trees are close to thickets, you can bet that the deer will be nearby. Areas around crab apple trees are the best spots for taking deer when the hunting pressure is on and all deer-feeding patterns have been interrupted.

It's been my contention for several years that my hunting buddy Frank has the best tree stand in the entire state of Massachusetts. Granted, the guy is a darn good deer hunter, but in the ten-odd years that his stand has been in place, Frank has taken at least six deer from it—and most have been bucks.

The stand helps Frank take advantage of everything a deer needs. Open hardwoods are nearby, to the south of the stand. To the north is the thickest hemlock thicket I've ever seen. And in the middle of it all is the stand, amid a nasty tangle of alders and briers. Near the briers are several crab apple trees. And though other apple trees bear fruit on a cyclical basis, crab apple trees almost always have fruit. So when deer season opens and other hunters head for the hardwoods, the deer head for the friendly confines of this thicket, which offers both protection and crab apples. I can't recall a single season in which Frank hasn't at least seen deer. That may not sound like a great accomplishment to many, but for the area in which we hunt, that's darn good. And more often than not, Frank will score on a dandy buck.

He did just that late in the deer season four years ago. Poor weather forced him out of his tree stand, so Frank decided to hunt a thick brier patch located between a power line right-of-way and a dirt road. The tangle is interspersed with crab apple trees, and it is so thick that few hunters ever enter it. However, the deer just love it. Sure enough, while slowly stillhunting through the briers, Frank pushed out a husky one-horned buck that had let the hunter get just a little too close. Until Frank had come along, there was little reason for that buck to leave the thicket. It is likely that the deer spent much of the season in or near that very spot—just holing up in the briers when its stomach was full.

This is a formula that has worked for us on numerous occasions, and if you just take a little time to sit back and analyze the comings and goings of deer in and around apple trees and orchards, it can work for you no matter where you hunt.

Deer-Calling Secrets

By Bob McGuire

A pair of eyes gleamed out of the darkness when our spotlight swept the field. Unmistakably, it was a whitetail. My partner carefully loaded his weapon while I silently brought the heavy video pack to my shoulder. "It's a buck; I see the antlers," I whispered. "We've got a fair chance to put him down, but make sure my camera's up before you shoot."

We made final checks on wind direction and equipment, and then put the light out. While we had gone through our rehearsed routine in total darkness, there seemed little hope that the deer would hold his position long enough for us to sneak within range. The night had been fraught with failures. Deer after deer had detected our approaches.

Now after a normal amount of fumbling and fouled camera cables, we found ourselves positioned for an attempt. Lights on. No deer. "Over there, to the left. He's headed for the ridge!" my partner said in order to guide my powerful video light to the fleeing buck.

"Mind if I call?" I asked. As videographer, it was not my place to direct our effort, but I had grown tired of fleeting glimpses and no film footage.

"You can call deer?" he asked, and with that response, I let out a piercing scream to imitate the fawn distress bawl. We turned off the light and dropped to the ground. I proceeded to unleash all manner of terrifying sounds. Unprepared for the loud noise and unfamiliar with the vocalizations, my partner promptly lapsed into belly-rolling spasms of laughter.

I was sure his laughter had caused the deer to run, so we turned on the light. There he was. The buck stood frozen in place. Slowly, ever so slowly, up came the gun. My partner took careful aim at close range, then *phiitt*, the dart struck home.

I documented this "hunt" on videotape, and my biologist partner carefully logged the details.

We had to keep the deer in sight, but we tried not to spook him. The darted buck might take flight and run for a mile, or perhaps bed down and succumb to the immobilizer drug within minutes. Our purpose was to collect samples from the interdigital foot gland for a scent research program that was being conducted by East Tennessee State University. The deer would be released unharmed.

Though our attention was focused on our quarry, we slowly became aware of other animals that were materializing from every direction. Slow movement of the light illuminated more than 20 deer within 50 yards. My calling had filled the field with deer, and the biologist had become a believer in deer calling.

In recent years, I have traveled all over the United States and called or rattled up deer for hundreds of outdoor writers, biologists, and hunters. Most were skeptical about calling until they witnessed the results. Veteran hunters, in particular, find it hard to believe that such a silent animal has such a complex vocabulary. Even as our understanding of the vocalizations increases, additional complexities arise and are compounded by variations in body language. One sound may have several different meanings when associated with differing postures or motions under different circumstances.

Fourteen different whitetail vocalizations are now recognized by biologists. Although opinions differ somewhat on the significance of certain sounds, there is basic agreement on the meaning of general categories of the sounds. In the early 1980s, biologist Larry W. Richardson identified seven distinct vocal and nasal signals while doing his master's thesis research at Mississippi State University. These sounds included the fawn's distress call, bleat, and nursing whine; and the buck's tending grunt, aggressive snort, snort-wheeze, and alert snort.

At about the same time, a graduate student at the University of Georgia was completing his Ph.D. dissertation research under the guidance of renowned deer biologist Dr. R. Larry Marchinton. In this comprehensive study, Dr. Tom Atkeson identified and recorded 12 different whitetail sounds and grouped them into the following widely accepted categories:

- Alarm or distress sounds, including the snort and the fawn bawl.
- Agnostic (aggressive) sounds such as the low grunt, grunt-snort, and grunt-snort-wheeze.
- Maternal/Neonatal (doe/fawn) vocalizations, including the low-pitch doe grunt, and fawn sounds such as the mew, bleat, and nursing wine.
- Sex-related sounds, including the buck's tending grunt.
- Contact calls or general vocal signals between deer that have become separated.

After studying the work of Marchinton and Atkeson, I spent considerable time observing and filming the University of Georgia deer herd, and my initial audio cassette featured many of the vocalizations recorded by the two Georgia biologists. In addition, I observed and recorded a prolonged low-volume sexual grunt and an agitated buck grunt similar to a distressed cow's *moo*. Although I have successfully called deer with each of the known vocalizations, it has become apparent that certain sounds work better than others for specific purposes. Much of my recent vocalization-response testing and filming has been done in conjunction with a research program at East Tennessee State University, where I maintain adjunct-faculty status.

In my own trophy hunting, I favor the bold, aggressive deer sounds such as the grunt-snort-wheeze. Starting with a low grunt followed by a rapid series of sniff-snorts and a prolonged hissing, this high-level aggressive threat is guaranteed to send every deer packing out of the woods in high gear—except, of course, the dominant buck. Dominant bucks come to this call more readily than to any other. Long ago, I had heard reports about this strange aggressive vocalization that sounds similar, in part, to air discharging from a tire punctured by an ice pick.

Veteran North Carolina bowhunter Lester Ballard once told me of a fortunate mistake he made while suffering from a severe winter cold. After a miserable morning spent fighting off sneezing seizures, he glimpsed a nice buck passing by at more than 100 yards. A sneeze came on, and Ballard nearly exploded his ear drum in an attempt to muffle the sharp sound. The buck voiced dominance with a series of grunt-snort-wheezes. The deer then retired to Ballard's freezer.

Preceding an earnest fight, one or both bucks that believe themselves to be dominant will make this threatening sound. Although rare in nature (as are serious deer fights), this sound accompanies each of my heavy-handed rattling performances. Trophy hunters who try this call go for broke because the sound brings in only dominant bucks; it frightens away all others.

The powerful magnetism of this call still amazes me, but even so, using it sometimes backfires. I remember an Ohio hunt where I was riding high on a series of calling successes. I was making subordinate vocalizations to a yearling six-pointer to coax him in for pictures. I had no intention of shooting the little deer. I concentrated on my performance, but I suddenly became aware of a high-racked buck easing along the adjacent field toward my tree stand. He was very close. Without thinking, I let out a grunt-snort-wheeze. It was a good rendition of the call that terrified subordinate bucks.

I had forgotten the little guy below me. He took off like a rocket because he thought the big deer had made the sound. Worse yet, the big guy tore down the woods in hot pursuit, perhaps believing that it was the yearling buck that had given that macho challenge.

I have directly called in dominant bucks more often with the grunt-snort-wheeze than with all other calling and rattling techniques combined. However, when a buck is already hooked up with a ready doe, this call and all other direct calls are of little use. No matter how dominant a whitetail buck may be, if he is tending an estrous doe, he will invariably drive her away from even the most timid rattling or calling. Old-world deer such as elk (wapiti) typically establish harems and accept challenges, but new-world deer such as whitetails tend single estrous does. When a boss whitetail is faced with a challenge while in the company of an estrous doe, he takes his lady and runs.

This forces hunters to change tactics during the peak rut in areas where hunting pressure has resulted in a heavily cropped deer herd in which there are few antlered bucks. In that situation, chances are that a dominant buck will be constantly in the company of an estrous doe. This is the case when the buck/doe ratio is below one to ten. Formerly a puzzle, it has become easy to determine when to call or rattle directly for the buck and when to avoid calling him directly. Where there is a low buck/doe ratio, ground scraping by dominant bucks apparently diminishes or ceases during the peak rut. This correlates with increased doe-tending activity. It also accounts for the fact that in some areas, rattling is least effective during the peak rut, while in other areas, rattling is most effective at that time.

Author Bob McGuire blows the Twin-Tube deer call and follows up with an angry grunt-snort-wheeze . . .

. . . and a dominant buck promptly replies to McGuire's challenge with a grunt-snort-wheeze of its own. Call, and they'll come!

Before attempting to call or rattle up bucks, therefore, trophy hunters should make sure that they have found revisited, fresh, dominant-buck scrapes. These active scrapes are made below overhanging branches, and they show fresh, rounded deer tracks. If the scrapes are old or show subordinate sign (sharp-toed prints), the odds are against successful rattling or direct buck calling. The total amount of actual scraping by the big doe-tending bucks, however, may not decrease. The dominant bucks may merely refrain from going out of their ways to check their scrapes because ready does are abundant. Many hunters are confused when the best-looking scrapes do not produce during the peak of the rut and big bucks start leaving their rounded-toe prints in field-edge scrapes or anywhere else an estrous doe might lead them.

How then does a hunter call in these tending bucks? It's another seemingly complex problem with a simple solution. Several years ago, I bow-hunted Ohio whitetails during the mid-November peak rutting period with Oregon elk hunter Larry D. Jones. Although he is one of the best all-around game callers I know, Jones, on this particular hunt, planned to witness some deer-calling on my part.

I was talking about the day's experiences with Jones when we were walking out of the woods one evening. After I detailed my unsuccessful calling, which had been directed at a dominant tending buck, Jones made a clever suggestion. "If you call the doe," he remarked, "that buck is bound to follow." How simple!

The next morning, that same buck was hooked up with a doe, probably the same one. She was leading him on laps around a large cut soybean field, a common tactic for estrous does.

Calling does isn't always a guarantee, but the calls are easy to make. A few loud fawn distress bawls, and the old girl approached without hesitation. Moments later, the buck followed and stepped within range of my arrow. Later, I recalled other times when I had called tending bucks with fawn distress calls without realizing why they came in.

A few months after Jones taught me that valuable lesson, I found myself hunting Alabama whitetails with champion turkey caller Ben Rodgers Lee. It was late January and the rut was peaking locally, yet the better scrapes did not show activity. The indicators warned me that odds were against successful rattling.

We filmed bowhunting to be broadcast later on national television. We wanted footage of bucks and does responding to calling and rattling. Ben was amazed at the violence I injected into my performances whenever we went after boss bucks. On one occasion, however, he was surprised by a complete change when I called a mature buck in to close range three times with much quieter calling.

The secret was that I was calling the estrous doe the buck was courting. She arrived in response to my fawn distress bawls, whereupon I held her in place with soft mewing sounds—fawn bleats. Although the buck took flight three times, he quickly returned when the doe would not run with him. Mewing is the best coaxer sound I know, especially for those last few yards to bring the deer within bow range.

Ben quickly spread the word about how I had called that buck in repeatedly, but we both knew that the doe-calling technique had turned the trick. Although my greatest successes with directly calling dominant bucks have been achieved with the grunt-snort-wheeze, I have recently experienced the best response through indirect calling, using the fawn distress bawl to attract estrous does with bucks following. For the deer hunter who wishes to master a single call that works with both buck and doe whitetails, nothing beats the wail of a crying fawn.

Until recently, I did all my deer calling with my mouth and vocal cords, but now I have begun using a calling device. When I was asked to design a two-tone sportsman's deer call for the Coleman Company, I collaborated with Tennessee trophy hunter Alan Altizer to first develop a good imitation of the fawn bawl. Quickly abandoning reed-type calls, we eventually settled on a stretched membrane over a mouthpiece that would produce the required high-pitched sounds through simple lip-buzzing—that is, blowing the call with the lips in contact with the membrane.

We field-tested that call on wild deer, and experienced so much success that we quickly agreed to cease calling for a day or so until we were prepared to videotape the responses of the deer. Accordingly, I retired to our vehicle while Altizer scouted for good buck sign. After looking out across the open hay meadows bordering both sides of the road, I was satisfied that no deer were nearby. I rolled up the truck windows and proceeded to fine-tune some diaphragms with a series of variable-pitch wails.

When I looked up from inside the vehicle, I was startled by a herd of deer streaking hell-for-leather toward the parked truck. Altizer later told me that he turned back when he heard my calls. He saw those deer jumping in unison from their center-field beds and racing for the road.

We resumed calling that day, though we had no cameras, and even brought in a fair-size bear to within 20 yards by using nothing more than that fawn distress call.

Currently, the most popular vocalization for calling bucks is, perhaps, the tending grunt. Although some observers believe this sound is only made by bucks when they are tending or trailing estrous does, I have filmed many grunting bucks that were definitely not in the presence of either estrous does or sign of estrous does. Regardless, there is un-

doubtedly some sexual significance, and bucks of all sizes are attracted to the sound although the real trophy deer do not respond as readily to this call as they do to the grunt-snort-wheeze threat.

A series of three deliberate low-pitch croaking grunts, each followed by several minutes of silence, has probably triggered the demise of countless bucks. This kind of calling even works on mule deer and antelope. In field-testing the new Twin-Tube Coleman call, we attracted several rutting antelope bucks. With mule deer, it worked best on solo bucks. Many of the whitetail vocalizations are apparently similar to those of the other two species.

I have used the tending grunt many times from my tree stand after observing a whitetail buck passing out of bow range. After making a series of short grunts, hunters should watch for a sexually stimulated response from a buck. If the buck raises his tail so that it is stiff and horizontal (or close to it), you've got his interest. Remember to call only when he is facing or looking away from you. Never call when he is facing or advancing toward your position. If you do, he will look for the source of the sound and may see something strange.

If the buck moves off into the wind, be prepared for a downwind circle. Spray out some sex scent; position yourself favorably; and focus your attention on the terrain or cover that would best accommodate his close approach.

Full-body decoys often work well with calling, and they sometimes provide the extra incentive needed to bring in those super-cautious trophy bucks that might normally circle downwind instead of coming straight in.

I do not profess to have mastered the entire whitetail vocabulary. As for calling techniques, I am happy with my successes, and am skeptical of a hunter who reports greater than 50 percent of actual direct-deer approaches in response to the hunter's calling or rattling. Undoubtedly, there are many better hunters than I who also utilize deer talk, but they just don't talk about it.

Perhaps the most important rule is to avoid practicing where you intend to hunt. Turkey hunters soon learn not to call shortly before the season opens in a place they will later hunt. The popularity of conventional elk bugling has probably also diminished its effectiveness. Experienced bulls do not respond to straight bugling as readily as they once did. Just as new calling techniques have evolved among elk and turkey hunters, whitetail hunters who wish to remain effective will be forced to develop new techniques. Mature bucks may soon become adversely conditioned to many of the calling techniques that are so devastatingly effective today.

The Twin-Tube deer call, designed by the author for the Coleman Company, is sold through retail outlets by Golden Eagle Archery, a division of Coleman. Cost is about $22. Hunters can also purchase the deer call, as well as a deer-calling video and cassette, from Bob McGuire Video Productions, PO Box 3213, Johnson City, TN 37602.

A Good Old-Fashioned Deer Drive

By John O. Cartier

Deer will certainly move in response to the sight, sound, or scent of hunters, but they'll move in the direction they want to go. There's no way you're going to drive deer the way that farmers drive cattle back to the barn. Deer stay alive by avoiding men. They almost never go in the directions that inexperienced drivers try to push them. This is the precise reason why most modern drives don't work nearly as well as the drives the old-timers put on generations ago did.

Back then, most deer hunters were parts of groups that stayed together year after year. They hunted out of camps that were set up in the same spots every fall. They camped in and hunted territory they knew very well because they had roamed the same hills, draws, and swamps for years, maybe decades. The danger of getting lost didn't exist. These men killed a lot of deer, and they knew precisely where they killed them. They knew how they could move the whitetails because they knew where the animals would be. Experience taught them how to move—drive—deer with very carefully planned and executed movements.

Today, deer hunting is usually not the serious business it was for the old-timers. The average hunter spends far less time at his sport; he hunts in various places he knows little about; and he seldom hunts as part of a group. As a consequence, he doesn't know where a given area's deer are most likely to be; he doesn't know the escape routes the animals are most likely to follow when disturbed; he doesn't know about prevailing wind currents; and he is naive when it comes to a host of other things that are normally essential to successful driving.

But he does have one tremendous advantage the old-timer did not have, and that's the enormous amount of new knowledge about how to hunt deer. New research findings have been a big help. Much of this knowledge was unknown a decade ago, and it was developed only through thousands of hours devoted to field research projects by private groups and government agencies.

Smart hunters who know how to combine the new information with the almost forgotten driving techniques of the old-timers have developed methods of moving deer that are truly amazing.

The most significant modern discovery is that deer will pay almost no attention to *known* noise, but will become instantly alert and very concerned with an *unknown* noise. Deer aren't always jumpy and on edge. More often than not they pay little heed to nearby sounds of human activity.

Consider that some sounds of human activity actually attract whitetails. The roar of a chain saw in winter often attracts the animals because the deer have learned to expect new browse in the form of treetops and sawed-off branches. The sounds of mechanical corn pickers tell deer that there will soon be waste corn on the ground. In areas where winter starvation problems develop, various groups conduct deer feeding projects. In such areas, the animals know that sounds of approaching trucks always mean that food is on the way. But an

unknown sound can grab a deer's attention immediately, and it will likely spook the animal into moving out in a hurry.

"I can move 80 to 90 percent of the deer out of a given patch of woods," Lyle Laurvick began. "And I can move 'em even if they're in an alder jungle so darn thick you can't see anything 50 feet ahead. You would think that today's whitetails in such a jungle would never move out, but I can drive 'em out of there in a hurry.

"All I need are four experienced hunters, each not only equipped with a good watch and a good compass, but with the ability to use the tools in a precise manner. I line the men up about 20 yards apart (distance between drivers depends on the thickness of the cover) and have them start walking in the same given compass direction at exactly the same time. Each man walks slowly for exactly three minutes, stops for exactly two, then continues with the same precisely timed stop-and-go procedure until the drive is completed.

"As soon as a smart buck hears the sounds of four walking men stop at the same instant, he becomes immediately aware of something drastically out of the ordinary," Laurvick continued. "The woods are full of natural noises, but no combination of four of them ever stop at the same instant. Each time the precise noises suddenly stop, the buck becomes more nervous because he is confronted with something he can't understand. The more jumpy he gets, the more likely he is to give up his bed and move."

There is another variation of the "unknown noise" drive that is very successful. After four or five men are lined up, one of them starts on a predetermined compass course and walks for three minutes. Then another of the five does the same thing, followed by the others as their times come. The movements are timed precisely so that only one of the drivers is moving at any given time.

The idea, of course, is to produce noises that a buck has never heard before. If he doesn't understand what's going on, he doesn't know whether or not he's in trouble. Confronted with this situation, a smart buck will almost always move out.

Now let's say we have a group of knowledgeable hunters who, like many of the groups of generations ago, know their hunting area so well that they're well aware of the escape routes deer are most likely to use. If this group posts hunters in the proper places, then executes drives of the type I've mentioned, they're almost bound to hang lots of venison.

Contrast this situation with the types of drives put on by the hunters who believe that the more noise they make, the better. They beat on pans, yell back and forth, whistle, and otherwise raise a

ruckus. Deer have put up with this type of nonsense for so long that they know exactly what's going on. They are so sure of what the drivers are doing that they seldom move from their beds.

If they do move, they're almost certain to go back between the drivers and escape to the rear of the drive. Veteran drivers claim that up to 95 percent of deer moved on a drive will employ this tactic. They also claim that the deer that do move are probably no more than 25 percent of the deer that are actually in the area being driven. So it's easy to see how your odds are so vastly improved when you use drives incorporating "unknown" noises.

Drivers who keep in contact with each other by using human sounds such as whistles or yelps are making a serious mistake. Such sounds let your neighbors in the drive line know where you are and they also alert the standers to your position, but they're guaranteed to make every deer within hearing totally aware of where each hunter is located. Such deer are well aware that they're much safer if they stay hidden in their beds than if they decide to move out.

This isn't guesswork; it's a fact that's been proved many times by radio-tagged deer. These modern studies were made with deer that were captured and equipped with collars incorporating tiny radio transmitters. The transmitters enabled researchers to keep constant contact with deer movements. In the studies made involving driving techniques, it was confirmed that deer almost never move out when they're confronted with noisy drivers.

A few of today's successful drivers insist that you can move deer with "unknown" scents, too. Here's how the theory goes:

A deer, suddenly faced with a scent it can't identify, tends to avoid the scent by moving away from it. This knowledge is especially valuable when drives are staged with a normally insufficient number of hunters.

Let's say that three hunters want to drive a swamp of branches-to-the-ground cedars. They know that the drivers don't stand a chance of getting a shot in the almost impenetrable cedars, but they also know that when deer move out of these particular cedars, they always use one of three escape routes that lead out through a ravine sparsely lined with aspens.

Two men will drive the cedars, and one will take a stand in the ravine. Because there are three escape routes, it would appear that the lone man on stand has only one chance in three of correctly guessing which route the deer will use when they move out.

"Not so," said Paul Kennedy, a hunting buddy who has been driving deer for about 40 years. "Now we know that we have a fair-to-excellent chance of making sure a smart buck will use the one escape route where we place our stander. The trick is to make the stand sites on the other two escape routes

Four experienced hunters equipped simply with watches and a compass can successfully drive deer.

undesirable to approaching deer. The popular lubricant WD-40 was just coming out in spray cans when we first developed this method of driving.

"We simply went to the two unused stand sites and sprayed some WD-40 on nearby trees before we began our drive. When we got the deer moving and they approached a new and unknown scent, they moved across to the alternate route that held no new surprises. We've put a lot of venison in our freezers by using that trick. WD-40 is pretty old hat now, and a lot of hunters use it on their guns, so its scent isn't unfamiliar to many of today's deer. We've long since switched to other new spray-can products for this technique. There's always some kind of new so-called 'miracle' gunk being introduced by manufacturers. Any product having a scent that's totally new to deer will work."

Kennedy added some other tips during our conversation. No matter what driving techniques you use, it seldom pays to drive long distances because whitetails won't go very far in any direction. A drive of more than 500 yards almost never pays off because deer have too many escape options. Standers should never walk in a straight line to their stand sites. Always take the long way around to your stand and come in from the opposite direction the cover area will be driven from. It is obviously pointless to drive an area where the deer have already become aware of the standers. Once on stand, the posted men should remain motionless until the drivers come out. The slightest movement will be noticed by a deer that's already spooked.

Kennedy emphasized that it's virtually impossible to drive large, unbroken stands of forest. He also feels that drives involving large parties of hunters become unwieldy. It's difficult to control a gang of more than six hunters.

"Stay away from the larger areas because you can't move the deer out of them," Kennedy pointed out. "The deer will just mill around in there, constantly aware of where the drivers are. The best areas to drive are those that are small enough to make it tough for deer to sneak around drivers without the real possibility of being seen. It's always best to select woodlands that are bound by lakes, open fields, and other such natural barriers. Deer don't want to expose themselves in such areas. Make it tough for them to move in any direction except where your standers are. You'll harvest a lot more venison if you use natural barriers to funnel deer toward your standers. In order to do this, you have to know the lay of the land like your backyard. This is the main reason why the old-timers were so good at driving deer."

All experienced drivers know that it's a waste of time trying to work drives upwind. Deer traveling that way will be sure to scent standers and sneak around them. It's almost as bad to drive downwind. In this case, the animals use their scenting capabilities to pinpoint the movements of approaching drivers.

It's best to make drives crosswind because this technique makes it much more difficult for the deer to scent either drivers or standers. The stronger the wind, the more difficult it is for deer to pinpoint the locations of anybody. Because high winds deprive deer of their sound/scent knowledge, deer become extremely nervous when they first become aware of the presence of drivers on windy days. When a drive is made against a very strong crosswind, drivers are more likely to get shots than standers. Deer just don't like to move in strong winds, so they're not likely to bolt until a driver almost steps on them.

I've experienced that dramatic moment several times, and believe me, it's one of the most exciting things that can happen to a deer hunter. Many years ago, back in the days when I smoked cigars, I was puffing on a half-smoked panatela when I almost walked on top of a bedded buck. When he blew out of there, it was almost like a bomb exploding. I threw my rifle to my shoulder in such a hurry that the stock smashed against my lighted cigar. Red-hot ashes sprayed against my face as I tried desperately to find the bolting buck in my sights. I never even got a shot off.

Just a few years ago, four of us were driving a small alder thicket. Near the end of the drive, Charlie Blanchard, who was just a few yards to my right, began angling toward me. At that precise instant, I almost stepped on another buck. The big bruiser must have had his total attention on me because he blitzed straight at Charlie. Man and deer saw each other at the same instant, but it was almost too late to avoid a head-on collision. Since then, Charlie has always insisted that the buck actually brushed against him as it went flashing past.

The more hunting pressure in any given area, the more reason to try getting your deer with a modern drive. The reason is simply that clever bucks become very nocturnal in direct proportion to the amount of hunting pressure. In heavily hunted areas, these bucks simply will not move from their beds except in dark-of-night hours unless they're forced to.

In such cases, the hunter on a stand during dawn and evening hours just isn't going to see the buck that won't be moving. The stalker can't stalk a buck that can't be seen, and the tracker can't track a buck that doesn't make tracks. Seasoned, gun-shy bucks are likely to be moved only by well-planned and organized drives.

Every driving situation is unique because conditions vary with each piece of terrain that lends itself to driving. For this reason, I can't tell you how to drive a certain area you may have in mind, but I can offer some suggestions that apply to all drives, regardless of the specific terrain on which they're conducted.

Of prime importance is the knowledge that the harder you appear to be trying to drive a buck, the less chance of success you'll have. This is why noisy

Illustration by Nina Wallace

Here's what a typical deer drive should look like. The bold lines are blazed trails that run due north, south, east, or west—no in-betweens. Trails are stopping and starting places for drives, and letters are reference points known to every member of the party. Watches must be synchronized to keep the drivers organized. The arrows denote the direction of the drivers (note the many different directions in which drives can be done). Drive direction must be altered according to the wind. Standers are denoted by black dots. Similar drives can be set up almost anywhere you hunt.

drives seldom work. The opposite is always true. The principle involved is that secrecy is always the best policy. The less the buck understands about your plan, the better. This is why the "unknown" noise and "unknown" scent drives can be successful. But neither of those drives will work if the buck has any suspicion at all of where your standers (point men) are located.

I've already touched on this point, but I want to emphasize that standers must reach their stand sites in total secrecy. The biggest mistake made by beginning drivers is that they don't give their standers enough time to properly reach the positions. Each person involved in the drive must know exactly where each stander will be and how long it will take each stander to get there under current weather conditions.

When you try to drive a buck, he can do only one of three things.

- He can sneak out of the area far ahead of the drivers, and likely before the standers get into position. This happens when the driving group is unaware of the importance of secrecy and advertises its presence with loud talking, slamming of vehicle doors, and other man-produced noises.
- He can sneak back behind the drivers by going between or around them. This is what deer often decide to do when a driving group attempts to drive a woodland that is too big or when the group spaces its drivers far apart. Proper distance between drivers depends on terrain. In dense cover, 20 yards is not too close; in rela-

tively open woods, 100 yards or more could be about right. Spacing is always determined on the basis of how close drivers should be to each other to prevent deer from sneaking back through the line unseen. If a buck wants to sneak back through the line of drivers but decides there is too good a chance of being seen, he probably won't try it.

A buck especially won't try it if he is faced with drivers who *are not* in a straight line. Knowledgeable drivers move forward in a formation more closely representing a U or V. The forward parts, or ends, of such drives tend to intercept deer that try sneaking around or through drives. Such animals are more likely to reconsider and move toward standers, particularly because they detect being surrounded.

- He can attempt to stay hidden and let the drivers walk by him. Whitetails almost always do this when drivers walk too fast. You should always move ahead with a leisurely pace. Deer are much more likely to move ahead toward standers if they know they don't have to hurry. They aren't too concerned with drivers who just seem to be messing around somewhere in the woods behind them. They'll take their time moving out along established escape routes. Deer almost never run at random; they go where they want to go. This again is why it's impossible to drive deer to specific locations. All you can do is get them moving and hope for the best.

With military-type precision planning, the odds are definitely improved in your favor. I've hunted with a group in northern Wisconsin that enjoys tremendous success. There are about eight men in this team of drivers, and they have hunted together almost every day of every firearms deer season since World War II. Everybody usually gets a buck. When a stander gets his deer, he becomes, or volunteers to become, a driver until all the other members of the group have filled their tags.

This group operates with as much military precision as I've seen in a group of hunters. They work precisely timed drives. An explanation of how they work is best made by studying the sketch that follows. The bold lines represent the driving area. Note that the area is about a mile from the closest roads, so far that most hunters aren't likely to bother with it.

The bold lines are blazed trails. They're not trails in the true sense of the word; they're marked by simple blaze marks on trees. All trails run in straight north, east, south, or west directions—no in-betweens. This is so because what might be 7 degrees off straight north for one driver might be read as 2 degrees off north for another. All drives go straight north, east, south, or west so drivers can stay organized with military-type precision.

All drivers have stand sites on a trail or within

sight of a trail. The trails are starting and stopping places for drives. The letters on the trails are reference points, and their precise locations are known to all members of the group. Each member also knows how long it takes, for example, to walk from point E to point H. With this knowledge, each driver knows how long it should take to make a drive, say, from line D/E to line I/H. All of this information enables drivers and standers to stay precisely organized. All members know at all times exactly where they are in relation to any given letter's spot.

The overall driving area is divided into rectangles for other reasons, too. Let's say the group finds several fresh deer tracks leading into one of the rectangular areas. Several of the hunters will very quietly go to stands on all four sides (trails) surrounding the rectangle. After the standers are in position, one or two men head into the rectangle, following fresh deer tracks. Sooner or later, the deer being tracked should move out of the rectangle, hopefully within sight of one of the standers.

The arrows in the sketch represent the paths of drivers. Note the great variety of directions the drivers can go. In other words, no matter which way the wind is blowing, there are always some drives that can be made within the overall hunting area. Note that each arrow direction could be reversed if the next day's wind blew from the opposite direction. The possibilities are almost endless.

You can set up a similar area for your own group. Start by selecting an area. Then begin preparing your hunting map by tracing over a U.S. Geological Survey map to get section lines, creeks, roads, power lines, and so forth. Then outline your overall hunting area in rectangles and spot your identifying letters.

I should add that the area shown in the sketch was chosen for two reasons. First, it's a jungle-like area where deer concentrate after the shooting begins in surrounding areas. The deer go there because the terrain is too thick and tangled for most hunters. Second, before freeze-up, there is a lot of standing water and muck. The group never hunts the area until the last week of the gun season. By then, many deer are concentrated in the driving area; the deer are easier to see against the usually snow-covered background; and the drivers are likely to have far easier walking over the frozen water and muck.

When you consider all those advantages, it's no wonder that this group of dedicated drivers figures that it's just natural that each member of the group gets a buck every fall. It's likely there's an area near you where your group can score with the same degree of success.

For your copy of John O. Cartier's HOW TO GET YOUR DEER, please send $24.95 plus $2.64 for postage and handling to Outdoor Life Books, Dept. DHY8, Box 2018, Latham, NY 12111.

The Hunting Lesson

By Patrick F. McManus

Over the years it has been my distinct honor and pleasure to introduce numerous persons to the sport of hunting the whitetail deer. It is odd, however, that a man can have a thousand successes and one failure, and it will be the failure that sticks in his mind like a porky quill in a hound's nose. Thus it is with my single failure, one Sidney Fipps. Even now, five years later, I torment myself with the question of where I went wrong. How did I slip up with Fipps?

The affair started off innocently enough. One fall day, with none of my regular hunting partners available for the following weekend, I strolled next door to Sidney's house to invite him to go deer hunting with me. I found him digging up bulbs in the garden and greeted him informally, namely by sneaking up behind him and dumping a basket of moldering leaves over his head. Not one to enjoy a good joke on himself, Sidney growled malevolently as he shook the soggy leaves from his balding dome and thrust blindly at me with the garden trowel.

"Sidney," I said, holding him at bay with a rake handle, "I am about to give you the opportunity of a lifetime. How would you like to go deer hunting with me?"

"Not much," he replied, digging some leaf mold from an ear. "In fact, my desire to go hunting with you is so small as to escape detection by any means known to science!"

"Don't like hunting, huh?" I asked. "Well, many people who have never been exposed to the sport feel that way about it. Listen, I can teach you all about hunting. One weekend out with me, and you'll come back loving it."

"No," Sidney snarled.

"If nothing else, you'll enjoy getting out in the crisp mountain air. It will invigorate you."

"No! No! NO!"

"Sid, I just know you'll enjoy the camaraderie of the hunting camp, the thrill of the pursuit, the . . . ."

"No, I tell you, no! *Go home!*"

". . . the free meat and . . . ."

"Free meat?"

"Sure. Just think of packing away all those free venison steaks and chops and roasts in the freezer."

"Free meat. Venison's pretty tasty, too. I tasted it once. Yeah, I wouldn't mind getting a bunch of free meat. Then, too, as you say, there's the hunting camp camaraderie, the crisp mountain air and the thrill of pursuit. But I'm willing to put up with all that stuff if I can get some free meat."

I would have patted him on the shoulder but I didn't want to get my hands all dirty with leaf mold.

"I can see right now you have the makings of a true sportsman," I told him.

"So, how do I get this free deer?" Sidney asked.

"Well, you just go out with me and get it. Of course, there are a few odds and ends you'll need to pick up down at Duffy's Sporting Goods."

"Like what?"

"Oh, let's see. You'll want a rifle, of course. Outfitted with scope and sling. A few boxes of shells. Seems to me there's something else. A knife! You need a good hunting knife. And a whetstone. I nearly forgot the whetstone. That should be about it. You have a good pair of insulated boots don't you? No? Oh, wool pants, you'll need wool pants and some good wool socks and a wool shirt and a down parka and some thermal underwear and an orange hunting vest and a red cap. Heck, that should do it. Good, you're making a list. Did I say gloves? Get some gloves. Oh, binoculars! And first-aid kit. And a survival kit, with a daypack to carry it in. Rope; you'll need a length of rope for dragging your free deer out of the mountains with. We could use my tent, of course, but it has a rip in the roof on the guest's side. You might want to buy a tent. A sub-zero sleeping bag, did I mention that? You'll probably want an insulated sleeping pad, too. Down booties are awfully nice to slip into when you take off your hunting boots, but they're optional. Then there's the grub, and that's it."

"Hmmmm," Sidney said, studying his list. "Just how big are these free deer, anyway?"

"Plenty big enough," I said.

"Geez," he said. "I don't know how I can afford to buy all the stuff on this list."

"Take some advice from an old, experienced hunter," I said. "Mortgage the house."

The day after Sidney purchased his gear I took him out to the gun club range and we sighted in his rifle. He grouped his last five shots right in the center of the bull's-eye. Then I showed him my technique of scattering shots randomly around the target because, as I explained, you never know which way the deer might jump just as you pull the trigger.

"How long before I learn to do that?" Sidney asked.

"Years," I said. "It's not something you master overnight."

The day before the hunt my old friend Retch Sweeney called up and said he would be able to make it after all.

"How come he's going?" Sidney snapped when I told him the news. They are not exactly bosom buddies.

"He's between jobs," I said.

"I didn't know he ever worked," Sidney growled. "When did he get laid off?"

"1957."

I explained to Sidney the absolute necessity of being ready on time the following morning. "We'll pick you up at your house at two sharp. Got that? *Two sharp!*"

"Right," he said.

"Don't bother about breakfast. We can grab a quick bite at Greasy Gert's Gas 'n Grub just before we turn off the highway and head up to our hunting area. Now remember, *two sharp!*"

We picked Sidney up the next morning at exactly 4:15. He was furious. Naturally, Retch and I were puzzled. Then it occurred to me that since this was Sidney's first hunt, he didn't realize that when hunters say "two sharp," they mean "sometime around four."

"Stop whimpering and toss your gear in back," Retch said kindly. "You better not have forgot nothin' either, because we're not turnin' around and comin' back for it! Now put your rifle in the rack next to mine."

"What do you mean, next to yours?"

"That ol' .30/06 right ther. . . . . Say, I wonder if you fellas mind swingin' by my house again. Just take a few minutes."

After Retch had picked up his rifle and I had returned to my house for my sleeping bag and then we had gone back to Retch's for his shells, it was 5 o'clock by the time we got out to the highway.

"Aren't we going to be awfully late with all these delays?" Sidney asked. "What time will we start hunting?"

Retch and I looked at each other and laughed. "Why, man, we're already hunting!" Retch said. "This is it. Gettin' there is half the fun."

We drove along in darkness for an hour, with Retch and me entertaining Sidney with bawdy jokes and detailed accounts of other hunting trips. "It was a tough shot, looked impossible to me at first," Retch was saying. "The deer was going away from me at an angle and. . . ."

I held up my hand for silence. "OK, now we got to get serious. We're coming to the most difficult and dangerous part of the trip. We get through this ordeal and we should be OK. It'll be easy going by comparison from then on. Now I want you guys to watch yourselves. If you start to feel faint or queasy, Sid, let Retch or me know, and we'll help you out."

"Cripes!" Sidney said, nervously. "What do we have to do, climb a sheer cliff or something?"

"Worse," I said. "We're going to eat breakfast at Greasy Gert's."

Dawn had long since cracked and spilled over the mountains by the time we arrived at our hunting spot. Retch looked out the window and groaned.

"What are you groaning for?" I asked. "I'm the one that had Greasy Gert's chili pepper omelette."

"It's not that," Retch said. "I see fresh tracks in the snow all over the place. If we'd been here an hour earlier, we'd have nailed us some deer."

"Listen," I said. "Did we come out to nail deer or to go hunting today? If we're hunting, we have to get up two hours late, forget a bunch of stuff we have to go back for and then stop for breakfast at Gerty's. You know how it's done."

"Yeah, sorry, I forgot for a second when I saw the tracks," Retch said. "I got carried away. Who

cares about nailing deer right off, for Pete's sake!''

"I do!'' Sidney whined. "I got $2,500 worth of gear with me and I want to get my free deer!''

It was clear that Sidney had a lot to learn about hunting, so I lost no time in starting on his first lesson. I put him on a stand and told him that Retch and I would sweep around the far side of the ridge and drive some deer past him. "We'll be back in an hour,'' I told him. "Don't move!''

Retch and I returned three hours later and found Sidney still on the stand. We tilted him over against a tree for safety until we got a fire going to thaw him out. "How come you didn't move around?'' I asked him.

"Y-you to-told me to stay on the st-stand. You said y-you would be b-back in an hour and for me not to m-move.''

"I'm sorry, I should have explained,'' I said. "When a hunter says he'll be back in an hour, that means not less than three hours. Furthermore, nobody ever stays on a stand like he's told to. As soon as the other hunters are out of sight, he beats it off to some other place where he's sure there's a deer but there never is. That's standard procedure. I guess I should have mentioned it to you.''

"Yeah,'' Retch said. "Anyway, next time you'll know. It takes a while to catch on to deer hunting.

Well, we might as well make camp. We ain't gonna get no deer today.''

"Oh, I got one!'' Sidney said. "See, he's lying over there behind that log. He was too big for me to move by myself. Right after you fellows left, he came tearing along the trail there, and I shot him.''

"Oh, oh!'' I said. "Better go have a look, Retch.''

Retch walked over to the deer, looked down, shook his head and walked back. "We're in for it now,'' he told me.

"How bad is it?'' I asked.

"Six points.''

"Cripes!'' I said.

"Did I do it wrong?'' Sidney asked.

"We'll have to wait and see,'' I said.

Sidney thought for a moment, then smiled. "Gee, wouldn't it be funny if I was the only one to get a deer and it was my first trip and all, and you guys were teaching me how to hunt? Not that I would ever mention it to the guys down at Kelly's Bar & Grill, but. . . . Is six points good? Say, let me tell you how I got him. It was a tough shot, looked impossible to me at first. The deer was going away from me at an angle, and. . . .''

"It's going to be worse than I thought,'' Retch said.

"Yeah,'' I said. "Ol' Sidney learns fast.''

PART 3

HUNTING MULE DEER

The Mule Deer

By Jack O'Connor

Written by the late Jack O'Connor, *Outdoor Life's* former shooting editor, this classic discussion of the animal's natural history is tailored to the needs of the hunter. It originally appeared in January 1960.

Whenever anyone assures me that all mule deer are morons, I think of the first really big buck I ever shot. I knew of a chain of hills where early in the season I had always seen a good many does, fawns, and young bucks. One year I turned down easy shots at two or three perfectly legal males, knowing that late in the season a big fellow would probably show up to boot out the small bucks and take over the harem.

So it came about that one afternoon when the Arizona season had only a couple of days to go, and when every morning white frost glinted on the grass and the brooks up in the mountains were frozen at the edges, I hit my little chain of hills again. By taking a game trail up the side of a wide canyon I had an easy walk to the top. When I got there I planned to work along the ridge and hunt the points and the heads of the draws.

I had hardly started up the trail when I saw a movement in the buckbrush and junipers about 400 yards ahead of me and toward the top of the ridge. It was a doe. Then I saw more shadowy gray forms, and I could tell that about a dozen deer were going over the top. Then a larger form detached itself from the group and sneaked off to the left. Even at a quarter of a mile or so I could see a big gray body and heavy, many-pointed antlers. Here was the

82

buck I had been looking for, the old boy himself. He had collected his harem and chased the young bucks out, but now that danger threatened he was abandoning the ladies and looking after his own sleek hide.

I felt that he'd cut over the ridge into the head of the next draw. So the moment he was out of sight, I ran over the ridge that separated the two canyons and stopped in a spot that gave me a good look at the far side. I hadn't got my wind back when I heard a stone roll, and in a moment I saw him slipping through the scrubby junipers and piñons with his head up and his great antlers laid back so they would get through the brush easier. If he kept on coming he would go by me on the opposite side of the draw, so I switched off the safety of my Springfield and waited.

It was the first time I'd ever been close to a really big trophy buck, and I'll never forget the sight he presented—the blocky, dark-gray body, the heavy brown antlers with the many points polished sharp and bright, the massive neck swelled from the rut, the maniacal look of lust and excitement in his eyes. I had the wind on him and I could smell the oily, rancid odor of the rutting mule deer, a smell at once fascinating and repellent, heavy, musky, greasy. He saw the movement when I lifted the rifle to my shoulder, and stopped less than 50 yards away. Winded, and shaking with excitement though I was, I couldn't very well miss him. There was nothing wrong with that buck's brains. In the grip of the strongest of instincts, he was yet smart enough and cool-headed enough to leave his does as decoys and try to slip out one side and around where the danger was.

The mule deer is no boob, but I must admit that he generally isn't as smart as his cousin the white-

An often-fatal habit of the muley's is to stop for a last look-see before bounding out of the hunter's range.

tail, or as hard to get. Part of this comes from the fact that he is more of an open-country animal and hence is easier to see and hunt. But part of it also comes from the fact that he does not lie as close, that he takes longer to make up his mind, and that he often is addicted to the fatal habit of stopping for one last look before he gets out of sight.

A whitetail will conceal himself in a patch of brush hardly big enough to hide a pheasant. If he thinks he can't sneak off unseen, he'll sit tight with hunters all around him. When he thinks he has to move, he's off like a rocketing grouse and he doesn't stop for a backward look. The mule deer, on the other hand, has a tendency to move off and reveal himself in the face of danger, to jitter around, unable to decide which way to run, and to stop for one good look. But old trophy bucks get cautious. They select their beds with care, and get almost as good as the whitetail is at slipping away from the hunter.

A very smart and close-lying buck mule deer I'll never forget was one I shot in northern Arizona in 1934. I had made a long trip to hunt an area I knew well, and I was after a trophy head. I turned down several small bucks and a couple of good average ones with four points to a side. About 2 P.M. of my last day I stopped on the brink of a canyon to eat a sandwich. I was still without a deer and was kicking myself for passing up the two four-pointers. Below me I could see the trail that led to camp about five miles away. I was going to have to start back, pack

O'Connor grabbed the horns as the buck sprang to life.

Illustrations by Doug Allen

up, and leave empty-handed.

After I finished my sandwich, I drank from my canteen, smoked a cigarette, and started to lead my horse down the side of the canyon which was too steep and rocky to ride down safely. I hadn't gone more than 30 yards when a tremendous buck got up from beneath a juniper below me about 300 yards away and took off. On my second or third shot he fell head over heels and lay in the scrubby sage. When I got to him I found he needed another shot. The bullet that dumped him had passed through the knee joint of his left front leg. He must have had most of his weight on this leg when it was struck, and the fall must have stunned him. He had seven points on one side, six on the other, and a spread of 34½ inches. A right fair buck. All the time he'd been lying there getting more and more nervous, and when I started toward him he must have thought he'd been seen. If I'd gone the other way, I'm sure I would never have known he was there. All mule deer aren't dumb.

The fact that they have adapted themselves to great varieties of climate and terrain also shows they have their share of brains. They are found from the Dakotas to the crest of the Coast Ranges, from the hot subtropical deserts of Sonora, Mexico, to the subarctic tundras of northern British Columbia. I have seen mule deer in country rough enough for mountain sheep and have, in fact, seen bighorns and deer feeding on the same hillside. I have likewise seen them in the cactus and brush on the level deserts of northern Mexico. When I was hunting antelope some years ago around Gillette, Wyoming, there were many mule deer in the brush coulees where little streams wandered through the antelope plains. When they were frightened they'd take right off across the sagebrush flats with the antelope.

In most areas mule deer have increased enormously in the past 20 or 30 years, so much so that they have starved on their winter range. They have invaded the suburbs in many Western cities, particularly in the winter when feed is scarce. In the north they have followed the Alaska Highway up into southern Yukon, where they have never been known before. So plentiful have the mule deer become in some states that in certain areas hunters can legally take two, and even three, deer.

The mule deer got his Latin name of hemionus from his large ears, hemionus being the Latin word for mule. In general, the muley is a different breed of cat from his whitetail cousin. Instead of having the whitetail's large, floppy tail—generally body-colored on top and snow-white beneath—the mule deer has a small, thinly haired tail of dingy white with a black tip. He does not throw it up when frightened, as the whitetail does. He always keeps it hanging down. The tail of the muley's near relative, the Columbian blacktail, is about halfway in size between the small one of the mule deer and the large one flaunted by the whitetail. It is black on top, and instead of tossing it up when frightened, as the whitetail does, he carries it horizontal.

In many ways the blacktail looks like a compromise between the mule deer and the whitetail. It's an odd fact that in areas where both mule deer and whitetails range, one occasionally comes across bucks that look like Pacific Coast blacktails. They are crosses between whitetails and mule deer. I have never shot one, but I have seen several that were taken in southern Arizona and northern Sonora.

The mule deer has a strongly marked face with a dark V on the forehead and a light muzzle, as compared with the whitetail's fairly uniformly dark face. All the points of the whitetail's antlers come off of one main beam, but the antlers of the mule deer are evenly branched. The brow tine of the whitetail's antlers is always conspicuous and large, but that of the mule deer is smaller and sometimes absent altogether. Pacific Coast blacktail antlers look like those of mule deer, and both differ so much from those of the whitetail that it is almost impossible to confuse them. In the West the brow tine is not counted, and only the points on one antler are referred to. A four-pointer by Western count would be a ten-pointer in the East.

An odd thing about the facial markings of mule deer that I have never seen referred to in print is that the latitude from which the deer comes can pretty well be told by the black line around the lower jaw. In the northern portion of the range in Alberta and British Columbia, the black line goes completely around. Somewhat farther south the line is divided in the middle, and at the lower end of the range—in the deserts of southern Arizona and northern Mexico—the line has degenerated into two dark spots on either side of the lower jaw.

In favored localities mule deer grow tremendous antlers, and a fine muley head is one of the most beautiful of all North American trophies. These big heads are found wherever there is plenty of lime in the food and water. Colorado has produced many great heads, and so have the limestone ranges of Alberta. Many spectacular ones have come out of Arizona's Kaibab National Forest north of the Grand Canyon. I have not hunted there for many years, but I believe I have seen a higher proportion of exceptional heads there than anywhere else. I once measured a Kaibab head with a spread of 47 1/2 inches and about 20 points to the side. Another region of fine heads that is little known is in Sonora south of the town of Altar, and I have seen some beauties from southern Idaho. In the latest edition of Records of North American Big Game, the world record typical mule deer head came from Arizona's Kaibab.

On average the mule deer is the largest of American deer, but many tales told of their size are on the giddy side. For the past 40 years I have been following up rumors of bucks that are supposed to have field dressed at 400 pounds and more, but I have yet to find an authentic instance of one. Apparently the very largest mule deer and the heaviest northern whitetail from Maine and Michigan are about the same size, with dressed weight running something over 300 pounds and live weight at close to 400.

For many years all deer brought into the hunting camps of Arizona's Kaibab were weighed, and in years of good forage the heaviest bucks would weigh something over 300 pounds hog dressed. The largest bucks I have authentic weights on all go about like that, with records running from 300 to 335 pounds. I have heard of many bucks that weighed more, but when I investigated I found the weight was estimated. I have shot two bucks that went 175 and 176 pounds in the quarters (the four quarters weighed without skin, head, or entrails). One was shot northwest of Flagstaff, Arizona, and the other down in the Sonora desert. The Arizona buck had been hit in the ham as he ran away from me and I had cut away 10 or 12 pounds of bloodshot meat. How much would they have weighed field dressed? I don't know. They might have gone 250 pounds or so and well over 300 on the hoof.

I have only seen one buck I thought would weigh 300 pounds field dressed, and it was shot in exactly the same area, Slate Mountain northwest of Flagstaff, where I killed my heaviest Arizona buck. He was distinctly larger than any other buck I've ever seen. But anyone who gets a buck that weighs 175 pounds field dressed has a large one, and anyone who gets one that weighs 200 has a very large one. A Western game warden I know has weighed hundreds of mule deer and says he has never seen one that weighed more than 225 pounds dressed. I have yet to see a buck mule deer anything like as large as a spike bull elk.

In most areas with which I'm familiar, the mule deer begin to show signs of the rut by the end of the first week in November, and by the middle of November most of the bucks have swelled necks and are starting to get interested in the does. The height of the rut for most Rocky Mountain mule deer is probably about the last week of November and the first week of December. Then each big buck collects as large a harem as he can and viciously defends it from other bucks.

The desert mule deer of southern Arizona and northern Sonora are not well into the rut until about the middle of January, apparently a provision of nature for the does to be in milk during the summer rains. The old bucks have a grim time. Each will have from four to 12 does, and the bunch will move endlessly, restlessly. Hanging around the outskirts will be from two to four smaller bucks. Now and then when one of these approaches too closely, the big herd buck will chase it away. Occasionally one of the hangers-on will do battle, but generally they turn tail and run. On many occasions I have seen a small buck slip in and cover a doe while the lord of the harem was chasing off another one, but I have yet to see the big, heavy-horned bucks in the act of mating. I have a notion that most of the breeding is actually done by the young bucks, and that big fellows have all the responsibility and little else.

At the height of the rut the old buck is a sight awesome yet piteous, and at that time he's easily killed. He has a wild and desperate look in his eyes—as anyone would who had 12 wives ready to two-time him—and he looks gaunt and ragged. Generally he has a point or two broken off his antlers and skinned and bleeding places on his neck. The ones I've seen have always been running around with their mouths open as if they had difficulty in breathing, and I have had them go by me within 20 feet and pay no attention to me.

A Mexican cowboy I once knew was sitting on a hillside one January day brewing a can of coffee and heating up some tortillas when he saw a desert mule deer doe trot by about 50 yards away. A minute or so later a big buck, following her trail with his nose to the ground, came into sight. The vaquero had a little Winchester Model 92 .25/20 carbine on his saddle. He unlimbered it and shot the buck in the neck. Before he could get to it a smaller buck came along on the trail. He shot that one and a moment later yet another—this an ardent little forkhorn. I went by his place a week afterward and he had jerky strung up everywhere.

Once the rut is over, the bucks leave the does and start putting some fat on their ribs. Sometimes one sees solitary bucks, but generally a couple will travel together, often a large buck and a small one. Occasionally before the rut I have seen several together, and one time near Slate Mountain I saw a herd of about 30 fine big bucks. But that was exceptional.

The gestation period of the mule deer is seven months, and in the Rocky Mountains the young are born in late May and early June. In the deserts, of course, they are born later. Young does generally give birth to single fawns, but mature does almost always have twins. In areas where food is plentiful and predators are not numerous, around 40 percent of the deer should be taken annually if the herd is to be kept within the limits of its food supply.

Coyotes and bobcats take fawns, and some are even killed by golden eagles. But the greatest natural predator of the mule deer is the mountain lion. Every one of these big cats, the most skillful deer hunters in the world, will kill from 100 to 150 deer a year—a lot of deer. Compared with the incredibly stealthy mountain lion, man isn't a very good hunter.

One factor in the astonishing increase of mule deer throughout the West has been the thinning out of the lion population in certain areas. In Arizona's Kaibab, which was for years open to lion hunting but closed for deer, the explosion of the deer population—with the result that tens of thousands of them starved to death and the range was permanently damaged—came about because there were too few lions. In the West today there are many problem-deer areas not only because there is a shortage of lions but because the coyotes have been poisoned off.

As is the case with most other game meat, mule deer venison varies enormously with the time the

The mountain lion has proven to be the greatest natural predator of the mule deer.

deer was taken, his condition, the manner in which he was killed, and what he'd been eating. No deer taken during and right after the rut is much good to eat, and no deer is good if he's been wounded and chased all over the country before being dispatched. The deer of some localities produce fine venison and of others they do not. I think the answer lies in their food.

The desert mule deer of southern Arizona and northern Mexico (like the bighorn sheep and whitetails that occupy the same country) are almost always fine eating. The answer probably lies in what they eat—mild and nourishing plants like jojoba, mesquite beans, leaves of the ironwood, and cactus fruit. Some mule deer in the Southwest spend the entire year on the winter range, and without exception these are poor eating because of the bitter plants, such as juniper and quinine brush, they devour. Deer that have fattened on mild morsels such as aspen leaves, mushrooms, and piñon nuts are as good as the best beef. I have shot several deer on the Salmon River upstream from Riggins, Idaho, and I have yet to find one that furnished first-class venison. On the other hand, all the deer I have taken off the Snake River upstream from Lewiston, Idaho, would melt in your mouth.

One of the worst bucks I ever ate was a fine, fat three-year-old I took in the piñon-juniper belt in northern Arizona, and one of the most delicious was an old-timer I shot in the Kaibab. He was hog fat with four inches of lard on his rump, and I think I must have taken him right after he came down from the summer range where he'd been feasting on mushrooms and aspen leaves. He was blind in one eye, and so old I think he'd lost his interest in the gals. Although I shot him on Armistice Day—a time when the necks of most of the bucks were swelled and some of them were showing interest in

the does—he gave no sign at all of the rut. The meat was so tender you could cut it with a fork. But once the rut is well under way, the venison is strong and musty.

Some of my most pleasant memories are of hunting mule deer. I have hunted them right at timberline in the Rockies, where they can be glassed and stalked like sheep. On those lofty ridges right at the limit of trees it has been my experience that the deer are almost always bucks—generally big ones—as the does and young bucks tend to summer lower where there is more cover. And I have stillhunted them down in the flat deserts of Sonora so close to salt water that I could see the blue Gulf of California by climbing a little hill. It's a great joy to sneak quietly along upwind in the frequently chilly hours of early morning watching through the cholla and palo verde for the glimpse of gray that means a deer. It is easy tracking country, and often I have taken up the fresh trail of a buck as he fed along.

But some of the most interesting hunts I have ever had have been on horseback for the great bucks of Arizona's north Kaibab. It is easy riding country for the most part—wide, shallow draws and long ridges clothed with a scattering of junipers. A couple of horsemen riding down a ridge will usually pull deer off the points. The action can be fast and furious when a big buck comes tearing across an open flat or trotting along a hillside flashing in and out of the junipers. That used to be a great deer country, and I presume it still is. Many times I've seen from ten to 200 big bucks in a day, and well over 100 deer, and the man who could pass up the ordinary heads had a good chance of finding a trophy to be proud of.

Once a friend and I were hunting there on horseback when we saw a tremendous buck just going over a ridge. The footing was good for horses, so

Hunting from horseback, the action can be wild when you see a buck slip from cover or rip over the flats.

we dug in the spurs and went after it. We chased it over about three ridges never having it in sight long enough to jump off and shoot. Then the buck (no dumbbell he) cut to the left up a draw and turned left again about 300 yards away in an effort to get into heavy timber. I jumped off my horse, grabbed my .30/06 out of the scabbard, swung ahead of him, and let drive. I saw him go down at the front quarters, and then he was out of sight.

We jumped on our horses again, took after him, and found him down. He looked not long for this world, but he was still breathing. Foolishly I decided to cut his throat. At the prick of the knife he came frantically alive. I dropped the knife and threw myself on his head, with a hand on each antler. The buck dragged me in a 50-yard circle, bumping me against every bush and tree around. When he finally collapsed I was skinned, dusty, and covered with blood. From that time on I have never tried to dispatch another animal by attempting to cut its throat.

Because mule deer are usually found in open, hilly country, and because they tend to move out ahead of danger, they are generally shot at longer ranges than are whitetails. As I look back on 40 years of hunting them, I'd guess the average range at which I've shot muleys has been well over 200 yards—maybe 250. I have shot a good many at 300 or a little over, but doubt very much if I've ever shot more than one or two at 400. Those I have taken in the brushy desert have, of course, been much closer.

I believe I've taken more mule deer with a .30/06 than with anything else, and because they usually open up quicker I like the 150-grain bullets better than the 180's. Compared with a moose or an elk, even a large mule deer is lightly constructed, offering no great amount of resistance to a bullet, and the heavier loads generally don't open up quickly enough to nail deer in their tracks. The .30/30 with the old soft-point bullet with plenty of lead exposed is good deer medicine up to about 150 yards, but beyond that distance it won't anchor a deer unless the shot is placed just right. With the 150-grain bullet in the .30/06 or .300 Magnum, or the 130-grain bullet in the .270, quick and spectacular kills are the rule.

Oddly enough I have killed more deer with fewer shots with the 7 × 57 Mauser than with anything else—all with 140-grain bullets. I believe I have killed 12 deer with 12 hits. In Mexico, over a score of years ago, I once had to shoot a desert mule deer twice with a 7mm, but a few years ago I let fly at a fat doe at about 300 yards and the bullet went through her and killed a spike buck on the far side. Both of the deer came rolling down the hillside at the same time.

Once I literally killed a big buck in his tracks with the 7mm. I was out with my wife, who had shot a buck earlier, when we saw this beautiful buck standing by a tree about 200 yards away across the canyon. I dropped into a sitting position and let one go. He collapsed like a paper deer in a puff of wind. When we went over we could see that his feet were still in his last tracks. I have a lot of respect for that little 7mm.

Much as I like old Odocoileus hemionus, I have to admit that he doesn't have as much in the way of gray matter under the antlers as an elk or a whitetail, and that he won't give the hunter quite as much of a run for his money. We all can't be geniuses, though, and the mule-deer hunter who confines himself to the hunting of big bucks will get all the action he could want. And when he gets a real trophy head he has something—the finest antlers worn by any American deer.

High-Low Trophy Bucks

By Kirt Darner, as told to
Rich LaRocco

One of the greatest myths in mule-deer hunting is that most really big bucks live way up in the high country. As a full-time forester in Colorado and a serious trophy deer hunter for more than 20 years, I've seen my share of record-class bucks in that stunning alpine landscape above timberline. But I've also seen dozens of gigantic muleys in middle-altitude oakbrush thickets, low-country river bottoms, and pinyon/juniper jungles. Indeed, altitude seemingly has little to do with where you might find your buck of a lifetime.

One of the largest mule deer that I've ever seen was standing right on a major highway less than half an hour's drive from my home in Montrose, Colorado. With ten record-class bucks to my credit, I knew what I was seeing. This behemoth's antlers were as big around as baseball bats and spread at least 40 inches. I'm positive that he would have ranked very high in the Boone and Crockett Club's record book.

I'd like to report that I returned to the area when deer season opened and tied my tag to his fabulous rack, but that was not to be. King-size muleys don't get that way by making mistakes, and that animal was no exception. Though I used all my hunting skills in an attempt to locate the old buck, I caught nary a glimpse of him, but I did see many of his huge, blocky tracks. As far as I know, nobody else figured out a way to outsmart him, either. For one thing, not many hunters were roaming about on his home range. Most of them were in the high country.

My true love is hunting above timberline, where I can enjoy the wilderness and almost always have a good chance to see oversize antlers. But I try to hunt where the biggest deer are, and sometimes

that is not so far up the Western mountainsides— nor so far from roads and civilization. In fact, I shot my largest buck only half a mile from a main highway in a valley. Through my binoculars, I saw orange-shirted hunters driving by in an almost continuous stream of trucks, cars, motor homes, and jeeps. They were all making for higher country while I was admiring a rack that was 38 inches wide and that had nine long points on a side. It turned out to be the biggest muley shot that year in the United States. I know of only two larger bucks shot since then.

My wife, Paula, and I spend several weekends every summer scouting for trophy deer. Invariably, we find the biggest bucks in three main zones: mixed conifers and alpine country, oakbrush mixed with quaking aspen and perhaps a smattering of conifers, and overgrown river bottoms that run up through sagebrush and pinyon/juniper stands.

I'm convinced that some bucks spend their whole lives in just one zone. In my opinion, some old muleys tire of migrating every summer to the high country, so they stay on so-called winter range all year long. On the other hand, it's my belief that some alpine deer would spend all year in the high country if snow didn't force them down. In very mild winters, big muleys sometimes do stay high throughout the year. Further, in some places, wind keeps the ridges relatively snow free, so the animals are able to feed above timberline right through the dead of winter.

Massive antlers seem to come most often from oakbrush/aspen terrain. However, some of this zone is heavily hunted, and many deer there don't survive long enough to grow really large antlers. In my

Don't forsake the middle-altitude oakbrush thickets, pinyon/juniper jungles, or low-country river bottoms in your search for impressive muleys. These hunters didn't—and their reward is a rack for the wall and venison for the freezer.

own case, the two biggest non-typical bucks that I've seen were in higher country. The larger one eluded me, but I was fortunate enough to kill the other one. He was a timberline monarch taken in Wyoming in 1982. The rack was still in velvet when I shot that monster in mid-September, so I had it mounted in velvet. For that reason, it cannot be officially measured, according to the rules of the Boone and Crockett Club, but the antlers roughly score 285 points, which would put it among the top 20 freak-horned muleys ever shot. Incidentally, I believe that other deer would have scored more than 300 points, which would have put it in the top ten. I saw him both before and after hunting season but could never locate him when it was legal to shoot.

Over the years, I've seen three or four bucks that I think were large enough to rank about No. 2 in the typical category of the Boone and Crockett records. Basically, a typical deer rack is symmetrical and has few abnormal or extra points. One of the gigantic typicals that I saw was in the transition zone between pinyon/juniper and oakbrush/aspen cover. Another was above timberline in Wyoming, but I'd already filled my tag. I saw another before the hunting season near a Colorado lake in the oakbrush/aspen zone.

So if king-size mule deer are found high and low as well as at medium altitudes, how can you decide where to hunt? And how do you hunt the area that you select?

One key to my success is doing a great deal of pre-season scouting. I realize many nonresident hunters cannot do this. However, it's just as important to do what I call *phone scouting*. Use your telephone to find out as much as you can about an area before you visit it. I killed my largest buck in an area where I'd never been before, but I had done enough pre-season research to know that record-class deer were there. I have made 20 or more long-distance phone calls to find out about one good hunting area. It's not so important to know the exact hillside where a big buck was killed, but you should know the best counties and mountain ranges. Then you should scout and become familiar with the area until you find the very best parts of it.

Taxidermists, outfitters, biologists, conservation officers, Forest Service rangers, loggers, other hunters, ranchers, and even backpackers can provide hot tips. If you really want to take a bragging-size muley, use the phone and don't worry about the phone bill.

As you research hunting areas, you'll notice that the best ones usually have one thing in common. For one reason or another, they're not heavily hunted. Sometimes the reason is remoteness. Most hunters stay within half a mile of roads, and virtually none venture five miles or more from roads. Other places get little hunting pressure because the terrain is steep and extremely rugged. That was true of the place where I killed my biggest Colorado buck. For two straight years, I took a deer with a

38-inch-wide or wider rack off that roadside hill and I never saw another person or even a boot track. Some areas are good because they are private and posted.

One of my biggest typical muleys came from a ranch in New Mexico. All I had to do to get permission to hunt there was ask. Most ranchers have negative attitudes toward hunters because of past conflicts and trespassing, but some only want to know who is hunting on their land or using it for access to federally owned forests.

A few private areas are being managed to produce trophy deer. The hunting is usually limited to those who pay for it, and permits are often expensive.

Lately, there has been a welcome trend in state wildlife management to set aside a few areas for trophy-deer management. In Idaho, Arizona, Utah, and Colorado, there are a few hunting units where permits are issued on a strictly limited basis, usually in a drawing. More bucks are able to survive to their prime because of the reduced pressure, and some huge trophy deer now live in these areas. If you want a good chance at a wall-hanger, read the hunting regulations for Western states closely to learn about these newly established areas.

If you're like most mule deer hunters, however, you'll end up hunting on public land that's open to everyone. How do you find a trophy buck there?

My advice is to concentrate your efforts on portions of the public land where few others hunt, such as the nearly vertical terrain that I've mentioned. I think that many sportsmen are actually afraid to kill a big-game animal far from roads because they know that packing the meat out can be a lot of work. Arrange to have horses available for packing or be prepared to debone the meat on the spot (where legal) and bring it out with a backpack. Even the largest mule deer can be easily backpacked by two hunters if they debone the meat; a single hunter can make it in two trips.

One night I walked into a camp in Archuleta County, Colorado, and met two fellows with a giant buck. The rack would have placed in the top 50 typicals ever taken, and I was impressed.

"Where did you get him?" I asked.

"Over in them rimrocks on that steep hill," one of the men replied, pointing into the darkness. "But we wouldn't want to shoot another one in that rough country. We shot him at 8 A.M. and didn't get him to camp until dark."

I told the men that a head like that is worth a day's work and suggested that they waste no time in getting the antlers measured for entry in the Boone and Crockett records.

"Well, I would have traded for a smaller one," one of them replied!

Rough country is exactly the kind of place to look for big mule deer. I've often wondered whether old bucks prefer that sort of terrain or whether that's the only place they can go to get away from hunters. I suspect the latter is true. If an experienced muley sees, hears, or smells a human, he goes where he rarely detects man scent and man noises. Nowadays, there are so many hunters in the mountains that few smart bucks linger anywhere except in the steepest, brushiest, rockiest, remotest places.

Once you're in good habitat, you must avoid making the kinds of mistakes that most other hunters make. Probably the most common one is moving too fast and too much. Some fellows look like they're in a marathon race to see who can get to the top of the mountain first. As they move along, making a lot of noise, they pass some of the largest mule deer in existence and spook others. If you know that you're in an excellent area, you shouldn't move more than 200 yards in an hour. It sometimes takes me that long to move half that distance.

The reason why you should move slowly is that you must see the buck before he sees you. After every step or two, use your binoculars to study the cover. Look for antler tips, the flick of a deer's ear, a hoof protruding from under a bush, a patch of hair. Don't look for an entire animal. If you see an entire deer, it's probably because you're moving too fast. Otherwise, you would have seen only a part of the animal first. Despite my slow-moving style, I've gone too fast many times. I can remember three Boone and Crockett-class deer that I might have killed if I'd been going more slowly.

One of my acquaintances who loves to hunt moved to Montrose in 1976, the same year I did, but he hasn't killed a trophy buck or a bull elk since. The reason is that he moves too fast. I can tell by listening to his stories.

One fellow I know, Alan Jones, came to Colorado to hunt with a group of seven or eight local hunters. He thought that they moved too fast, so one day he went to a rocky knob and spent the day sitting. That night after dinner, he asked how to determine if a mule deer has a 30-inch rack from a distance. His companions told him.

"Well," he said, "I saw one today."

"You should have busted him," a friend said.

The next day, Alan went back to the knob, saw the buck again in the same oakbrush jungle, and made a good 100-yard shot. The spread was 35 inches and the rack was good enough to make the record book.

I've noticed that hunters who are in excellent physical condition often have little success because they spend all of their time making tracks, while hunters who are out of shape stop to catch their breath often and sometimes kill record-class deer, as a result.

Some hunters think that binoculars are useful only at long distances, but they are also a lot of help in dense brush. Once, while waiting near a water hole in southern Colorado, I spotted a flicker of movement in some thick oakbrush across the pond. Through my binoculars, I could see a deer, but I didn't realize that it had antlers until two bushes more than three feet apart moved on both sides of the animal. Then I made out a huge rack. One shot put the buck down. His antlers spread 42 inches

and, though he didn't carry enough extra points to get into the records, the rack is still one of my favorite trophies. If I hadn't been using binoculars that day, I might have been able to see a deer, but I wouldn't have seen the antlers.

Using binoculars properly is especially important if you hunt above timberline or in other wide-open country. Most hunters look through their field glasses for only a few moments before moving on. They scan a hillside so fast that they seem to be watching a low-flying hawk. This is no way to spot big bucks.

Whenever possible, put your binoculars on something steady, such as a rock. If you must sit, prop your elbows on your knees and use your hands and head to support the binoculars solidly. Train the glasses on the terrain that you want to glass and hold them absolutely still while studying the cover. Move only your eyes. After examining a portion of the hillside, move the glasses slightly and start the process all over again. Do not scan a hillside by continuously moving your binoculars. It's far better to hold the glasses still and move your eyes.

Here's something that illustrates the importance of glassing. One day, I was using my binoculars to study a slope when I noticed a white spot on a background of gray oakbrush. I soon realized that it was the throat patch of a smart old buck. As soon as I saw him, he must have realized it because he slowly lowered his head and put his chin on the ground. That made him almost impossible to see, even though I knew where he was and had memorized the shape of the tree next to his bed.

I estimated the outside spread at a bit more than 30 inches, and he carried five points on each antler. I wasn't interested in killing him, so I backed slowly away and left him. Then I went back to camp, described where the deer was bedded, and sent a friend to the hillside. About an hour later, he came back.

"Well, he must be gone," my friend said.

I didn't believe that, so I took my pal back to the hill and showed him the buck, which hadn't moved.

"Should we make him run?" my friend asked.

"No, you might not get a good shot if you do that," I said. "Let's just sneak a bit closer and act as if we don't see him. Then you can shoot."

We walked toward the deer until we got about 200 yards away. Significantly, the mossyhorn again lowered his head until his chin was on the ground. I'm sure he was convinced that we couldn't see him, but my buddy shot him right in his bed. It was a little sad to me. That old buck had survived many previous hunting seasons by holding tight and refusing to move. He had probably seen dozens of hunters glassing that hillside in one quick scan before moving on. Most likely, he thought we would do the same.

If you want a buck worthy of a taxidermist's skill this year, don't hunt where everybody else hunts. Go high or low and hunt smart. Somewhere out there is a king-size muley for you!

Smarter Than The Average Muley

By Rich LaRocco

"Out-of-staters aren't giving these mule deer credit," Utah outfitter Kim Bonnett was telling me. "They still believe those stories about muleys being stupid, and that attitude is a real handicap. If the hunters just knew how smart a big old mule deer buck is, they'd stand a lot better chance of outfoxing one."

I nodded in agreement. If there's one thing I've learned in the past few years of hunting trophy-size mule deer, it's that a big buck is unbelievably wary and difficult to hunt. I'm convinced that most truly large muleys end up dying of old age, and I'm not alone in this thinking. I've hunted with or interviewed some of the best hunters in the West, and virtually every one of them agrees that once a buck deer reaches trophy class, he'll most likely die of some cause other than a hunter's bullet.

San Stiver, a Nevada wildlife biologist who is also an ardent bowhunter, provided me with an example. In the mid-1970s, during the depths of the West-wide mule-deer decline, Stiver was hired to study a mule-deer herd in the Schell Creek Range. He captured and radio-collared several deer, including one massyback that he estimated to be six or seven years old. During the first year, the old sultan's six-by-four antlers were about 30 inches wide. The next year's rack was even bigger, with at least eight points on each antler and an estimated outside spread of 34 inches.

Stiver wanted to find out how the buck had managed to elude hunters. One day, using a radio receiver with a directional antenna, he walked within 30 yards of where the animal was bedded out of sight on a rocky finger ridge. The muley burst from his bed and leaped off the far side of the ridge. Stiver ran forward and discovered that the animal had fled into a thicket below. Straight across was a barren slope, so the biologist began throwing rocks and making noise in an attempt to drive the buck into the open. More than a dozen deer exploded from the corner, including several forkhorns, three-by-threes, and four-by-fours, but no big buck.

The biologist ducked low and hid to watch. After holding like a bobwhite quail for 22 minutes, the buck finally broke from his bed, crashed from the brush, and galloped out of sight over the open ridge.

"He never looked back, either," Stiver recalled. "He came out at full stride and got out of sight so quickly that I doubt I could have killed him even if I'd had a rifle."

When the hunting season opened, Stiver followed the buck at a distance to see where it would go and how it would act. One day, he pinpointed the animal's location in a small basin of mahoganies. The radio signal was steady, meaning that the buck was stationary. A group of about 15 hunters entered the basin and began walking slowly through it about 15 yards apart.

"I just knew that I was going to watch that old buck die," Stiver said. "I knew which patch of mahoganies he was in, and when the hunters reached it, I expected the deer to jump up at any moment and get shot. The hunters walked within seven or eight yards of him. The signal never modulated at all, and I started to wonder whether he might have already died. Using my receiver, I walked right up to within ten steps of that old buck before I saw him. The instant I made eye contact, he busted off."

The tale has a sad ending. When the buck's thoughts turned to love and he dropped his guard during the rut, a poacher killed him, perhaps at night with the aid of a spotlight. The culprit cut off the radio transmitter and stashed it in sagebrush. Said Stiver: "That old buck was smart enough to avoid hunters during the season, somebody had to take an unfair advantage to kill him."

Stiver says that big mule deer are most vulnerable at two times: during the beginning of the season, when so many riflemen are in the field that a buck sneaking from one hunter often exposes himself to another hunter; and during the last part of rifle seasons that extend into November and early December, when the rut is under way. Otherwise, he says, most old muleys are fairly safe.

One reason why fewer record-class mule deer are killed nowadays may be that most states have ended rifle hunting during the peak of the rut. A glance through Jack and Susan Reneau's book, *Colorado's Biggest Bucks and Bulls*, shows that many of the largest deer killed in Colorado were taken during special late seasons. The same is true in Utah, Idaho, and Wyoming, where most late-season rifle hunts have been discontinued. The bulk of rifle seasons in the Rockies are now in October, probably the toughest month of all to hunt big bucks.

The late summer and early fall are also good times to see superb bucks in open terrain, especially if the antlers are still covered with velvet. Each hair in the velvet is connected to a nerve, and bucks evidently stay out of brush to avoid irritating these nerves. Also, flies bother bucks in velvet, so the animals seek out high, windswept ridges to escape bothersome insects.

Several of the largest trophies listed in the Boone and Crockett Club records were taken during late-August or early September hunts. As mentioned in the preceding chapter, well-known trophy deer hunter Kirt Darner killed his biggest muley in full velvet in September 1983 in Wyoming, one of the few states that offers general rifle hunting in September. Rocky VanderSteen, another Westerner with a roomful of 30-inch-class mule deer to his credit, took his largest buck in 1984 during a September hunt in Wyoming. Most Western bow seasons take place in August and September, and many bowhunters see large numbers of mature bucks. But when October comes, the animals drop into heavy brush or black timber, and the smart bucks become difficult to find. Even in fairly open country, mature deer seem to know how to stay out of sight by finding a tiny patch of cover, a shady spot under a ledge, or a shallow cut where they can lie below ground level.

Kelly Beckstrom, a neighbor of mine who has hunted throughout Utah, told me that he once saw several mule deer hiding effectively in a cut alfalfa field.

"The alfalfa couldn't have been more than eight or nine inches deep," he said. "But there were several does out in the middle of the field, lying as flat as they could with their chins on the ground and their ears held down low. They looked like little mounds of dirt or some rocks, and I'm sure that I would have missed seeing them if one of the does hadn't got nervous and flipped her ears up. My hunting partner and I couldn't believe that they could hide in that stuff."

Rocky VanderSteen told me of glassing a Utah buck feeding in a shallow depression in a sage and wheatgrass meadow. Suddenly, two hunters on horseback rode out of the timber and headed across the meadow directly toward the depression. "Gee, he's a dead buck," Rocky muttered under his breath. But the buck must have heard the horses because he suddenly threw up his head like a startled racehorse and saw the hunters. If the deer had raced for cover, he might have been killed. Instead, he dropped flat, thrust his head and antlers against a bush, and held his chin to the ground. The hunters rode within 20 feet of the buck and never saw him. After they'd ridden by, the rascal sneaked back into the trees.

Watching through binoculars, I once saw a buck pull a similar trick on two bowhunting companions. The deer, which sported a 30-inch typical rack, was browsing on oakbrush when my two pals surprised it at a range of about 60 yards and passed within a few paces. The buck moved just enough to keep a thick bush between himself and the hunters.

Another friend, Bill Christensen, is part-owner of a 10,000-acre Utah ranch that is home to some huge mule deer. While scouting the spread last summer, at least three hunters saw a tremendous mule deer that they thought would make the record book. Yet, even with 40 different hunters spending an average of two days each combing the place, not a single person saw the buck after Labor Day. Two of the hunters did glimpse a monstrous non-typical that might have made the record book, a buck that had never been seen before and hasn't been seen since.

Kim Bonnett, who outfits hunters on a large private lease in southern Utah, told me that he showed his guides at least a half-dozen extraordinarily big muleys on his place last summer. Yet, not one of those bucks was seen during the season—even with 20 guided hunters on the property. Bonnett, who has killed several 30-inch-plus mule deer including one record-book head, estimates that at least 90 percent of truly large bucks are never seen by anybody. He said that last summer he saw 30 to 40 bucks with antler spreads exceeding 27 inches. Of the seven bucks in that class that were killed by his

Photo by Wyman Meinzer

Big, the muley is—but dumb he's not. How else do they live to grow such fine antlers?

To nail a trophy muley, try hunting from high vantage points where you can hunt unseen.

Photo by Rich LaRocco

clients, he's confident he had seen none of them previously.

Seeing a big buck during the hunting season, let alone killing one, is simply more difficult than some writers make it out to be. A story Kirt Darner told me illustrates the point. One day, he was talking to a female lookout in a fire tower in Colorado about an exceptionally big buck in the area.

"You know," she said, "that big old buck is really smart. I've watched him pull tricks you wouldn't believe. Twice, I was watching him feed when hunters came within 50 or 60 yards of him. That old buck just lay on the ground and put out his head like a German shepherd on the front porch. His antlers were laid back so that you could hardly see him. He'd wait until the hunters had passed, and then he'd go back to feeding."

If mule deer are so wary, what can a hunter do to outsmart one?

San Stiver says that the key is to sneak into a basin or canyon without exposing yourself, then sit and glass for hours, using high-quality binoculars and a spotting scope.

"I've found that I can see more deer by glassing one basin thoroughly in a day than by walking through seven or eight basins," he said. "Long-range surveillance is the real secret to seeing big bucks before they see you. Most hunters blunder into basins or canyons and let the deer see them first. A guy who makes that mistake gets the impression that there are no deer."

Stiver's advice is especially true in open country.

I lease a large ranch in a desert-like mountain range in Utah, where I outfit hunters and charge an access fee to do-it-yourselfers. One year, a hunter from North Carolina who was accustomed to hunting brushy country and a hunter from Nebraska who knew how to hunt open country spent the same three days hunting on their own in the same part of the ranch. The North Carolinian saw only 12 does and went home in a huff, while the Nebraskan reported seeing 75 bucks, including 20 four-by-fours, and killed a buck that had unique, odd-shaped antlers with heavy bases.

The difference, I'm sure, was in hunting technique. The Nebraskan climbed to high vantage points and thoroughly glassed territory where he hadn't shown himself, while the other fellow undoubtedly just walked on ridges and in draws, exposing himself to dozens of deer. The Nebraskan also made sure that he was in prime lookouts at dawn and dusk, when deer are more likely to be standing or moving and are much easier to see than when bedded in shadows during the day.

Incidentally, neither hunter saw the huge non-typical or the really big typical that were living in that same part of the ranch. A hunter who arrived a few days later spotted them and missed several shots. I hunted during the November muzzleloader season, spying the non-typical only once in three days. My poor shooting allowed that old nine-by-nine mossyback to survive another autumn.

In some terrain, glassing is impractical because of dense brush or heavy timber. If possible, hunt thick cover when snow is on the ground. That way, if you run across a set of big tracks, you can follow them and perhaps eventually get a shot. Snow also makes the deer much easier to see, and it concentrates them. If you have a choice to hunt either early or late in the season, go late because of the increased likelihood of snow on the ground, as well as of cooler weather. In unseasonable heat, big bucks are almost totally inactive during daylight hours. An old buck is normally hog-fat under his insulating winter coat and avoids exertion as much as possible during an October heat wave. A deer that spends almost all of the daylight hours bedded in dense cover is extremely difficult to hunt and is even more likely to hold tighter than usual. For instance, in the fall of 1985 it was so hot during October in western Colorado, southern Idaho, and Utah that far fewer large bucks than normal were taken. One outfitter in southern Colorado told me that his clients took only one buck, compared with a usual kill of 30 to 40 bucks. Hunters in southern Idaho and Utah reported similar problems, yet when the weather cooled after the rifle season ended, many trophy-size deer were seen.

Lloyd Kindsfater was hunting with a friend, Jack Groves, in Colorado when he found out just how tightly a big muley can hold. As the story was told in Jack and Susan Reneau's book, Kindsfater was watching Groves walk up a draw when a movement in the brush about 250 yards away caught his eye. It was a huge buck bedded behind a log, with only about eight inches of its back showing. Groves passed within 30 feet of the deer and hiked up to his friend. Together, they watched the animal for 20 minutes before Kindsfater decided to try a shot with his .300 H&H Magnum. His first shot missed. Incredibly the old buck didn't move, completely trusting his natural camouflage. Neither did he move after the second shot. The third bullet struck home, and the record-book buck collapsed. Stories such as that make a hunter wonder just how many of those old muleys may have watched him hike by in the mountains.

When bucks are in heavy cover, an organized deer drive sometimes is effective. It takes experience to recognize where standers should be positioned and how to force deer into moving, but the best way to find out is to try. A variation on this is to take a stand overlooking a trail or terrain feature where deer may move when pressured by other hunters in the area. This tactic is particularly effective on the first morning of the season. I would guess that at least one-third of mature mule deer are shot either by standers on opening day or by participants in organized deer drives.

There's a saying in my part of the country that a driver can't move a big buck unless he kicks the buck in the rear. Indeed, most bucks hold tight and avoid detection, but sooner or later a driver gets so close to a buck that it flushes. Probably more than one-half of the big muleys taken on drives are shot by the drivers rather than the standers.

Long drives seldom work well because the deer usually detect the direction of the drive and try to circle to one side. On one day last year, three guides and I tried to force deer up a long canyon toward some hunters positioned at the top. Brad Smith of Preston, Idaho, was actually crawling on his hands and knees through heavy mahogany brush when I saw two deer leap to their feet less than 40 yards from him. One of them quickly circled and disappeared back into the dense brush behind Brad before I could get a good look at its head. The other one panicked and smashed directly through the center of a dead mahogany before stopping. It was a beauty, with odd-shaped, wide-flaring antlers. Instead of running directly up the canyon, the buck trotted about 150 yards, then circled uphill and left the canyon well below our standers.

Even if you're alone, you can hunt dense cover with fair success. There are two ways to do this: Either stillhunt slowly and silently, watching carefully for any sign of a buck, or walk through quickly and then quietly backtrack parallel to your original route. Mule deer normally hide until potential danger has passed; they then get to their feet and investigate. If you come sneaking back 50 or 100 yards to the side, you may catch a buck intent on your original trail. A walking or standing buck is ten times easier to see than a bedded buck.

Probably the best advice I could offer would be to respect a muley buck just as you would a big old whitetail or blacktail. As is the case with whitetails, even in areas where big bucks are known to exist, most hunters never see one. Hunter success in most parts of the West is well below 50 percent, and the vast majority of the deer shot are yearling bucks. Plan to hunt hard and long for a chance at a mature animal.

Don't set your standards too high, either. Unless you're perfectly willing to go home with your deer tag in your pocket, it would be silly to set your sights on a 30-inch-plus giant. Even the best hunters in the very best areas don't get a wall-hanger every year. The exceptional hunters such as Kim Bonnett, Rocky VanderSteen, and Kirt Darner usually hunt several states a year and spend hundreds of hours and dollars researching and scouting hunting areas, and even they have dry years. VanderSteen told me of once hunting in his favorite area in Wyoming for nine straight days without seeing a single mature muley buck.

You can improve your chances by hunting in the best places, which you can find by research or by hiring a reputable outfitter. But no matter whether you're hunting in virgin wilderness, on the best private ranch in the West, or in the exact canyon where several enormous bucks were seen a few weeks earlier, don't expect to take the trophy of your dreams without a lot of effort and a large pinch of outright luck. Remember, it's precisely because big muleys are hard to hunt that they have been so highly prized.

A Scent For Mule Deer

By Clyde Cowan

"If you wear scent glands from a mule deer buck, other bucks will follow you," said John Gottfriedsen, my Okanagon Indian hunting partner.

I tried it, and a forkhorn buck followed my tracks to within 20 feet of me during the first half-hour I hunted.

Dr. Valerius Geist, the well-known animal behaviorist, helps explain why a buck would follow another buck's scent in the book *Mule and Black-Tailed Deer of North America*, compiled and edited by Olaf C. Wallmo. Dr. Geist writes, "On first meeting a large unfamiliar buck, subordinate males try to sneak behind him and sniff his hocks."

Scent glands are the business cards, ID badge, and resumé of a mule-deer buck. If you wear the scent glands, you've got the credentials.

Dr. Geist goes on to indicate that a muley buck trusts his nose more than his eyes when it comes to identifying another buck.

Indians from several tribes in British Columbia use scent glands to hunt mule deer. John said that his brother used to tie a buck's scent glands to his bootlaces so that they dragged on top of the snow. Bucks would follow him and snort.

I first tried hunting with mule deer scent in 1983. A friend killed a buck, and I asked for the scent glands. The buck was heavy-bodied and had a rut-swollen neck and gnarled antlers past their prime.

I didn't know which glands to use, so I skinned out one tarsal and one metatarsal gland from a hind leg.

Thirty-six hours later and 40 miles away, I tied a piece of gland to each foot and went hunting. Laced at my instep, the tufts of hide and hair brushed the top of the fresh snow. It was early November.

With the dawn at my back and wind in my face, I hunted one end of a bench on a mountainside. No deer.

I retraced my steps quickly to check the other end of the bench. I'd gone about 100 yards downwind when I came to a brush-filled gully. The deer trail dipped into a narrow slot through brush and Christmas trees. As I entered the narrow place, the forkhorn buck forged toward me from the other end with his nose to my tracks in the snow. A second after I saw him, he lifted his head and looked at me. Then he slowly raised his front legs like a rearing horse, pivoted on his hind feet in the narrow trail, and dropped again with his rump toward me. He turned his head.

It was a beautiful morning to find a big buck, and I had several weeks of season left, so I didn't shoot.

The forkhorn walked off the trail. I knelt to look through a hole in the brush and saw the buck with his head down in a posture similar to mine. He was looking back at me and seemed embarrassed, as though he'd been caught eavesdropping.

Tracks in the snow showed that he had followed

Photo by Thomas W. Kitchin

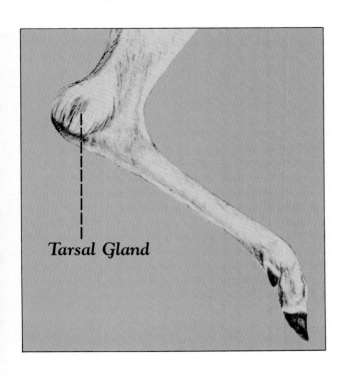

Tarsal Gland

me for 100 yards before we met. No buck had ever followed my tracks like that, so I scored one for the scent glands.

A quarter mile eastward along the bench, the open mountainside flowed down into a narrow meadow with some thick timber fringing the far drop-off. As I reached the meadow, a doe and a fawn bounded into the timber along the rim. I paused for a minute or two and then moved out into the meadow. Just then, the doe led her fawn buck out of the timber and toward me. She came in a crouch, with her neck low and her nose stretched out to smell me. She was downwind, and I was in the open.

She would come within 25 or 30 yards and bound away for two or three jumps. Then she would circle for a few steps, as though to line up the breeze exactly, and crouch toward me again. She repeated that three times and then slowly worked her way up the mountain, stopping often to look back at me.

Tarsal glands are located on the insides of the hocks (rearward-bending joints) of the hind legs. The odor of the gland's secretion identifies individual deer to others.

99

By that time, I was impressed with the effects the scent glands were having. I wanted to see how the next deer would act, but a sudden blizzard cut visibility to near zero and I headed home.

During the next week, I didn't hunt but I did look for information on mule-deer scent. There isn't much around.

I got the best help from Dr. Geist's chapter in *Mule and Black-Tailed Deer of North America*. He describes does acting much like the one I saw in the meadow. He writes, "A strange buck coming to a female group may cause a female to sneak quietly around him on her belly, sniff his tarsals, and bound off."

There are two sets of scent glands on a deer's hind legs: tarsals and metatarsals.

The tarsal glands cover the inside of each hock. They're palm-size tufts of hair that look as though they're stained with tar during the rut. Tarsal hairs have special chambers, scales, and comb-like features to hold and disperse scent.

The metatarsal glands lie on the outside of each hind leg, below the hocks. They look like a long tuft of hair with a part down the middle. On the skin under the "part" in the metatarsal is a ridge of black, waxy secretion. To humans, the waxy stuff stinks; it's a lot stronger than tarsal scent. Under the hide, the metatarsal looks very much like a tight cluster of blisters.

To use the glands for hunting, skin off the hide with the glands in it. The glands looked big enough to make several scents, so I cut each into three pieces with hide and hair still attached.

From the first buck, I kept one section of each gland fresh, and sealed the others in separate plastic bags in the freezer. I punch a hole in each piece of hide, thread a two-foot length of clean parachute cord through it, and cinch the hide in the middle of the cord with a square knot. The long ends of the cord are free to tie the gland to my belt, boot, or wherever I choose. I usually wear one of each kind when I hunt.

About two weeks after I first used the glands, my boss, Jack Teeter, came up to hunt for a couple of days. We both like big antlers, but with empty freezers we decided to take any legal deer.

The first day, we hunted an area where there was a two-deer limit—one buck and one doe. I gave Jack a set of scent glands and tied a pair to my ankles. Sometimes, when you demonstrate a new hunting technique, it really works.

We had walked 75 yards from the Bronco, whispering about our hunting plan, when a deer snorted behind us. He caught us moving in the middle of an old road.

We turned around, and the deer snorted again. Jack darted to the left and I went right to get two different angles of view through the timber. Two does and a buck were staring at us from only 40 yards away.

I shot one doe. The forkhorn buck kept right on snorting and stepped behind a log. Jack shot twice, and the buck and doe both dropped out of sight.

As I approached my doe, Jack saw a forkhorn stroll away on the road. It stopped to sniff and stare at him several times. He thought that he'd killed a buck, so he didn't shoot. It was the same buck that had snorted. Jack had clipped the log and missed the animal. We had fired three shots, killing both does, and the buck was still curious.

Jack dragged his doe next to mine and shook his head. He has a Columbia blacktail in the Boone and Crockett Club record book and several big muleys to his credit so he's seen a lot of deer. "I've never seen deer act that way," he said.

"They were downwind, and they smelled the scent glands," I told him.

"That must be it," Jack said. "Something made them stand in the open and snort."

The next morning, we hiked to the mountain where I'd first tried mule deer scent. With snow nearly knee-deep at that elevation, I tied the buck glands to my gaiter tops. I hung another set from my belt to spread a scent layer at the nose level of any deer downwind of me.

The deer had moved to the foot of the mountain, so we hunted a belt of timber below the bench. We didn't find much deer sign, so we split up. Then I hit a patch of young spruce where fresh deer trails laced everywhere.

I spotted several very fresh rubs presumably made that morning because there were fresh shreds of bark on top of the new snow.

On impulse, I rubbed the buck glands I wore on my belt on a fresh buck rub. That threw a new factor into the experiment, but it was a prank I couldn't resist. I then brushed the buck glands against every rub I found.

Jack was hunting a quarter-mile away, and I went to get him. I didn't see a deer track on the way through the heavy timber.

Jack and I headed back toward the concentration of deer in the spruce saplings by following my tracks through the timber.

After reading this far, you are probably thinking that I was expecting to see a buck on my trail, but remember that was only the third time I had worn scent glands. I just wasn't prepared. I was bulling along under spruce boughs when a movement ahead caught my eye and Jack hissed, "Buck!"

Two deer were easing toward us 15 yards away. The nearest one lifted his head from my tracks and stopped. The second one had his head down and bumped into the first one. Then the lead deer swung to my right, and I had the impression that he had a good four-point rack. I crouched to my right, and Jack went left. I saw a deer's side and one stained hind leg when the animal stood still for a moment 20 yards away. I knew it was a buck but I wanted more ID than just a look at his stained hock, and I never saw his head.

The deer that turned left was a buck, too, but Jack didn't get more than a glimpse.

We hunted on into the open area, but all of the deer had cleared out with the two bucks we had spooked. However, I found several buck rubs made after I had walked through a half-hour before. The new rubs were always within a few feet of the ones against which I'd rubbed the glands. One buck had attacked the trees with a frenzy, shattering low clusters of spruce limbs and kneeling in the snow to gore saplings. Maybe I had violated mule deer ethics, or maybe I had insulted or challenged him when I touched his rubs with scent from another buck. We didn't know his motive, but he thrashed a lot of little trees.

For the last few days of the season, I wore scent glands whenever I hunted, but I didn't take a buck.

After deer season, we stored the scent glands in sealed plastic bags in the freezer. We wondered whether they'd smell right to a buck after a year in storage.

The next season, I killed a whitetail buck right away. I shot a mule-deer doe when she stood up and sniffed at me while I tracked past upwind of her bed. Several deer responded and confirmed what I'd learned but didn't add much new information. I collected the glands from a dominant buck that another hunter had killed and froze them.

To start my third fall of hunting with scent glands, my two sons and I returned to the mountain with the bench. It was early October and dry. We all wore the glands tied to our belts to give off a scent in the air rather than drag them in the dust and rocks.

David, 12, didn't carry a rifle. Travis, 15, had a license and a gun.

I was glassing along the face of the mountain from the ridgetop when I saw a buck with heavy, dark antlers. He stood facing me about 1,000 yards away. He was looking at something below him and closer to me. I moved the glasses down a bit and saw Travis.

The buck stayed above Travis while the boy angled up the mountain. The deer followed his scent on the morning thermals that flowed up the mountain, and I was sure the buck could see Travis part of the time.

The buck stopped on a steep rockslide below a cliff while Travis climbed up ahead of him toward a notch in the ridge. I'd left David in that notch to warm himself in the sunlight. I could see both boys and the deer. When the boys greeted each other, I expected the buck to sneak over the ridge and into a vast timbered basin. I was too far away to do anything but watch.

When Travis walked up to David, the buck flicked his ears toward the boys but didn't move. The buck stood at their level about 200 yards away. The ridge soared from the notch until it topped out several hundred feet above him. He kept his ears locked on the boys.

I eased behind a juniper, slipped back over the ridge, and started running toward the boys and the buck. I didn't expect the deer to stay put until I got there, but you certainly don't put antlers on the wall without trying.

When I reached the notch, I sent Travis up the ridge to look down for the buck and also to watch the top in case he tried to sneak over. I dropped down 75 yards and crawled out on a rock knob to get away from the face of the mountain so I could see along it. The buck hadn't moved. He stood on the rockslide, still stretching his nose and ears toward the place where he'd last seen Travis and heard both boys. Travis couldn't see the buck under the cliff, so I padded a juniper limb rest for the 200-yard shot and held on his brisket; I wasn't sure that I had hit him until we found him.

The massive animal had lost an eye a year or two before, but the wound was completely healed. We boned him out, and he set a new weight record for us at exactly 120 pounds of trimmed lean meat.

That mule deer seemed exceptionally curious for an older buck. He had seen Travis, smelled him, and followed him. He had listened to the boys talk. There was lots of time for him to ghost away, but he stayed long enough for me to cover one-half mile of rough country and make a shot. We're convinced that the buck scent he smelled caused him to follow Travis and hang around.

After hunting with scent glands for three seasons, I'm positive that they do attract mule deer. I still don't know whether tarsal or metatarsal glands work better, so I always wear a piece of each. Any trace of blood scent on the skinned hide doesn't seem to bother deer. After long storage, the glands freeze dry. Flexing them a bit after they thaw pumps up their scent output.

From my observations and what Dr. Geist writes, here are some tentative conclusions:

- The bigger the buck, the more likely you are to get a response when you wear his scent glands. Use glands from a dominant buck if you can get them.
- Scent glands are more effective if they come from a buck that lived outside the range of the deer you're hunting. You have the scent of a mysterious stranger.
- Young bucks are quick to follow the scent trail of an older buck. I suspect that a dominant buck will also check out any strange buck scent, but he may be sneaky about it.

To really test how deer react, it would be best for one man to wear scent glands and stillhunt through an area of deer concentration, while another observed the reactions of the deer from a high point.

This year, I plan to drag scent glands through a prime deer area and then hang them on a bush in a place that I can watch. I want to see whether a buck will follow the trail and smell the bush.

Whether a buck follows you or simply hesitates for a moment to take another sniff, wearing scent glands could let you get a shot.

Muleys In The Timber

By Walter L. Prothero

"Look at that!" my hunting partner said. He was looking across the plateau at a huge buck that had just come out of a ravine less than 100 yards away. The buck stood in the sagebrush and stared at us for a moment as I brought the Jeep to a halt. We watched the buck as he trotted across the open flat and then across the four-wheel-drive trail in front of us. Then he went down into the aspens on the north slope of the plateau. We had both killed bucks earlier, so we couldn't shoot. I like to think we wouldn't have done so, anyway. It seems less than sporting to shoot a deer so close to the car.

That was the last really big buck I've seen out in the open during the season. The year was 1972, if memory serves. These days, big bucks just aren't seen in open country when hunters are about. The bucks that do show themselves never grow to trophy proportions. Bucks that live long enough to have a good head do so by becoming survival experts. And with the large numbers of hunters now afield, survival means hiding.

In the 1960s, I used to take a trophy buck—often with an antler spread in excess of 30 inches—every year, most often by catching the buck browsing early or late or by spooking him out of the brush and onto the opposite open slope of a ravine. In those days, I wouldn't go into the timber; the hunting there was too hard and required too much concentration. It was many years before I could finally bring myself to hunt in the timber, and then I did so only after several years of shooting small bucks and not even seeing anything that could be considered a trophy animal.

The first time I hunted the timber, I was practically dragged into it. I had seen a big buck browsing at the edge of some timber late one evening. He was too far away to risk a shot in the poor light, and it would have been dark by the time I could make a stalk. But he was the biggest buck I had seen in years. In camp that night, I couldn't get the vision of that big, heavy rack out of my mind.

I returned to the stand of timber at first light, found the tracks, and began to follow. I was wearing blue jeans, and the snow and subfreezing temperatures had frozen them hard from the knees down. Occasionally, the frozen cuffs scraped together. At that point in my hunting career, I hadn't yet realized how keen a deer's senses are, and the thought of wearing quiet wool pants hadn't even crossed my mind. I followed the big tracks as they twisted and turned down through the spruces on the steep slope. Occasionally, I had to force my way through a thick growth of willows around a spring. Then I found his bed. Though it was below freezing and the snow that had thawed while he lay on it had

Photo by Tim Christie

Where, the hunter wondered, did the big deer spend their days? It could only be in the timber. The bulb turned on.

frozen again, his droppings were still soft. I didn't think he had left the bed more than an hour before. The tracks led across the slope, through several shallow ravines where he had stopped to browse, and into some willows where he had battered one sapling almost barkless with his antlers. The brown strips of willow bark lay on the snow. Then he had gone on, meandering at times, moving straight and purposefully at others.

I followed the trail for several hours. It was cold in the timber; the rifle hung from the sling on my shoulder, and my hands were plunged deep into my coat pockets. I stepped across a small stream. The willows that bordered it scraped against my hard-frozen pants, and there in the gloom was the buck. He was lying down and staring at me. Then he was up and gone in one motion. I didn't even have time to pull my hands out of my pockets.

That encounter still did not impress on me the importance of hunting the timber. I had spent too many years hunting the old way on open slopes where the bucks browsed placidly. To me, that timber buck was just a random occurrence.

The following year, I hunted the same country and concentrated on the rolling hills and shallow ravines on top of the big plateau. The land was open, and you could take your time, take a rest for your rifle, and pot the buck at your leisure. The mainstay was marksmanship. I saw a few bucks that season in the open country but nothing that could be considered a big buck. There were big tracks, though, and it was beginning to dawn on me that they had been made at night.

Where, I wondered, did the big deer spend their days? It could only be in the timber. That realization came suddenly and with force. The bulb turned on.

Full of enthusiasm, I moved into the timber, certain that I was making the right move. I walked down the same trail I had followed the preceding year when I had gone after that big buck. There were big tracks in the shadowy gloom. One set was on the trail I was following; others crossed it. I moved quietly on the needle-duff, remembering the year before, carrying the rifle almost as I would carry a shotgun when approaching a covey of quail. Then the buck was there in the deep shadows, wraith-like, his nose working to find out what had made him uneasy. At the shot, so out of place in the silent timber, the buck dropped without a quiver. I gloated, not at the buck—a very good four-pointer (Western count)—but at the realization that I had finally found out where the big bucks were.

Stalking and tracking big bucks in the timber forced me to learn new skills. I had to become more of a hunter. No longer could I rely on my rifle's ability to hold a five-inch, 300-yard group. I had to move quietly and with the wind in my favor. I had

to strain to see as far into the shadows as possible to detect the buck before he saw me. I had to be ready at all times with the rifle in my hands. I had to learn to pay more attention to sign. I learned to tell one set of tracks from another. I began to be able to tell how long ago the buck had browsed or urinated or scraped, and to tell whether the buck was traveling or looking for a place to bed. I had to move slowly, perhaps spending all day to get through a stand of timber and blowdowns less than a mile long. In the old days, I was known for covering large expanses of country.

Stillhunting or tracking in the timber makes a man a complete hunter. It's not enough to be good at tracking, or to hunt quietly, or to be a good shot, or to know the country and to see well. The best timber hunter does all of these well and all at the same time. Falling down in just one at any given moment can mean the escape of a trophy buck.

Another advantage of hunting the timber is that you can do it all day, even when the deer have bedded down. One afternoon, I was following a large set of tracks through a stand of spruce and fir. The area was full of deer tracks, and it was difficult not to lose the ones I was following in the maze. I was concentrating so hard on moving quietly and following the tracks that I nearly stepped on the buck, who apparently had been snoozing. He jumped up less than five yards away and crashed off through the blowdowns, frightening me out of my wits. Had I been more aware and looking ahead as I moved through the timber, I might have collected that buck.

Stillhunting can be just as effective in the timber as tracking. It is helpful, though, to know a particular stand of timber. Most stands include good areas for bedding, frequently used game trails, and places where the deer can grab an afternoon snack. If the stillhunter knows where these different areas are located, he stands a better chance of taking a buck.

One stand of spruce and fir I am particularly familiar with is located in northern Utah. The surrounding country sustains heavy hunting pressure. I've been hunting it for years. In the timber, which is on a slope that faces north, is a steep ravine. One side of the raving faces west, and the soil is so shallow that no large trees grow on it. Bitterbrush, some mountain mahogany, cliff-rose, and forbs—all good deer browse—grow there. Above the ravine, there are large evergreens. The bucks, if undisturbed, lie beneath the trees. They are only a few yards from food or, in the other direction, thick, impenetrable blowdowns and timber. If I'm not following a set of tracks, I usually stillhunt toward that open slope. I've killed one good buck there and missed chances at several others.

Every hunter who has spent some time in the timber knows a lot about the wind. It's always good to keep it in your face, and it is always nice if the buck you are following is cooperative and moves

The buck, still uneasy, stepped slightly forward, his nose working, his ears cocked, until his neck was clear.

into it. As often as not, however, it doesn't happen that way. A buck is as apt to move with the wind as into it, and he often beds in a place that is nearly impossible to approach without letting him scent you. In such situations, you have to anticipate what the buck will do. It helps to know the lay of the land, the game trails, deer habits in the area, and the normal wind direction at various times of the day. The wind normally blows uphill with the warming temperatures after sunup and becomes more dense and blows downhill with cooling temperatures.

Suddenly, mule-deer hunting has become complicated. Now the hunter not only has to know the habits of the deer but the intricacies of the country as well. To me, that is the best of all possible hunting. You choose some timber where deer are abundant and hunt it year after year, learning all a hunter needs to know about it and disturbing it as little as possible so the bucks don't move out.

Every hunter, though, has to hunt a stand of timber for the first time. Most hunters, due to lack of time or commitment, will never really learn a patch of timber. Even so, there is a way to go about it. If there are big deer tracks that aren't too old, and even though the buck is moving with the wind, there is still a decent chance of taking him.

Late one season, I was following a set of big tracks in snow that had fallen earlier that morning. The breeze was quartering in from behind me over my left shoulder. I had been hunting in timber for several years and knew that the buck, if he behaved anything like most of the other big bucks I'd hunted, would make a buttonhook not unlike the one a football receiver makes as he runs his pass pattern. I guessed that the buck would do this below his trail to be downwind and to one side of it so he could scent anything following him. The best chance I had was to make loops downwind of the trail, returning to the track every 100 yards or so— a pretty fair distance when you are stalking very slowly in timber—to be sure I hadn't passed the buck in his bed. If I did it right, I figured I had a good chance to get a shot. It was nearly midday, and I was sure the buck had bedded down.

I was in my third loop downwind of the trail when I sensed that something was about to happen. I didn't discount that feeling or try to rationalize it away. I stopped, my thumb on the safety and the rifle held a little higher so I could bring it up more quickly, and looked carefully around for perhaps 20 minutes. Then I took a step forward and saw some branches that looked suspiciously like antler tines. Then an ear twitched and the "branches" moved. I eased the rifle up, forcing myself into that quiet, controlled state you shoot from if you do it right. I waited, hoping the buck would step clear of the blowdowns. He was uneasy. He probably had heard some faint noise I had made, or perhaps he was relying on some sixth sense of his own, but he hadn't located me. I was downwind, so he could not smell me. Then the buck, still uneasy, stepped silently forward, his nose working, his ears cocked, until his neck was clear.

That was a good buck, five points to the side (12 points Eastern count) and very fat. He was also quite old. His molars were worn nearly to the gum. He'd gotten old by staying in the timber, at least during hunting season.

Another method of hunting in timber is taking a stand along a well-used trail. I am not much of a stand-hunter because it's sheer torture for me to be inactive for very long, so I seldom employ this method. One season, I was hunting with a lady friend. I knew where there was a heavily used trail through the timber, and I posted her behind a big fir tree above the trail. An hour or so after I'd left her, I heard a shot. When I returned, she was standing over a fat forkhorn. The buck had walked down the trail below, and she had killed him cleanly. A moment after her shot, a good four-point had run up the trail and almost trampled her. Apparently, the second buck had been confused about the direction of the shot that had echoed through the timber.

Often, large stands of pine or spruce/fir have open areas within them that offer the resident deer excellent food without their ever having to leave the safety of the timber, even at night. These areas may be steep, shallow-soiled slopes exposed to the south or west that don't hold enough moisture for large trees, or they may be openings around water that have been kept clear of trees by beavers. Occasionally, they may be fairly large meadows. When you find a place like that and see a good set of tracks, you've got a fair chance to take a good buck if you hunt carefully.

I know of several such places, one of them in Montana. It is near the northern boundary of Yellowstone National Park. It is on a low mountain covered on its north and east slopes mainly by fir and spruce, and on its drier and warmer south and west slopes with lodgepole pine. On top of the mountain is a sagebrush opening that drops into an open ravine, which is dry except in the spring. The ravine is thick with good deer browse, and it slopes gently to the east before being swallowed up by the timber. The whole area is perhaps 300 yards long and maybe 200 wide. It is an excellent place to find big bucks. I've photographed deer there a number of times, but I haven't hunted there yet. Indeed, I wouldn't want to disturb the place and chase the bucks out; they might never return. I don't think I could kill a buck there without a twinge of bad conscience.

Hunting the timber has given me a new enthusiasm for hunting big mule-deer bucks. It is a little like an old man suddenly finding his wife attractive again. After years of watching trophy hunting deteriorate, of seeing or hearing about fewer and fewer big bucks, all of a sudden I've found a way to get at big heads again.

Foiling The Great Escape

By Rich LaRocco

Sometimes, a hunter knows when everything is perfect. That's how Mike Crane and I felt on opening morning of the Idaho mule-deer season as we waited along the rim of a rugged, heavily timbered canyon. We'd begun hiking well before first light so that we could circle around to a saddle at the head of the canyon. From experience, I knew that most hunters started hiking up from the bottom at dawn, pushing most deer ahead of them. If everything went according to plan, we'd have chances at several bucks as they beelined along their escape route across the saddle.

"There's one!" Mike said in a low but excited voice. "A four-pointer!"

Sure enough, catfooting about 150 yards below us was a slate-gray, heavy-bodied buck.

"He's a beauty," I whispered. "But I think we'll see bigger ones."

Soon the buck crossed the saddle and disappeared from view. Moments later, a branch cracked down in the canyon, so we searched the cover below us until our eyes teared from the strain. Suddenly, three more bucks appeared below. They drifted by so quickly that we barely had time to decide whether to shoot.

"The last one's a good one," I said. "You want him?"

Mike never took his binoculars from his eyes. "I guess not," he said. "We have all season. Besides, the morning's hardly started."

In the next half-hour, Mike and I passed up five more four-by-four bucks. A few minutes later, an-other branch cracked below, and a hunter walked into view. Hoping to learn something useful, we hurried ahead to intercept him at the saddle.

"See anything?" Mike asked.

"Heck no," the man replied. "I guess the bad weather last winter killed all of the bucks. I haven't even seen a fresh track all morning. You have to be lucky to get a deer around here anymore."

Mike and I aren't the sort of hunters who like to share our favorite areas, so we didn't volunteer any information about the bucks we'd just watched. Besides, our hunting technique wouldn't be so deadly if everyone did it. Someone has to push the deer to use their escape routes. Waiting on an escape route is the most effective mule-deer hunting technique we know, but it works only when other hunters cooperate. For all I knew, this hunter could be the same man who had pushed my trophy buck to me two years earlier at the same spot. That animal had carried long, deep forks, a wide spread, and an extra tine on one antler—the sort of rack few sportsmen can pass up.

Stand hunting on an escape route is effective in almost any deer habitat. The technique is equally effective on blacktails, whitetails, and mule deer. Once you learn to identify an escape route and can find a way to reach it without alerting the deer you intend to hunt, ambushing deer in this way can be a sure fire way to put venison in your freezer year after year. In cases where you can't depend upon unknowing hunters to spook deer your way, you can organize simple drives to intentionally force bucks to use their escape routes. I know whitetail hunters in Pennsylvania who use the same drives year after year to kill bucks sneaking along the same escape routes.

Learning to recognize these routes in your hunting area can take years, but some principles apply wherever deer live. First, realize that an escape route is not necessarily a trail or a path. When alarmed, bucks often abandon well-beaten trails and move through dense cover or across topographic features that offer a quick way to vacate an area. Where I've hunted whitetails in New York, the escape routes led directly through the thickest, orneriest, thorniest brush imaginable. In open terrain, typical of much mule-deer habitat, bucks often exit a canyon or draw through low spots in ridges, called saddles. In some places, an escape route might cut through a swamp or across a river, along the edges of cliffs, or even out across a sagebrush flat. There is a common denominator among escape routes. In almost all cases, an escape route allows a buck to exit an area quickly without exposing himself at close range to an approaching source of danger. A buck does not always flee along the same route, even when danger approaches from the same direction. Normally, however, an escape route used

once will be used again and again. Locate a good flight path, and you'll find yourself enjoying a buck bonanza.

The best way by far to locate a good escape route is through experience. That's one good reason to hunt the same area several times rather than jump from one hunting spot to another. If you spook a deer, note carefully the exact course it follows.

A few years ago, I was invited to spend the first day of bowhunting season on the New Jersey estate of Jeff Anderson, an inventor of hunting equipment. Jeff's property bordered a large tract that was hunted hard by a police force from a nearby town. Jeff was intimately familiar with the whitetails on his place, and he knew the routes that deer would use to reach a dense thicket near his house. Sure enough, several whitetails pussyfooted beneath my tree stand right along the route Jeff had pinpointed. The deer did not walk along trails, but right through the brush and the dry, fallen leaves. That evening, I shot a small whitetail while waiting along another escape route. George Ollert, one of Jeff's friends, arrowed a six-pointer along still another exit path Jeff had identified. That deer stayed well off the closest trail and sneaked through brush so dense that George had to wait until the buck was directly

Photo by Harry L. Thompson

Usually, an escape route used by deer once will be used again. Locate a flight path, as the hunter on the facing page did, and you could find yourself enjoying a buck bonanza.

below him before he could see it clearly enough to shoot at it.

Mule deer often follow ridges to flee from hunters. Kirt Darner, the well-known trophy deer hunter from Colorado, told me he has taken four of his big bucks on such ridges as they were trying to elude other hunters.

"Today, there's hardly any place that's not getting hunted," Darner said. "So, you really need to know where the deer are going and the routes they use to get there. The big bucks don't take long to get on an escape route and bail out of country where they feel pressured. You need to learn these routes when you're scouting before the hunting season. Sometimes, I'll intentionally spook deer on scouting trips just to see where they go."

Darner added that many hunters make the mistake of positioning themselves across a canyon from an escape route rather than waiting on the same slope. The result often is a difficult long-range shot. Also, big bucks seldom cross large openings and are difficult to see and identify at long range.

"I talk with a lot of hunters every year," he said, "and most of those who have seen big bucks tell me something like, 'Boy, I wish I'd been over there.' If they'd been more familiar with the habits of the bucks in their area, they would have known where to be. One advantage outfitters have over most hunters is that they know their territory well and know where the deer go."

In most of the West, bucks move uphill to get away from hunters. But in some places, roads run along the tops of ridgelines or mountains, and deer flee downhill. In an area I hunted for ten years, bucks run three to four miles down several extremely rugged, steep canyons early on the first morning of deer season. Three years ago, I walked two miles down one of these canyons, crossed a ridge, and took a stand in another canyon just at dawn. Through my binoculars, I could see several orange-jacketed hunters start hunting a mile or more above me. By 10 A.M., I'd counted 34 different bucks sneaking, running, or trotting down the canyon past me. About half of these bucks followed an escape route across a saddle in the ridge about 300 yards below me, and all of the others fled along a shelf on the slope about 200 yards above. The big buck I shot didn't show up until about 1 P.M. A high-antlered sultan with nine points on one antler and seven on the other, he apparently had held tight until most hunters had left the area before he dared to use his escape route. Later, I talked with some of the hunters who had unknowingly helped me. None had seen the deer I killed, and most had seen no bucks at all.

That same route, incidentally, has provided me with some of my best bowhunting action. On the first day of bowhunting season two years ago, I watched seven bucks walk past within bow range. Last year, working as a guide in the area, I waited there with a client from Texas when a heavy-antlered buck with an outside spread of at least 30 inches walked by and stopped only three or four paces from us. Unfortunately, my hunter was so excited that he shot high, or a photograph of him with his Pope and Young trophy would be gracing these pages. He had never killed a deer with a bow and arrow, so when a yearling buck walked out a few moments later, he tried another shot. The arrow flew 45 yards, zipping completely through the little buck's chest cavity and causing the deer to collapse within view.

If you're hunting a new area that you haven't scouted thoroughly, you can sometimes guess the location of escape routes just by observing terrain, cover, and sign and interpreting it with a dose of horse sense. Escape routes usually lead away from open terrain and toward dense cover; away from roaded areas and toward roadless, rugged topography; away from public, heavily hunted places and toward posted or lightly hunted areas; or away from open woods and toward woods with a heavy understory. Escape routes usually follow heavy cover but often trail along the edge of dense cover. Deer vacating open terrain such as sagebrush flat often run inside shallow draws or gullies, where they are often invisible to anyone standing on the flat. When fleeing crosshill, deer prefer to walk on a bench or shelf. If a buck is forced to climb uphill to leave an area, he'll usually top out in a saddle or where brush or trees provide cover. Where deer are forced to cross a road, they'll usually do so where adequate cover borders both sides of the road.

Don't wait exactly on an escape route, but to one side of it. I learned this lesson the hard way. While hiking down a steep mountainside, I happened to glance across the slope and saw a nice buck staring back at me. He was standing on the rim of a draw that was an escape route where I'd seen many deer cross the mountain in previous years. After he ducked out of sight into the draw, I knew that I could intercept him at one point if I could run fast enough. Up the mountain I returned, huffing and puffing like a first-time marathoner. Once on top, I jogged to the point where I'd seen deer cross before and waited in the shade of a white-barked aspen. In less than a minute, the big buck appeared not 15 feet away and on a course that would take him within slapping distance. Though I didn't move at all, the buck immediately saw me and broke into a dead run. My hurried shot went wide. If I'd stopped 30 or 40 yards short of the escape route, I'm sure that I would have had an easy shot at a slow-moving animal.

A group of hunters can sometimes be successful by working together to force deer onto escape routes. Greg Pink, a bowhunting friend from Montrose, Colorado, has used his knowledge of escape routes in his area to organize many productive drives. In any given canyon, he'll place a hunter at each of the two or three places where deer will most likely exit, and then he'll have a couple of hunters walk through the cover where he has seen deer during previous hunts. In the case of bowhunting,

If the big bucks have been eluding you, it's time to switch tactics and hunt escape routes.

it's vital to know exactly where the escape routes are because the maximum practical range for most bowhunters is less than 50 yards. Pink's hunting party has taken many respectable bucks this way, including a few outstanding enough to rank well into the record books.

"The first time you run a drive, something usually goes wrong," he said. "But after you do it a few times, you pretty well get to know where the escape routes are and where to put the drivers to get the bucks moving. You also need to learn how to reach the best stands without first spooking the deer. Big muleys are really hard to hunt if you go after them one-on-one, but if you can find a good escape route and have someone push the deer to it, you stand a pretty good chance of scoring."

Most hunters organize drives that are too long, or they try to push bucks into large openings where the shooting would be easy. If big bucks know they're being followed for a long distance, they'll usually circle and refuse to leave heavy cover. A large buck, whether it's a whitetail, blacktail, or mule deer, will seldom allow himself to be forced into a wide opening.

I was reminded of this last year by an incident

that happened on a ranch where I was outfitting mule-deer hunters. One of my clients was a movie producer who wanted his film crew to get some good footage of him shooting a trophy buck. He wanted the buck to be shot in an opening, rather than in the maple brush, so that it could be easily seen. About ten friends and guides helped to drive deer to an open sagebrush slope, where the camera crew was set up in complete camouflage. Though four or five small bucks crossed the open slope, the only large buck the drivers saw refused to expose himself in the open. One guide attempted to spook the buck into the opening four different times, but each time the animal wisely circled back into dense maple brush. The producer ended up shooting a forkhorn.

Contrary to what you might think, escape routes don't necessarily lead into the wind. My theory is that when a buck is sufficiently alarmed to use an escape route, his main concern is leaving the area and not what may lie ahead. If he must move with the wind or crosswind, he'll rely on his superb hearing and eyesight to detect danger ahead.

To avoid detection while waiting near an escape route, wear quiet clothing and avoid coughing, sneezing, or rustling about. If you see a buck moving toward you, make no sudden movements, even if you're in a tree stand. If possible, hold your gun or bow almost in shooting position as you wait on stand. Also, it's a good idea to wait for a buck to walk slightly past you or look away from you before you try to shoot.

Be prepared to react quickly if you see a deer. Bucks sometimes fairly fly along their escape routes, and if you can't instantly find your safety, you might be too late. I almost failed to kill my first buck for just this reason. My father had lent me his venerable Army-issue .30/06 with a safety that turned around the end of the bolt. I was waiting in a tree-choked saddle that connected two huge canyons when someone shot three times about 200 yards above me. Soon, I could hear the pounding of a deer's hoofs, and then a steer-fat buck that must have weight at least 250 pounds galloped into view. At the time, I did most of my hunting with a shotgun that had a safety in the trigger guard, and I felt for the safety there but couldn't find it. Finally, just as the deer passed, I remembered where the safety was and twisted it off. By then, I was so flustered that my first shot went high. My second shot was too far back, but it slowed the buck enough so that I was able to follow up with a spine shot. Now I know enough to be totally familiar with my rifle before I take a stand, and I mentally prepare myself for mind-racing action. When I hunt on escape routes, I rarely prepare in vain.

Perhaps you disdain stand hunting, preferring instead to stillhunt or glass for bucks in their beds. If you have venison and antlers to show for it, fine. If the bucks have been eluding you, though, it's time to switch tactics and start learning how to foil the great escape.

PART 4

GUNS AND SHOOTING

Carmichel's Guide To Hunting Cartridges

By Jim Carmichel

The debate never ends. Knockdown power, bullet energy—what are they? How do we compare one cartridge or bullet to another? Ever since hunters first observed the awesome effect of a powder-driven projectile, they have never tired of speculating on the relative effectiveness of bullets of different sizes and weights traveling at different speeds. The very earliest firearms literature, as you might guess, is filled with all sorts of opinions about killing energy. The speculations are based on everything from black magic to the alignment of stars.

Modern writers have been no less inclined to dream up various ways of comparing cartridge performance, some of which seem to be based on rationales no more substantial than the Mephistophelean theorems of medieval times. A particularly intent hunter/mathematician of the last century boarded himself up in a fog-shrouded Scottish castle and spent more than a decade formulating an exacting means of comparing bullet effectiveness. Finally emerging from his self-imposed entombment with the figures victoriously in hand, he met up with an old-time hunting pal with whom he shared the results of his revolutionary efforts. Predictably, an argument ensued. The disagreement deteriorated into a common brawl, during which the furnishings and inventory of a fair-sized pub were

Photo by Stanley Trzoniec

smashed and/or consumed. The mathematician achieved revenge by withholding his discoveries and, apparently, the formulas.

During this century, there have been some notable attempts to categorize cartridge performance. One much-discussed example is John Taylor's tables of "Knock Out," or "KO," values, in which he attempted to index the relative punch of dangerous-game cartridges. Unfortunately, Taylor's KO tables are frequently supported or condemned by lost souls who haven't even read his book, *African Rifles and Cartridges,* and don't realize that Taylor's KO values are just what he says they are—a means of assessing, for example, how long an elephant will remain unconsious if hit by a head shot that misses the brain. On the same page in which he describes his KO theory, Taylor allows that theoretical mathematical bullet energy may be a better guide to the relative effectiveness of bullets on non-dangerous game animals.

The theoretical mathematical energy that Taylor is talking about is what we usually refer to simply as kinetic energy, by far the most widely accepted measure of a bullet's power. This is the index we see listed as foot-pounds in ammo makers' ballistic tables. A foot-pound, simply stated, is the force generated by a one-pound weight falling one foot; or, conversely, it is the energy required to lift a one-

pound weight to a one-foot elevation. To get this into shooting perspective, we can say that the 2,900 foot-pounds generated at the muzzle of a .30/06 rifle is equal to the force of a 2,900 pound weight falling one foot.

Ballisticians prefer the foot-pound system for comparing cartridge performance for some very good reasons. First of all, it is the industry standard of comparison. Second, it is easily calculated. Third, the relative energy levels of various cartridges tend to correspond to actual performance in the field. The foot-pound energy index is not without a host of critics, however, especially shooters who prefer large-diameter, slow-moving bullets. As these critics very correctly point out, the foot-pound system is heavily skewed in favor of high-velocity cartridges. With the accepted formula for calculating bullet energy, if you double the weight of the bullet, leaving all else the same, you merely double the energy level. But if you double the velocity, you *quadruple* the energy. That's why big-bore fanciers stomp and sputter and dream up calculations that favor heavy bullets. One such set of calculations that I recently reviewed led to the conclusion that a thrown brick is the way to stop a charging Cape buffalo!

A once-popular means of comparing cartridge effectiveness that was favored by fans of large, heavy bullets was the so-called, and often confusing,

POINT-BLANK TRAJECTORIES AND REMAINING ENERGY LEVELS
OF 100 POPULAR RIFLE CARTRIDGES

Caliber	Bullet Weight (Grains)	Bullet Type*	Muzzle Velocity (Feet Per Second)	50 Yards	100 Yards	150 Yards	200 Yards	250 Yards	300 Yards	350 Yards	Range at Which Bullet Is Three Inches Low	1,200 Foot-Pounds (Deer, Antelope)	2,000 Foot-Pounds (Elk, Bears to 600 Pounds)	2,800 Foot-Pounds (Large Bears, Moose)
.223 Remington	55	HPPL	3,240	1.0	2.6	3.0	2.1	0.4	4.8		282	0	0	0
.22/250 Remington	55	HPPL	3,730	0.7	2.3	3.0	2.7	1.4	1.2	5.3	324	100	0	0
.224 Weatherby Mag.	55	PE	3,650	0.8	2.3	3.0	2.7	1.3	1.4	5.5	322	120	0	0
.220 Swift	52	HPST	4,000	0.6	2.1	2.9	2.9	2.1	0.3	2.6	355	170	0	0
.243 Winchester	80	HPPL	3,350	0.9	2.5	3.0	2.4	0.5	2.8	7.9	302	200	0	0
.243 Winchester	100	PSPCL	2,960	1.1	2.6	3.0	2.0	0.5	4.5		284	250	0	0
6mm Remington	80	HPPL	3,470	0.9	2.4	3.0	2.6	0.9	2.1	6.7	311	220	0	0
6mm Remington	100	PSPCL	3,130	1.0	2.5	3.0	2.3	0.3	3.1		299	300	0	0
.240 Weatherby Mag.	87	PE	3,500	0.8	2.3	3.0	2.7	1.3	−1.3	5.2	324	320	85	0
.240 Weatherby Mag.	100	PE	3,395	0.8	2.4	3.0	2.6	1.2	−1.4	5.3	322	415	140	0
.250 Savage	87	PSP	3,030	1.1	2.6	3.0	1.9	−0.8	−5.3		278	155	0	0
.250 Savage	100	PSP	2,820	1.2	2.7	2.9	1.4	−1.8	−7.1		263	160	0	0
.257 Roberts	87	PSP	3,170	1.0	2.6	3.0	2.2	−0.1	−4.0		289	190	0	0
.257 Roberts	117	SPCL	2,650	1.4	2.9	2.7	0.5	−3.8				140	0	0
.25/06 Remington	87	HPPL	3,440	0.9	2.4	3.0	2.5	0.6	−2.7	−7.9	303	225	50	0
.25/06 Remington	100	PSPCL	3,230	1.0	2.5	3.0	2.3	0.4	−3.1		299	285	65	0
.25/06 Remington	120	PSPCL	3,010	1.1	2.6	3.0	2.1	−0.2	−4.0		289	360	95	0
.257 Weatherby Mag.	87	PE	3,825	0.7	2.1	2.9	2.9	2.0	0.0	−3.0	351	415	175	5
.257 Weatherby Mag.	100	PE	3,555	0.8	2.3	3.0	2.8	1.6	−0.7		335	455	190	1
.257 Weatherby Mag.	117	NP	3,300	0.9	2.4	3.0	2.5	0.9	−1.9	−6.1	315	465	195	5
6.5 mm Remington Mag.	120	PSPCL	3,210	1.0	2.5	3.0	2.4	0.5	−2.9	−7.7	302	390	155	0
.264 Winchester Mag.	100	PSP	3,320	0.9	2.5	3.0	2.4	0.4	−3.1		299	270	80	0
.264 Winchester Mag.	140	PSPCL	3,030	1.1	2.6	3.0	2.2	0.0	−3.6		299	475	205	10
.270 Winchester	100	PSP	3,480	0.3	2.4	3.0	2.6	0.9	−2.1	−6.7	311	295	85	0
.270 Winchester	130	BP	3,110	1.0	2.5	3.0	2.3	0.3	−3.1		299	435	170	0
.270 Winchester	150	SPCL	2,900	1.2	2.7	2.9	1.6	−1.6	−6.7		266	295	115	15
.270 Weatherby Mag.	130	PE	3,375	0.8	2.4	3.0	2.6	1.2	−1.4	−5.3	323	570	295	95
.270 Weatherby Mag.	150	NP	3,245	0.9	2.4	3.0	2.5	0.9	−1.9	−6.0	316	690	380	155
.284 Winchester	125	PP(SP)	3,140	1.0	2.5	3.0	2.2	0.1	−3.5		294	370	150	0
.284 Winchester	150	PP(SP)	2,860	1.2	2.7	2.9	1.7	−1.1	−5.6		274	395	155	0
7/30 Waters	120	FP	2,680	1.4	2.9	2.7	6.5	−3.9	−11.2		242	145	0	0
7mm Mauser	140	PSP	2,660	1.3	2.8	2.8	1.2	−2.1	−7.4		260	325	55	0
7mm/08 Remington	140	PSP	2,860	1.2	2.7	2.9	1.8	−0.8	−5.1		278	410	140	0
.280 Remington	150	PSPCL	2,970	1.1	2.6	3.0	2.0	−0.5	−4.5		284	435	195	25
.280 Remington	165	SPCL	2,820	1.2	2.7	2.9	1.4	−1.8	−7.0		264	355	160	15
7mm Remington Mag.	125	PP(SP)	3,310	0.9	2.4	3.0	2.5	0.7	−2.5	−7.1	307	410	195	40
7mm Remington Mag.	150	PSPCL	3,110	1.0	2.5	3.0	2.2	0.2	−3.4	8.5	296	485	245	75
7mm Remington Mag.	175	PSPCL	2,860	1.2	2.7	2.9	1.9	−0.7	−4.8		281	575	285	80
7 mm Weatherby Mag.	139	PE	3,300	0.9	2.4	3.0	2.5	1.0	−1.8	−6.0	316	570	300	110
7 mm Weatherby Mag.	154	PE	3,160	1.0	2.5	3.0	2.4	0.6	−2.4		307	625	340	130
7 mm Weatherby Mag.	175	RN	3,070	1.0	2.5	3.0	2.3	0.3	−3.0	−7.8	300	660	380	175
.30 Carbine	110	SP	1,990	2.1	2.9	0.1	−7.1				176	0	0	0
.30 Remington	170	ST	2,120	1.9	3.0	1.5	−3.1				199	115	0	0
.30/30 Winchester	150	SPCL	2,390	1.7	3.0	2.1	−1.6	−8.7			212	120	0	0
.30/30 Winchester	170	SPCL	2,200	1.8	3.0	1.8	−2.3	−9.6			206	140	0	0
.300 Savage	150	SPCL	2,630	1.4	2.9	2.6	0.3	−4.4			238	280	65	0
.300 Savage	180	PSPCL	2,350	1.6	2.9	2.4	−0.2	−5.2			231	305	50	0
.300 Savage	180	RM	2,350	1.7	2.3	2.2	−1.1	−7.3			218	300	35	0
.30/40 Krag	180	PSPCL	2,430	1.5	2.9	2.5	0.2	−4.3			238	345	90	0

*HPPL, Hollow Point-Lokt; PE, Pointed Expanding; HPBT, Hollow Point Boat Tail; PSPCL, Pointed Soft Point Core-Lokt; PSP, Pointed Soft Point; SPCL, Soft Point Core-Lokt; NP, Nosier Partition; BP, Bronze Point; PP(SP), Power-Point (Soft Point); FP, Flat Point; RN, Round Nose; SP, Soft Point; ST, Silver Tip; SJHP, Semijacketed Hollow Point; FMJ, Full Metal Jacket.

Caliber	Bullet Weight (Grains)	Bullet Type*	Muzzle Velocity (Feet Per Second)	Trajectory (inches)							Ranges at Which Cartridges Retain Three Levels of Energy (Yards)			
				50 Yards	100 Yards	150 Yards	200 Yards	250 Yards	300 Yards	350 Yards	Range at Which Bullet Is Three Inches Low	1,200 Foot-Pounds (Deer, Antelope)	2,000 Foot-Pounds (Elk, Bears to 600 Pounds)	2,800 Foot-Pounds (Large Bears, Moose)
.30/40 Krag	220	ST	2,160	1.8	3.0	1.9	-1.7	-8.1			214	330	85	0
.30/06 Springfield	110	PSP	3,380	1.0	2.5	3.0	2.2	-0.2	-4.5		285	225	85	0
.30/06 Springfield	150	BP	2,910	1.1	2.7	2.9	1.9	-0.7	-4.9		280	435	185	5
.30/06 Springfield	165	PSPCL	2,800	1.2	2.7	2.9	1.5	-1.5	-6.4		268	405	180	15
.30/06 Springfield	180	PSPCL	2,700	1.3	2.8	2.8	1.3	1.9	7.0		263	460	205	20
.30/06 Springfield	220	SPCL	2,410	1.6	2.9	2.4	-0.3	5.5			229	330	140	5
.300 Winchester Mag.	150	PSPCL	3,290	0.9	2.5	3.0	2.4	0.6	2.7	7.5	304	465	260	115
.300 Winchester Mag.	180	PSPCL	2,950	1.1	2.6	3.0	2.1	-0.1	3.8		291	645	355	145
.300 Winchester Mag.	220	ST	2,680	1.3	2.8	2.8	1.3	2.0	7.3		261	540	300	125
.300 H&H Mag.	150	ST	3,130	1.0	2.6	3.0	2.2	0.1	3.6		294	460	245	90
.300 H&H Mag	180	PSPCL	2,880	1.2	2.7	2.9	1.8	-0.7	5.0		279	535	280	95
.300 H&H Mag.	220	ST	2,580	1.4	2.9	2.7	0.8	-3.0	9.0		250	490	260	95
.300 Weatherby Mag.	150	PE	3,545	0.8	2.3	3.0	2.7	1.5	-0.8	4.3	334	645	400	225
.300 Weatherby Mag.	180	PE	3,245	0.9	2.4	3.0	2.5	0.9	-1.9	6.0	315	750	465	265
.303 Savage	190	ST	1,940	2.1	2.9	0.6	-5.4				184	70	0	0
.307 Winchester	150	FP	2,760	1.3	2.8	2.7	0.6	3.8	-11.1		243	205	70	0
.307 Winchester	180	FP	2,510	1.5	2.9	2.5	0.0	-5.1	-13.0		232	250	80	0
.303 British	180	SPCL	2,460	1.6	2.9	2.4	-0.4	-5.8			227	230	65	0
.308 Winchester	110	PSP	3,180	1.1	2.6	3.0	1.8	-1.1	-6.3		271	200	60	0
.308 Winchester	125	PSP	3,050	1.1	2.6	3.0	1.9	-0.6	-5.0		280	295	105	0
.308 Winchester	150	PSPCL	2,820	1.2	2.7	2.9	1.5	-1.5	-6.5		267	345	130	0
.308 Winchester	180	PSPCL	2,620	1.4	2.8	2.8	1.1	-2.5	-8.1		256	425	170	0
.32 Winchester Special	170	SPCL	2,250	1.8	3.0	1.9	-2.0	-9.2			209	145	0	0
8mm Mauser	170	SPCL	2,360	1.7	3.0	2.0	-1.6	-8.6			212	150	15	0
8mm Remington Mag.	185	PSPCL	3,080	1.1	2.6	3.0	2.1	-0.2	-4.1		287	490	290	150
8mm Remington Mag.	220	PSPCL	2,830	1.2	2.7	2.9	1.7	-1.1	-5.7		273	580	345	180
.338 Winchester Mag.	200	PP(SP)	2,960	1.1	2.7	3.0	1.9	-0.8	-5.1		278	495	295	150
.338 Winchester Mag.	225	SP	2,780	1.2	2.7	2.9	1.7	-1.1	-5.6		274	680	400	205
.338 Winchester Mag.	250	ST	2,660	1.3	2.8	2.8	1.0	-2.6	-8.3		255	700	320	175
.340 Weatherby Mag.	200	PE	3,210	0.9	2.5	3.0	2.4	0.7	-2.4	-6.9	308	695	455	280
.340 Weatherby Mag.	250	NP	2,850	1.2	2.7	2.9	1.6	-1.3	-6.1		270	530	360	220
.35 Remington	150	PSPCL	2,300	1.8	3.0	1.8	-2.5	-10.8			203	95	0	0
.35 Remington	200	SPCL	2,080	2.0	3.0	1.0	-4.8				188	115	0	0
.351 Remington SL	180	RN	1,850	2.2	2.8	-0.1	-7.3	-19.6			174	40	0	0
.356 Winchester	200	FP	2,460	1.6	2.9	2.4	-0.5	-6.0	-14.8		226	255	95	0
.356 Winchester	250	FP	1,160	1.8	3.0	1.8	-2.1	-9.0	-19.5		208	300	105	0
.358 Winchester	200	ST	2,490	1.5	2.9	2.5	-0.1	-5.1			232	290	115	0
.358 Winchester	250	ST	2,230	1.7	3.0	2.1	-1.4	-7.6			216	355	105	0
.350 Remington Mag.	200	PSPCL	2,710	1.3	2.8	2.8	1.1	-2.5	-8.3		255	395	205	65
.375 Winchester	200	FP	2,200	1.8	3.0	1.6	-2.9	-11.1	-23.9		201	160	20	0
.375 Winchester	250	FP	1,900	2.1	2.9	0.5	-5.6	-16.0	-31.3		183	175	2	0
.375 H&H Mag.	270	SP	2,690	1.3	2.8	2.8	1.1	-2.4	-8.0		257	550	345	200
.378 Weatherby Mag.	300	NP	2,925	1.2	2.7	2.9	1.8	-1.0	-5.5		275	640	440	310
.38/40 Winchester	180	SP	1,160	3.0	-0.2	-12.1					116	0	0	0
.38/55 Winchester	255	SP	1,320	2.8	1.5	-5.9					135	0	0	0
.44 Remington Mag.	240	SJHP	1,760	2.4	2.6	-1.7	-11.8				159	65	0	0
.444 Marlin	240	SP	2,350	1.8	3.0	1.6	-3.3				197	170	80	0
.444 Marlin	265	SP	2,120	1.9	3.0	1.1	-4.3				191	190	70	0
.45/70 Government	405	SP	1,330	2.8	1.4	-6.3					134	110	0	0
.458 Winchester Mag.	500	FMJ	2,040	1.9	3.0	1.5	-3.0	-10.8			200	640	360	220
.460 Weatherby Mag.	500	FMJ	2,700	1.3	2.8	2.8	1.1	-2.4	-8.0		257	827	575	445

"pounds-feet" theory. Obviously, one reason it was so confusing was that it was frequently confused with foot-pounds of kinetic energy because of the similarity of names. The pounds-feet theory does not favor velocity as much as kinetic-energy calculations do. For example, when using standard kinetic foot-pounds calculations, a 180-grain bullet from a .30/06 leaving the muzzle at 2,700 feet per second develops 2,913 foot-pounds of energy at the muzzle. By comparison, a 405-grain .45/70 bullet that leaves the muzzle at 1,330 feet per second has only 1,590 foot-pounds of energy. But if we apply the pounds-feet theory, the .45/70 has a relative index of 76.95 compared with 69.40 for the .30/06.

The "pounds-feet" theory was done asunder by the arrival of modern cartridges, which demonstrated that the shock generated by a relatively small but high-velocity bullet was a better killer than the big holes made by slow-moving bullets.

Back in the early 1960s, P.O. Ackley, the well-known gunsmith and cartridge experimenter, wrote a book called *Handbook For Shooters & Reloaders,* which includes a chapter on killing power. Ackley discusses the various theories of bullet energy, much as I have done in this article, and also includes a section by Paul Van Rosenberg on the relative effectiveness of different cartridges on big game. Ackley describes Van Rosenberg as an experienced big-game hunter and ballistics engineer, and Van Rosenberg's comments indicate this to indeed have been the case. Among Van Rosenberg's more interesting recommendations is the establishment of more-or-less specific energy levels that a cartridge must provide to perform well on game. He feels that 1,200 foot-pounds of energy is adequate for game such as deer, antelope, sheep, and goats. For elk and small bears, he recommends 2,000 foot-pounds as adequate, and he sets 2,800 as the adequate energy level for large bears and moose. Of course, Van Rosenberg speaks of the *remaining energy at the target,* not at the muzzle.

By necessity, Van Rosenberg's recommendations must be regarded as generalizations, and there are plenty of exceptions to them. For example, the energy level of the .30/30 Winchester with a 170-grain bullet drops below 1,200 foot-pounds inside 150 yards. Yet, we know by experience that a .30/30 easily kills deer at 200 yards and even a bit beyond. Just the same, we can make some interesting comparisons of different cartridges and bullet weights by imposing Van Rosenberg's performance levels and seeing how—or, rather, where (at what ranges)—they stack up.

The accompanying table, computed at Outdoor Life Magazine's Briarbank Ballistic Laboratory, shows the critical ranges for 100 cartridges and bullet weights. By comparing the different energy/range figures, you'll get a pretty fair idea of what to expect in the way of *relative* performance on big game.

Also included is an expanded version of "The Nonthinking Man's Trajectory Table." The table shows the 3-inch (plus or minus) point-blank range of most American big-game calibers. By 3-inch point-blank range, we mean that, within the recommended ranges, the bullet never rises above or falls below 3 inches of your line of sight. From the practical hunter's standpoint, this is more than adequate bullet placement because it is well within the vital-area size of all big-game animals.

These figures are the best-ever means of comparing the useful hunting ranges of various cartridges. All data are based on a line of sight 1½ inches above the bore line. This is typical of most scope-sighted rifles. To make use of the table, simply sight your rifle in at any of the ranges shown so that the bullet impact, in relation to point of aim, matches the impact point at that distance (assuming that you're using factory-loaded ammunition and a rifle that is in good condition).

For example, the table shows that the .270 Winchester with a 130-grain Bronze Point bullet is 2.5 inches high at 100 yards. Accordingly, simply adjust the sight on your .270 so that the bullet hits 2.5 inches above point of aim at 100 yards. From that point on, the bullet will hit within 3 inches (vertically) of where you aim out to more than 250 yards.

One column of the table lists the range at which the bullet is 3 inches below line of sight. All the way out to that range, stated in yards, you can hold dead on and forget about trajectory when you're big-game hunting or when you're shooting most varmints. What could be simpler?

By consulting the retained-energy figures and the point-blank ranges, you can provide yourself with a very good idea of the performance of any listed cartridge. Some have such a looped trajectory that the practical hunting ranges at which they can be used are very short. At the other extreme are some of the magnums that retain, for instance, enough energy to kill deer dead at very long ranges. But at those ranges (more than 300 yards), even expert riflemen would seldom attempt a shot. In other words, by using both sets of figures, you can quite closely determine how far you can kill efficiently in terms of both on-target energy and ability to make a hit. Perhaps best of all, the combined figures give someone who's buying a new rifle a reliable means of determining which cartridge or cartridges are best for his form of hunting.

Hitting what you shoot at is the big weakness in the assumptions behind most cartridge-performance tables. Argue as we may about the relative performance of various cartridges, the major factor is the man behind the gun. When it comes to killing game, I give bullet placement a relative importance of 70 percent. The other 30 percent can be divided between bullet energy and terminal bullet performance any way you want to split it up.

For your copy of JIM CARMICHEL'S BOOK OF THE RIFLE, please send $34.95 plus $2.64 for postage and handling to Outdoor Life Books, Dept. DHY8, Box 2018, Latham, NY 12111.

Smoothbore Deer Hunting: Buckshot

By George H. Haas

For close-range shooting in thick cover, buckshot is better than any rifle bullet.

A repeating shotgun loaded with buckshot shells is a fearsome firearm. There are nine .33 caliber lead balls in the 12-gauge 2¾-inch 00 Buckshot load, a very popular cartridge. With four shells in the magazine and one in the chamber of a repeating shotgun, the gunner can trigger off 45 projectiles in five shots. Each ball is one-third of an inch in diameter, and the muzzle velocity is about 1,300 feet per second. Because nine projectiles are launched with each pull of the trigger, they leave the muzzle at least as fast as rounds from a submachine gun, and most submachine guns have only a 20-round magazine capacity.

Big-bore shotguns loaded with buckshot have been used to kill polar and grizzly bears, African horned game, and lions. Buckshot-loaded shotguns are often used by game wardens and professional hunters when following up a wounded leopard in heavy cover. A heavy buckshot load is more than enough to kill a leopard or even a lion if the shot is taken at close range, and a good shotgun is quicker to put on target than any rifle.

The awesome reputation of buckshot makes it puzzling for a first-time user when he finds that, for deer hunting, it is quite ineffective at ranges that exceed, at most, 60 yards (with the most powerful loads). And a deer is a rather small animal that is actually quite easy to kill.

The accompanying drawing shows the actual size of buckshot used in the United States. A single .36 caliber lead ball (000 Buck, called *triple-Oh*), the largest available, weighs about 71 grains. At a muzzle velocity of, say, 1,300 feet per second, energy at 100 yards has dropped to 84 foot-pounds. The reason for this sharp drop is that a round ball has a very poor aerodynamic shape. A pointed rifle bullet would retain its energy much better if fired at the same velocity. The 84 foot-pounds of energy is

about the same energy retained by a .22 Rimfire Long Rifle bullet at 100 yards, and shooting deer with a .22 Rimfire is forbidden by all states.

In the 3-inch, 12-gauge 000 Buck load, there are ten shot of .36 caliber. Multiplying 84 foot-pounds of energy by ten, we come to the conclusion that, roughly, the 100-yard energy of this heavy deer load is only 840 foot-pounds. This is quite a bit less than the 1,200 foot-pounds of energy that is generally considered satisfactory on-target energy for a deer-hunting rifle. This very powerful shotgun deer load is obviously not effective at 100 yards, and yet, many inexperienced hunters will fire it at a deer at that range and expect an instantaneous kill. These great expectations, usually harbored by hunters who have previously used only centerfire rifles, are the reason why buckshot loads have a bad reputation for wounding deer.

Even if you could hit a deer with 840 foot-pounds of energy in a heavy buckshot load at 100 yards, you probably would not kill the animal. You would have to hit the deer with all ten shot, and that's difficult. For best results, you would have to hit the vital heart/lung area with all the shot, and that is impossible. Remember that the heart/lung area of a deer is approximately the size of an 8½ × 11-inch sheet of typewriting paper, if you have a broadside shot. You'd be very lucky indeed if you managed to put three of the ten pellets in that area at 100 yards, and three of these pellets would yield only 252 foot-pounds of energy. Penetration would be shallow because of low energy and because of the blunt, rounded shape of the projectiles. Of course, the other seven shot might connect with the deer, and it's faintly possible that one or two would hit the spine, cut an artery, or penetrate the brain, but one simply cannot depend on it.

On the average, what is the extreme effective range of buckshot loads when used in deer hunting? Exact ranges are impossible to determine because so many factors enter into the "equation." But approximations can be developed by considering each factor in turn. This will also give a lot of useful information about these deer loads.

The diameter of buckshot ranges from .36-inch in a 000 load down to .24-inch in a No. 4 load. The larger and heavier the projectile, the longer velocity and energy are retained during flight since muzzle velocity in buckshot loads does not vary a great deal from load to load. For this reason alone, most hunters opt for 000 or 00 Buck and ignore the smaller sizes, but that may be a mistake.

A few years ago, 00 Buckshot, then the largest size, had a poor reputation for accuracy. The most popular load was the 2¾-inch 12-gauge shell with nine shot. In tightly-choked guns, patterns were so wide and spotty that the hunter was lucky to hit any part of a deer with three or four pellets, much less put enough lead in a vital area to make a sure one-shot kill. For that reason, many experienced shotgunners opted for the smaller sizes, particularly No. 4, the smallest in 12-gauge guns. In the standard factory-loaded 2¾-inch shell, this load contains 27 pellets. At reasonable ranges, the hunter could, therefore, expect to hit a deer with ten to 12 pellets, and in most cases, four or five of them would hit the vital heart/lung area when shooting broadside. For a then-unknown reason, the small No. 4 Buckshot produced denser, more even patterns than the 00.

But the smaller pellets had less retained energy out at 45 or 50 yards; so penetration was less, and many gunners would not shoot a deer with No. 4 in a 12-gauge at any more than 30 yards or so. Some hunters compromised by using No. 1 Buck in the standard 12-gauge shell (16 pellets) or No. 0 (12 pellets). This is one dilemma of using buckshot. Heavier pellets have greater individual energy, but there are fewer of them than there are of the smaller sizes when loaded in the same capacity shell. The problem is often to find an acceptable compromise between retained energy and the number of shot that hit the target.

The problem was partially solved when buffered buckshot loads were introduced. In these shells, spaces between the projectiles are filled with granulated plastic. This prevents most shot deformation caused by firing, by bouncing of shot against bore,

and by "jostling" of shot during passage down the barrel. The buffering also greatly improves pattern density and uniformity of buckshot fired from tightly-choked guns. All major manufacturers of buckshot cartridges now offer buffered loads. Not using them limits the effective range of your shotgun quite a bit.

It used to be said that large buckshot formed tighter, more even patterns when fired from open-choked shotguns. But with buffered loads, tight patterns are produced by 000, 00, and 0 Buckshot when fired from tightly-choked shotguns. Smaller sizes in 12-gauge guns are no longer so common.

Buckshot loads are made in 10 gauge, 12 gauge, 16 gauge, and 20 gauge. Twenty-eight-gauge and .410 shells, smallest of them all, are not available with buckshot charges. The small number of buckshot of any size that these two shotguns could fire made them completely ineffective for deer hunting.

The nominal bore diameters (some manufacturers vary slightly) of the six shotgun gauges are shown in the drawing.

In other words, the largest bore available today is larger than three-quarters of an inch, and the smallest one that is useful with buckshot to any degree is bigger than the bore of a .50-caliber American machine gun.

The larger the gauge, the greater the number of shot in the shell, all other things being equal. With the mighty 3½-inch 10-gauge Magnum, the only two buckshot loadings at present are charged with 18 00 Buckshot or 54 No. 4. Both are manufactured by Federal Cartridge. With the small size of No. 4 Buckshot, the loading is obviously intended more for fairly close-range shooting at moving deer. The very heavy 00 Buckshot load is best for use at longer ranges.

Before you go out and buy a 10-gauge gun, however, you should note that they are expensive, very heavy (11 pounds or so), bulky, and that the recoil is punishing for most shooters. Shorter, less powerful 10-gauge loads are available.

Twelve-gauge loads are available in many different sizes of buckshot from 000 down to No. 4. Twelve-gauge shotguns are chambered for the 2¾-inch shell or the 3-inch Magnum. These lengths, as with all shotgun shells, refer to the unfolded length of the case after firing. The 3-inch 12-gauge has a greater capacity than the shorter case. If you have a gun chambered for the 3-inch shell, you can also fire the shorter shells in it. The short shell is loaded as a Magnum (more shot and more energy) or with "standard" 2¾-inch charges. This gives the shooter three broad classes of 12-gauge buckshot (and birdshot) loads to choose from and makes for a great deal of flexibility. If you have a gun with 3-inch chambers, you have the option of firing progressively lighter loads if the heavy ones prove too much for you or if the gun does not handle them well.

The heaviest 12-gauge 3-inch Magnum is loaded with ten pellets of 000 Buckshot, and a dozen other

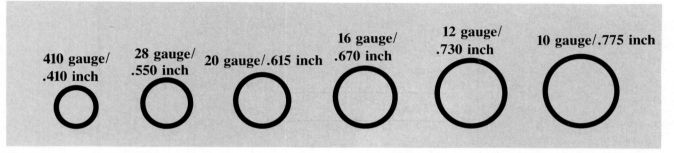

Buckshot diameters in inches: No. 000 buckshot was introduced only a few years ago. It adds several yards to the maximum effective range of buckshot. For deer, however, 00 buck in a 12-gauge gun is the more popular.

The 28-gauge and .410 bore are too small to be effective with buckshot or slug loads in big-game hunting. The 12-gauge is by far the most popular, but very heavy buckshot and slug loads are now available in 10-gauge. Some manufacturers vary from the bore dimensions given here by a thousandth of an inch or several. By coincidence, the 12-gauge bore is almost exactly the diameter of a U.S. dime, but a dime will not actually enter the muzzle of most 12-gauge guns because of choke constriction.

12-gauge loadings are currently available. These include 000 Buck, 00, No. 1, and No. 4. Obviously, you can easily change your load quite a bit to suit changing hunting needs. Even if you do not have a 12 that will take 3-inch shells, there are eight different 2¾-inch loads.

A great variety of 12-gauge shotguns is available. Pump, semi-automatic, double-barreled, single-shot, and even bolt-action 12-gauge guns are on the market in countless model variations. Prices range from moderate to a king's ransom. With the other gauges, particularly the 10 and the 16, the variety is extremely limited. In 20 gauge there is a good variety of guns, but the 20 has severe limitations when used with buckshot.

Sixteen-gauge guns are being phased out. Very few of them are being made, even in Europe. If you're buying a new shotgun for any purpose, it's best to avoid the 16 because the variety of loads available in this gauge constantly declines. Currently, the only 16-gauge buckshot load is 12 pellets of No. 1 Buck, a compromise between a long-range and a short-range shell.

The choice in 20-gauge buckshot loads is limited, too. You can use a 20-gauge 3-inch Magnum of No. 2 Buck (18 pellets) or a 2¾-inch load of No. 3 Buck (20 pellets). The larger buckshot sizes are not available in 20-gauge shells. It's obviously best to avoid using a 20-gauge gun with buckshot because of this lack of versatility and because the small number of pellets in the available sizes severely limits effective range.

In leafing through ammunition tables for useful buckshot loads, you'll find odd gaps. For instance, using 00 Buckshot in a 20-gauge gun might seem like a good way to increase effective range, but doing so is not possible. Too few 00 projectiles could be loaded in the small case.

One of the most important considerations is the choke of the shotgun. Without going into great detail, most modern shotguns are choked Extra Full, Full, Improved Modified, Modified, Improved Cylinder, and Cylinder. Extra Full is the tightest choke available, and a shotgun bored Cylinder has no constriction at the muzzle. Choke is intended to concentrate the shot into an even, dense pattern at long ranges. With buckshot, the objective is to place as many shot as possible in the small vital area of a deer and, for this, the obvious choice is the tightest possible choke.

The usual method of determining the degree of choke is to fire at a large paper target at a range of 40 yards. If a 30-inch circle drawn on this target encloses more than 75 percent of the pellet holes, the choke is Extra Full. Full is 65 to 75 percent; Improved Modified, 55 to 65 percent; Modified, 45 to 55; and Improved Cylinder, 35 to 45. A Cylinder bore usually throws a 25 to 35 percent pattern. Many authorities differ on the precise percentages for each degree of choke, and most American guns are labeled simply Full, Modified, Improved Cylinder, and Cylinder.

But a 30-inch circle is much larger than a deer's vital area, and percentages taken with buckshot will probably not match the choke marking on your gun barrel.

The only way to check out your shotgun is to put up a full-size paper target of a deer of the type used by bowhunters and fire at it with various buckshot loads. If full-size deer targets seem expensive to you, buy only one and cut out the deer's image. Then trace the outline on large sheets of paper.

Start out at a reasonable range, say 30 yards, and fire a few shells. Then increase the range in 5-yard increments until the pattern disperses to such a great degree that putting three pellets in the heart/lung area becomes merely a matter of chance. Most hunters agree that if you hit the heart/lung area with at least three pellets, you'll make a quick kill. If you hit the heart, death is almost instantaneous, and if three pellets pierce the lungs, you won't have to track the deer very far. The point at which you simply cannot put at least three pellets into the vital area should be considered your maximum effective range with that particular load. Doing all this will also give you a good idea of where your pattern is actually going in relationship to your shotgun sights. With buckshot, it's best to use the single-bead or double-bead sighting equipment that is installed on bird hunting guns.

Don't be surprised if the results are terrible. In some guns marked Full, the 00 Buckshot pattern is so thin at only 30 yards that it is completely useless at that short range. Because of all the variables that go into buckshot performance, a beat-up, barbed-wire-scratched pump gun that cost only $90 second-hand may fire a better buckshot pattern than a fine new shotgun. Choke markings on barrels are often meaningless. You may find that a Cylinder-bored Skeet gun fires a tighter, more even pattern than an Extra Full, long-range duck gun.

If one load does not work, try another. Dropping down one size in the diameter of the buckshot may improve the density of the pattern, and doing just the opposite may have the same result. Sometimes, a very heavy Magnum load does not perform well in a given shotgun. You may even find that you have an old-fashioned doughnut pattern in which most of the shot tends to impact at the edge of the pattern, leaving the center empty. Holes in the pattern are to be avoided because the hole may coincide with the small heart/lung area.

In patterning buckshot, it's also wise to remember that you may fire at a deer that is facing you, and in that case, the maximum heart/lung area is only six or eight inches wide. If you're wise, you won't fire at a deer that is facing straight away from you because the penetration of buckshot is very limited. Even the largest shot entering from the rear will often fail to penetrate all the way to the vital area. In patterning on a full-size picture of a deer, pay very little attention to hits in the head and neck area. They're a matter of good luck, at best, unless you are firing at close range.

Some shotguns simply will not handle any buckshot load well. If such is the case with your gun, it's best to beg, borrow, or buy another that patterns well. Wounding a deer with buckshot so that it gets

Maximum Ranges For Buckshot Loads

Guage/Shot	Yards
10-gauge, 3½-inch Magnum, 00 Buck	60
12-gauge, 3-inch Magnum, 000 Buck	55
12-gauge, 2¾-inch Magnum, 000 Buck	50
12-gauge, 2¾-inch standard loading, 00 Buck	40
16-gauge, No. 1 Buck	35
20-gauge, 3-inch Magnum, No. 2 Buck	30
20-gauge, 2¾-inch shell, No. 3 Buck	25

away to die in agony is wrong, whether you do it with a shotgun or a rifle.

Because good buckshot performance depends on so many different factors, some of them not clearly understood, it's obviously impossible to determine precise maximum effective ranges for these loads. Experience and testing on paper targets counts more than mere calculation. But some generalizations can be made. Listed at left are maximum effective ranges for buckshot-loaded shotguns using the heaviest buckshot loads—those with the largest projectiles. It is assumed that buffered loads are used and that the gun fires a dense, even pattern.

With smaller buckshot, you must shoot at shorter ranges under most circumstances, but sometimes you'll come across a shotgun that throws very dense, very tight patterns with it. At medium ranges, these patterns enable you to put more shot on target than you can with the larger sizes of buckshot. In other words, you increase the total energy by increasing the number of pellets rather than the size (and weight) of each projectile. If you have such a gun, hang on to it. They're hard to find.

Many hunters will disagree with the maximum ranges I've cited. Some old-timers have never fired the new buffered loads or are unfamiliar with Magnum shells. They say that these ranges are too long. Other hunters have killed deer at longer ranges, and they will say the ranges are much too conservative. But these maximums are intended only as a general guide. Test your gun until you yourself find out what the best load is and its maximum range. Never exceed it.

Range estimation is obviously important when using buckshot. If you're shaky in this area, practice regularly by estimating ranges to distant objects and pacing them off. Those who regularly hunt with centerfire rifles are often very accurate when estimating ranges in excess of 100 yards; but when it comes to telling the difference between 50 and 65 yards, or 25 from 30, they simply can't do it.

The recoil of heavy buckshot loads is so great that some shooters simply cannot handle it. This is particularly true when these loads are fired in lightweight bird hunting guns. The heavier the gun, other things being equal, the less the felt recoil. If recoil does bother you, using a gas-operated semi-automatic shotgun helps a bit because the gas mechanism helps dampen the impact. A thick recoil pad on the butt of the shotgun helps, too. The worst gun for heavy loads is probably a side-by-side double-barreled shotgun with a European-style splinter forend and a high, sharp comb.

Recoil can have a subtle effect on accuracy. Many heavy, powerful men say that the recoil does not bother them at all. Yet, I've seen such people make astonishing misses at quite close ranges when using these loads, even though they are very accurate with light bird hunting cartridges and when shooting Trap and Skeet. The only possible conclusion is that, unknown to themselves, they do fear the recoil of heavy shells and do flinch when they pull the trigger. If you're a good shot with light loads, yet miss a great deal with heavy ones, this is probably the case with you. If so, you have no choice except to use lighter loads and limit the range at which you fire.

In many parts of the South, deer are hunted with shotguns and dogs. The gunners are posted in place on stands, and the huntsman and his helpers take the hounds around to the other side of the cover and drive deer to the standers. This form of hunting often takes place in very heavy cover where nothing can be seen beyond 20 or 25 yards. For this type of hunting, the emphasis is on more pellets in the load instead of long-range killing capability with the use of heavy buckshot.

You must be able to see the deer or you cannot fire with reasonable accuracy. If you can see the deer, it is obviously only a short distance away, and there are holes in the cover for the buckshot to travel through. You're better off with, say, 27 pellets of No. 4 Buck in a 12-gauge gun than you are with only eight 000 Buckshot. Besides, most Southern dog packs include at least one good tracking hound that can be used on leash to go after a wounded deer. Of course, every decent hunter wants to put the deer down with one shot, but if you don't succeed, following the deer by means of a hound makes is possible to get in another shot or track it to the place where it has died.

Outside the South, almost every state and Canadian province forbids hunting with hounds, and if you actively hunt deer with a shotgun, you'll eventually find that big buckshot works better, on the average, than smaller sizes. With hounds, the deer are almost always moving when the shot is taken. In stillhunting, if you're skilled, you'll get standing shots, often at rather long range. For this, large sizes are more effective.

But many deer are shot from tree stands and ground stands, and some of these shots may be only a matter of 20 yards, if that. In this situation, many hunters rely on the smaller sizes, feeling that the advantage of more shot outweighs greater penetration. Actually, if the deer is very close, large-diameter buckshot does very well. If, on the other hand, you do get a shot at long range from a stand because the deer simply refuses to come closer, you're equipped for it. It's also true that a few large buckshot ruin less meat than half a handful of smaller shot.

One way to be ready for what comes along is to use a double-barreled shotgun and load one barrel with heavy buckshot and the other with lighter (smaller) shot. For a moving shot at close range, trigger the big buckshot. The disadvantage is that you only have two shots to fire, and if the deer is at long range, you only have one effective load. Most hunters, therefore, prefer to use a pump gun or a semi-automatic and load it with the kind of shell best suited to the type of shot they are used to getting.

One dodge is to load a repeater with short-range loads but put a heavy, long-range load in the chamber. If a long-range standing shot is offered, fire the heavy load. If the gunner doesn't score at long-range, the thinking goes, he wouldn't get another shot anyway because the deer often gets beyond maximum range very, very quickly once a shot is fired. If, on the other hand, a moving animal appears at close range, the heavy load is fired and followed as quickly as possible by the shot-range load or loads. If the heavy shell puts the deer down, well and good; but if the deer keeps going, you'll get a target quickly with the other shells. Sometimes it works just fine. Sometimes it doesn't.

Simply patterning your shotgun and determining maximum range is sufficient training for firing at stationary deer. For moving deer, you have to acquire many of the skills of a wingshooter, and this is particularly important for those who participate in deer drives with dogs or human drivers. Fortunately, practicing for moving targets is a lot of fun, and the name of the game is Skeet.

It's true that the ranges in this clay-target game are very short, but the principles of lead are the same and the velocities of the shot do not differ from heavy buckshot loads. Skeet is better than Trap shooting because the angles vary more. Shoot starting from a low-gun position. You can't walk around in the woods with a shotgun already mounted on your shoulder, and by all means, use your regular hunting shotgun rather than a specialized Skeet gun. But load your gun with No. 8 or No. 9 Skeet shells. You won't shoot high scores, but you'll become a better deer hunter.

For your copy of THE OUTDOOR LIFE DEER HUNTER'S ENCYCLOPEDIA—from which this chapter is excerpted—please send $49.95 plus $2.64 for postage and handling to Outdoor Life Books, Dept. DHY8, Box 2018, Latham, NY 12111.

Gear For The Muzzleloader

By Rick Hacker

Buying a muzzleloading hunting rifle is probably the most expensive part of the sport, but as any first-time charcoal burner soon finds out, the rifle is merely an excuse to immerse himself in a tepeeful of accessories that help increase the chances of success during the hunting season.

Of course, it can be argued that all you really need to bag a buck with blackpowder is a rifle, powder, a ball, and a cap or flint. But there is more to it than that. A stripped-down car will get you to work and back, but that same car loaded with options can make driving much more pleasurable, practical, and even safer. The same thing is true with the myriad of items now available to the muzzleloading hunter. Not all of these items are new inventions—some have been around as long as the sport itself; others are ingenious variations of age-old themes; and still others are worthless contraptions that serve no useful purpose to the hunter other than to separate him from his money. A prime example of the last category is the "artificial flint." Considering that real flints cost only 30¢ apiece and can even be found along certain riverbanks, it has always eluded me as to why a flintlock shooter would want to put something that looks like a Zippo lighter on his gun. (Of course, that is only one writer's opinion, and for all I know, the chap who invented this gizmo is probably a millionaire by now.) Nonetheless, there are thousands of accessories available today for the blackpowder hunter. You don't need all of them, but here are a few that may be worth a second glance if you are serious about "making meat" with your smokepole this fall.

SPEEDLOADERS

This is one of the most useful items for any big-game hunter. Whereas it normally takes from 30 seconds to a full minute to reload your blackpowder rifle, a speedloader can help cut that time considerably. This is accomplished by prearranging the powder and ball in such a manner that no more than two or three steps are needed to reload for a fast second shot—often in 15 to 20 seconds, with practice. Some of the devices available are Butler Creek's waterproof Quick Loader, the Leding Speed Loader for Maxi-Balls, and the Dead-Eye Dan's Quick Loader from the F.P.F. Company for round balls or conical bullets.

RAMRODS

Yes, I know that all muzzleloading rifles come with a ramrod. But these ramrods are usually made of wood and are not always strong enough for re-

1) Uncle Mike's fringed soft-leather case; 2) Uncle Mike's bullet bag; 3) Dixie Gun Works "possibles bag"; 4) Speer, Buffalo Bullet, and Hornady bullets; 5) Uncle Mike's stainless takedown ramrod; 6) Kane Gun Chap camo covering; 7) Leding Loader Speed Loader for Maxi-Balls; 8) Butler Creek waterproof Quick Loaders; 9) F.P.F. Dead-Eye Dan's Quick Loader; 10) Uncle Mike's short starter's; 11) Winchester Sutler leather sling; 12) Navy Arms Enfield musketoon nipple protector; 13) Dixie Gun Works powder horns; 14) Mountain State Muzzle-loading Supplies patch knife.

peated use; they are generally intended only for field situations. For more extensive shooting-range use and rugged treatment, Uncle Mike's makes a stainless-steel takedown version, and Mountain State Muzzleloading has the Super Rod—an unbreakable, synthetic, brown-colored, threaded, brass-tipped ramrod that replaces the ramrod issued with your rifle. The Super Rod is probably one of the best choices for the hunter. And for an in-camp backup, Ox-Yoke Originals has a solid-handled, one- or three-piece Writers Rod. I recommend all three of these rods. However, a word of warning: Do not buy rods made of fiberglass because they are abrasive and will gradually wear away the crown on your frontloader's muzzle, thereby destroying accuracy.

NIPPLES

Most caplock rifles come with either blued-steel or stainless-steel nipples. By far, I prefer the corrosion-resistant stainlesss-steel variety. But no nipple can equal the Hot Shot stainless-steel nipples made exclusively by Uncle Mike's, as they produce a hotter flash from any brand of cap. Every one of my percussion hunting rifles and shotguns is equipped with the Hot Shot, and for serious hunting, yours should be, too. These nipples greatly reduce the chance of a misfire.

CASES AND SCABBARDS

Transporting a frontloader in a vehicle or on horseback, or just leaving it around the hunting camp, can plague an otherwise unmarred gun with dings, scratches, and even rust. Cases are the obvious answer, but because most muzzleloading hunting rifles sport barrel lengths that range from 28 to 41 inches, it is often difficult to find a suitable all-around product. Dixie Gun Works and Uncle Mike's both offer soft-leather cases that can accommodate everything from short-barreled Hawkens to lengthy Kentuckies. For even more protection, a new Cordura scabbard (with optional hood) from Uncle Mike's will protect muzzleloaders with barrel lengths up to 36 inches. The scabbards are also adaptable for carrying your frontloader on horseback or in a vehicle. And the cases are rustproof and waterproof.

SLINGS

Because slings and swivels were not originally part of the 19th-century designs, most of today's recreated muzzleloaders (aside from the military models) have no provisions for them. Yet, hunters who have to do a lot of climbing or carrying often require this modern-day feature. Uncle Mike's is the most widely accepted supplier of Quick Detachable Sling Swivels for muzzleloaders. The swivels affix to the ramrod ferrule under the barrel and are screwed into the buttstock in the conventional man-

ner. Uncle Mike's also manufactures a leather Muzzleloader Slinger that uses no screws or metal parts, as it is virtually laced onto your rifle. The only drawback is that the Slinger must be slipped off the ramrod before you can reload.

CAMOUFLAGE COVERING

This is a new development in the frontloading field, and it has nothing to do with Rambo-itis. For years, I have been admonishing hunters with rifles adorned with bright-metal patch boxes and other brass fixtures to dull the metal before taking the rifle afield. Until recently, when hunting wary-eyed animals such as deer, turkeys, and waterfowl with a muzzleloading shotgun, mummifying your muzzleloader with camo tape was the only practical answer. Now there is an alternative—the Gun Chap, a zip-on, Velcro-enclosed camo cover made by Kane Products. The Black Powder Model is available for Thompson/Center Hawkens and Renegades, but with a little fitting and stretching, it can be made to work on other similarly contoured half-stocks. (Versions for several other rifles are available.) Besides camouflaging your muzzleloader, the Gun Chap will also protect the wood and metal from scratches and from collecting moisture.

LUBRICANTS

This category offers more products to choose from than any other area of the blackpowder market. (When I first started shooting blackpowder guns back in the 1950s, I used plain old Crisco with excellent results.) Normally, I stay away from formulas that promise to do everything from lubricating patches to cleaning the bore. Beware of products with low melting points, as the liquid grease can seep into your powder and render it inert. Lubes for patches are a little looser in consistency than those used to fill the grooves and hollow bases of conical bullets, and it is not a good practice to interchange the two.

NIPPLE WRENCHES

If you ever plan to clean your rifle, or if you want the option of being able to pour some extra powder behind an inert charge so you can fire your gun, you'll need one of these handy devices. The three most commonly encountered versions are Uncle Mike's Deluxe Wrench, with nipple/vent pick and storage space inside the handle for two extra nipples; an inexpensive but serviceable wrench/screwdriver combo (sometimes subject to breakage); and a lightweight aluminum wrench equipped with a sliding handle.

SHOOTING BAG

This over-the-shoulder pouch is often called a "possibles bag," because practically every possible

Nipple wrenches, from left: Uncle Mike's; Dixie Gun Works; and Ozark Mountain Arms (being used).

CLEANING JAGS, TIPS, AND WORMS

All of these smallish devices are designed to screw in to the threaded tip of your ramrod to perform a variety of functions (in the event the threads don't match, Uncle Mike's even markets a thread adapter kit). Some of the most popular items are the standard screw-type "worm" for removing stuck round balls from the rifle's bore; the corkscrew "Patch Puller" from Warren Muzzleloading and Manufacturing; several versions of cleaning-patch jags; Uncle Mike's phosphorus bore brush; and Mountain State Muzzleloading's new breech brush for cleaning the hard-to-reach bottom of your barrel.

ADJUSTABLE POWDER MEASURES

These come in a variety of tubular sizes, and they are almost always made of brass. The best ones have a convenient swing-away funnel and will be adjustable for a wide range of grain increments. (My favorites offer the versatility of being adjustable from 10 to 120 grains.)

POWDER-CAN SPOUTS

From Blue & Gray Products and Butler Creek come these handy pouring spouts that fit right over the mouths of blackpowder and Pyrodex containers. They are used for filling your flask or horn.

CLEANING AIDS

Although using soap and boiling water is still the best solution, there are a number of products that make cleaning your muzzleloader less of a chore. For long-barreled percussion Kentuckies, Uncle Mike's Barrel Flusher Kit is by far the best. Hoppe's and Mountain State Muzzleloading both make a handy bronze-bristled brush for reaching into lock crevices. The most convenient item on the market is Ox-Yoke Originals' Complete Kit Bag, which has virtually everything and anything you'll need, including rod, solvent, oil, patches, brushes, and many other surprises. In addition to all of this paraphernalia, the muzzleloading hunter may want to take advantage of a number of foul-dissolving sprays, such as SS1/TDP, that are ideal for interim cleaning at camp.

CAPPERS

Unless you are extremely nimble and have very thin, long, double-jointed fingers, your percussion rifle will need one of these. Cappers make putting a cap on a nipple—the last step in readying your rifle for shooting—a quick and easy job. The two most practical designs are the straight-line capper and the Tedd Cash Capper, both of which are copies of the originals. There are also cappers made of plastic, but I have not found them to be as durable

shooting accessory can be carried in it. Many versions and styles are available, from handmade elkskin prototypes to inexpensive cloth "haversacks" styled after those used in the Civil War. Mass-produced traditional-style leather models are also available from blackpowder-supply companies such as Dixie Gun Works, Uncle Mike's, Navy Arms, and Mountain State Muzzleloading. Also new on the scene for the blackpowder hunter who doesn't want to "go primitive" are the black or camo Sidekick Fanny Packs and Belt Pouches from Uncle Mike's. Whichever design you choose, make sure it has separate compartments for all of your accessories and a closable flap to keep items from accidentally falling out.

POWDER HORNS AND FLASKS

These are the traditional devices used to carry blackpowder in the field for those who disdain premeasured charges. Metal flasks make noise, but they are equipped with spouts calibrated in grain measurements, making it convenient to load a separate charger with the required dosage. Horns, on the other hand, do not reflect light. In addition to the regular horn or flask for the main charge of 3F or 2F (depending on the caliber), flintlock shooters will require a smaller container for the priming charge (4F). A separate charger must be used in any case, as the main charge of powder should never be poured directly from the horn or flask into the muzzle. Warren Muzzleloading and Manufacturing the even makes a miniature brass funnel for filling the flasks.

WHERE TO GET IT

Miscellaneous Muzzleloading Supplies

Blue & Gray Products, Inc.
R.D. 6
Box 362
Wellsboro, PA 16901

Connecticut Valley Arms, Inc.
5988 Peachtree Corners E.
Norcross, GA 30071
(catalog: $1)

Dixie Gun Works, Inc.
Box 130
Reelfoot Ave.
Union City, TN 38261
(catalog: $3)

Mountain State Muzzleloading
Supplies, Inc.
Rte. 2
Box 154–1
Williamstown, WV 26187
(catalog: $4)

Navy Arms Co.
689 Bergen Blvd.
Ridgefield, NJ 07657
(catalog: $2)

Uncle Mike's
Box 13010
Portland, OR 97213
(catalog available for $1,
but sells to distributors
and through retail stores only)

Warren Muzzleloading and Mfg. Co.
Rte. 21 N.
Ozone, AR 72854

Other Specialty Supplies

Butler Creek Corp.
290 Arden Drive
Belgrade, MT 59714
(Quick Loaders for conical bullets or
round balls)

F.P.F. Co., Inc.
(Dead-Eye Dan's Products)
Box 211
Van Wert, OH 45891
(Quick Loaders for conical bullets or
round balls)

Kane Products, Inc.
5572 Brecksville Rd.
Cleveland, OH 44131
(camo covering for muzzleloaders)

Leding Loader, Inc.
Box 1129
Ozark, AR 72949
(speedloader for conicals)

Lyman Products Corp.
Rte. 147
Middlefield, CT 06455
(round-ball and conical-bullet molds
and molding kits)

Ox-Yoke Originals, Inc.
130 Griffin Rd.
West Suffield, CT 06093
(pre-cut patches, cleaning items)

Thompson/Center Arms
Box 2426
Farmington Rd.
Rochester, NH 03867

as the brass ones. Before buying your capper, make sure it can smoothly feed the proper-size caps for your rifle. There also are special large-size cappers for muskets.

SHORT STARTER

This tool is not always needed, but it's handy when you have the time to use it. A short starter makes quick work of getting your greased ball or bullet past the constricting muzzle and started down the bore so that it will be easy to ram home with your ramrod. Although all designs are basically the same, one of the best I have found is the extra-short and easy-to-carry Hunter's Model made by Warren Muzzleloading and Manufacturing.

NIPPLE PRIMER AND PAN CHARGERS

These devices are used to dispense the amount of powder necessary to ensure ignition of your main charge. The nipple primer is for use with percussion rifles, and one is available from Dixie Gun Works. The flintlock pan charger is made by Uncle Mike's, Dixie Gun Works, Thompson/Center, and many others.

SHOOTER'S PACK

Containing everything you need for your front-loader (excluding powder and percussion caps) in one box, these handy kits are put out by Lyman Products and Connecticut Valley Arms, and they

come with instructional books on getting started in muzzleloading. The drawback is that you can't choose specific brands within each kit.

BULLETS

For those hunters who have neither the time nor the patience for casting their own bullets, a number of swaged, ready-to-shoot brands are on the market. Hornady offers the most extensive list of round balls (in calibers ranging from .32 to .58), and the company offers them in easy-to-use dispenser packs. Thompson/Center offers its Maxi-Balls in 20-shot packs, and I highly recommend the pre-greased, super-effective bullets put out by the Buffalo Bullet Company (with seven styles available in .45, .50, and .54-calibers). But if you want to cast your own bullets, Lyman Products has the most complete array of blackpowder roundball and conical molds and molding kits. And unless you use a speedloader or the Hornady punch-out card, a bullet bag or starter block will keep your lead projectiles in one place.

STORAGE BOX

This the one accessory you will not be able to live without. It is a large, transportable, closable, and, hopefully, unobtrusive container in which to dump all of your plunder after each hunting season. This way, you will know exactly where everything is the next time you feel like making smoke—that is, if you don't lose the box!

The Rifle/Scope Connection

By Bob Bell

Hunters and guncranks spend countless hours bragging and arguing about their favorite rifles, cartridges, and scopes. That's understandable. It's easy to become attached to an accurate outfit that gives dependable performance in the field as long as the shooter does his part. But something is being overlooked.

It's basically the quality of the barrel and the bullets that makes it possible for today's outstanding cartridges to perform as well as they do, and it's the high quality of today's hunting scopes that gives the aiming efficiency needed for the long, tough shots. That explains the popularity of rifles, loads, and scopes as topics for discussion. But the item that tends to be ignored, though it's the one that makes it possible for the others to perform, is the scope mount. Without a proper mechanical link between the rifle and the scope, the shooter is better off with iron sights because his scope will never be in zero.

Think for a moment about what happens when a high-power rifle is fired. Almost instantaneously, the forces generated by the firing cartridge slam the motionless rifle rearward with a force many times

the normal pull of gravity—approximately 800 g's in the case of a hunting-weight .375 H&H Magnum. Yet an instant later, because of the rifle's weight, the resistance of the rifleman's body, and the quick dissipation of energy when the bullet's exit from the muzzle releases the gas pressure remaining inside the bore, the rifle's rearward motion is stopped and a rebounding effect takes place.

The scope sits above the action, held by whatever kind of mount has been fitted. The vast majority of scope mounts are attached with small screws. During the violent moment of firing, with the gun's recoil forces originating beneath it, the scope tends to remain motionless due to inertia. The jerk of rearward movement tends to shear off the screws that bind the mount to the gun. If the screws did shear, that would leave the scope floating around in thin air. For obvious reasons, most of us prefer this not to happen. The fact that it's a rare occurrence these days is due to the designs of available mounts, the quality of their materials, and the precision with which they're fitted.

We should point out that handgun hunters have an even tougher job of keeping a scope on a gun. A full-power .44 Magnum load generates 2,500 g's when fired in a medium-weight outfit such as the Thompson/Center Contender, and some 1,700 g's in the heavier Ruger Super Blackhawk. Thirty years ago, when we installed rifle scopes on Smith & Wesson's new .44 Magnum revolver with conventional mounts, the recoil routinely sheared off the four mounting screws after a few shots. There has been significant progress since then.

Knowing in a general sense what happens when a gun is fired, it becomes obvious that a scope mount must have various qualities. For instance, it must be strong. Today's most popular big-game scope is the 3×-to-9× variable, which often weighs more than one pound. In addition, the large size of its lenses means that it must be mounted higher than a small scope, thus, more leverage is exerted upon it when the rifle is fired. This, in turn, puts more stress on the mount. Yet, the mount must hold the rifle and scope motionless in relation to each other. It must not do this just once, it must do it every time the rifle is fired—hundreds if not thousands of times for a big-game rifle over the years, when zeroing in, load testing, and plinking are considered. And make that many thousands of times for a varmint rifle. The mount must also hold the scope solid if the rifle is dropped or subjected to a blow—both of which are good possibilities on any big-game hunt. If the mount allows any change in the physical relationship between the rifle and scope, the outfit is no longer in zero and the shooter's chances of hitting his target are small.

A good mount must also position the scope to give proper eye relief (the distance between the rear of the scope tube and the shooter's eyebrow), so that it is easily usable by riflemen of different sizes and shooting styles. The distance it places the scope above the action and the barrel is also important.

These factors are complicated because the eye relief of scopes of different makes and magnifications can vary by one inch or more; because the position of the adjustment turret differs from scope to scope, as does the length of straight tube between the enlarged objective and ocular ends; and because the power-selector ring near the eyepiece of variable scopes has to be accommodated.

There was a time when only a gunsmith could mount a scope because drilling and tapping of the action to receive mounting screws was required. Many years ago, however, manufacturers began supplying rifles with threaded mounting holes, so shooters have become accustomed to installing scopes themselves. This means, though, that mount bases must be manufactured to tolerances precise enough so that a person of average mechanical ability will be able to install the bases without the cost of a gun-shop visit. Furthermore, a mount should not add a significant amount of weight to the outfit, and its appearance should be pleasing—or at least nor jarring—to the owner.

Since scopes began to gain general acceptance in the 1930s, mounts have gone through a cycle of development. Scores—maybe hundreds—of variations have been made. Some gained lasting popularity; others, some of perhaps equal quality, disappeared. In the early days, when most shooters had little faith in the durability of a "glass sight," they wanted instant availability of iron sights, too, so side mounts were developed. The base of a side mount was screwed, pinned, or even soldered to the left side of the action. It was easy to vary ring heights so that the scope either sat right against the action, as most experts came to advocate, or was high enough to permit the use of conventionally

Griffin & Howe side mounts are screwed to the side of the receiver. Version at left is offset for top-ejecting rifles; one at right centers scope low over bore.

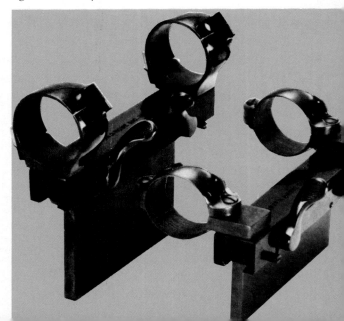

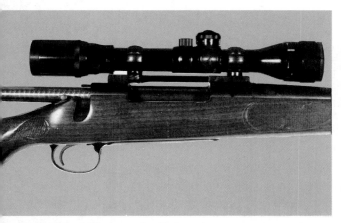

Redfield Jr. bridge mount with low rings puts scope as close to the rifle as rifle's bolt and size of front lens will allow.

mounted iron sights. Side mounts were often locked into place by finger-operated levers and so were quickly detachable, leaving the top of the action uncluttered. This, too, made iron-sight use possible. Few side mounts remain on the market, but the high-quality Griffin & Howe and Jaeger mounts are still with us.

Top mounts are far more common nowadays. They gained popularity because they are much easier to install even if holes have to be drilled, which is rarely the case nowadays. The mounts position the scope low, though rarely as low as is possible with a side mount. With some designs, it is possible to remove the scope quickly by detaching the rings from the bases(s). However, this leaves the base solidly screwed to the action, and its thickness makes it difficult or impossible to use some iron sights.

Top mounts usually attach to a bolt-action rifle in two places—on the receiver ring and on the bridge. The base can be a one-piece unit that spans the action opening like a bridge, or it can be two pieces. The former, typified by the Redfield Jr. mount, is perhaps easier to install and, of course, is self-aligning when the machined base is secured with the mounting screws. It usually has a recoil shoulder machined into the bottom to contact the rear of the receiver ring. When contact is made—which isn't always the case, usually due to differences in action dimensions—this is an additional strength factor because it decreases the shearing force of recoil transmitted to the mounting screws.

It is easy to build a windage adjustment system into top mounts. The Redfield type does this with opposing screws in the rear of the base that swing the rear of the scope in a horizontal arc around a pivot unit in the front of the base. In the days of noncentered scope reticles, this was a great convenience because it made it possible to zero the rig without ending up with the crosswire intersection way off center. Even now, it's a good idea to do as

much adjustment as possible with the mount rather than go to extremes with the scope adjustments, for the closer you stay to the optical center of the scope with the crosshairs, the better the image you'll get.

Dispensing with the middle of the base bridge by using two bases saves a bit of weight and provides more room beneath the scope for loading a bolt gun's magazine. Hardened-alloy, Weaver-type, two-piece bases save even more weight but do not have the windage-adjustment capability. These essentially are dovetail blocks, each with a transverse channel to accept a bolt that locks the scope rings into place. Though usually less expensive than bridge mounts and perhaps not as handsome, it's been my experience that Weaver-type mounts replace closer to zero than do the bridge types, if it's ever necessary to remove the scope while leaving the bases on the rifle.

One of the most refined two-piece mounts was designed by the late Len Brownell. The left side of each dovetail block is notched to accept teeth on a lever-locking unit of the rings. Finger levers make them quickly detachable. This allows scope removal and replacement with a high degree of accuracy.

Three other basic types of mounts are also available today. Two of these, the Pachmayr and Ironsighter types, were developed to counteract the effects of driving rain or snow on scopes, or to serve as backups if the scopes were damaged. The older unit is the Pachmayr Lo-Swing, which allows a low-mounted scope to be quickly swung to the side and out of the way so that iron sights can be used. Originally, it was a rather simple hinge arrange-

Kimber double-lever mounts allow easy removal of scope and rings from bases. Finger levers tighten the mortises in the rings on matching dovetails in bases.

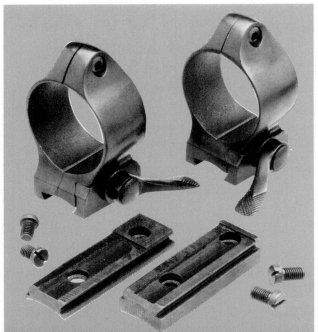

ment, but this developed into a highly sophisticated unit that permits the basic zeroing to be done in the mount.

The Ironsighter and numerous similar designs are popular as solutions to the bad-weather problem common to much big-game hunting. Essentially, they are a pair of metal figure-eights, the two upper circles holding the scope and the bottom ones providing a view of the iron sights. These designs are convenient, but the excessive height of the scope above the action makes it difficult to get full support for the face from a conventional stock. This introduces some problems, but countless hunters feel that the instantaneous availability of both scope and iron sights more than compensates for the drawbacks involved.

From the beginning, one of the biggest problems in installing a scope has been attaching the mount to the action. In most places where the base(s) must go, the metal is not very thick. Yet, holes must be drilled there to accept the mounting screws. For example, examine the left siderail, the top of the receiver bridge, and the receiver ring where the top bolt lug of a Model 98 Mauser action locks into place. This means that the screws must have fine threads, and this, in turn, normally means using small-diameter screws. The 6/48 size became standard many years ago, partly because it was the one often used to install receiver sights back in the 1930s, and some early install-it-yourself scope mounts did use preexisting holes.

Nevertheless, it's asking a lot of such tiny screws to expect them to hold a scope solidly against the heavy shear forces exerted by recoil. For that reason, recoil shoulders are machined into some scope bases to take up some of the shock. Two popular manufacturers, Sako and Ruger, have taken things a step further by producing rifles that completely eliminate the need for mount-attaching screws. These rifles have integral dovetails machined into the receiver bridge and receiver ring that accept the

scope-mounting rings. The designs are not the same. Sako's has a tapered dovetail, wider in the front than the rear. If recoil causes any movement at all, which is highly unlikely, it simply forces the rings tighter into the bases. The Ruger dovetails are straight-sided but have a cross-locking bolt and a projection on the base of each ring that fits into a depression in the dovetail and, thus, also acts as a recoil shoulder.

The Sako and Ruger approaches to scope mounting are significant advances. They eliminate the biggest weakness in scope mounting just by getting rid of those dinky 6/48 screws. However, the built-in-base approach sometimes brings on other problems. Both the Sako and Ruger bolt-action rifles are made in several action lengths to match the lengths of different classes of cartridges. When the position of the scope mount rings is determined by the length of the action, though, there are times when the physical and optical properties of some scopes are incompatible with a particular rifle. The rings must fit around the straight section of the scope tube, but the lengths of the enlarged tube ends and the positions of the adjustment turrets and power selector ring, if any, to some extent determine scope placement on the rifle. Even if you can get the scope on the gun, its position may not give the proper eye relief needed for safe and rapid aiming. This same problem sometimes exists with conventional bridge mounts of the Redfield type, but most of these are available with special extension rings that allow about one inch of fore or aft scope movement.

Another problem can arise when mounting one of the new small hunting scopes, at least on the Ruger. These compact or miniaturized models seem logical choices for the Ultralight Model 77 Ruger rifle, say, but some cannot be installed. For example, on my short-action Model 77 .308, the 2½× Leupold Compact, with its straight objective, is easily installed in the factory mounts. The 4× Compact also fits if the eye relief happens to suit you as you

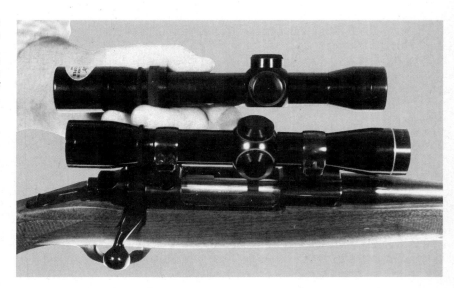

With Ruger Model 77 integral bases, use of some scopes is impossible. With the .308-length action, the 4× Leupold works, provided eye relief is right. But this Burris Mini variable won't work because its power-selector ring would be in the way of rear mount ring. There are other impossible rifle/mount/scope combinations.

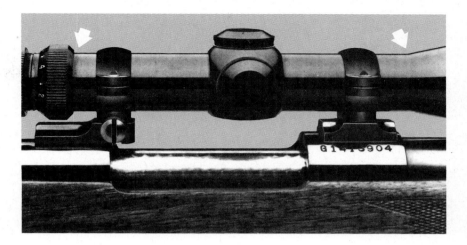

Arrows point to features that limit scope's fore-and-aft positioning. With this rig, scope can be moved only a short distance when trying to achieve proper eye relief.

get it when the rings are tightened. The straight portion of this tube will accept the factory-spaced rings, but the enlarged ends make it impossible to slide the scope either forward or back to adjust for eye relief. And if your scope preference should be the 2×-to-7× Burris Mini—a logical choice in the minds of many—you're out of luck. The rings just won't fit between the selector ring and the enlarged objective. So, it pays for a prospective scope buyer to give some thought to getting it on the rifle before he plunks down his money. Some combinations just don't make it. Assemble the rifle, scope, and mount and check their compatibility, rather than shelling out and then trying to make the installation.

Once a suitable combination is chosen, it's time to assemble it into one unit. With today's factory-drilled threaded mounting holes or integral dovetails, this is no big problem.

Mounts and screws come with a protective film of some kind. Use a solvent to remove this from the screws, the threaded holes, and the inner surfaces of the rings. You want to eliminate all slippage. Using a substance such as Loc-Tite on the threads helps eliminate screw loosening, but I rarely have this problem when the screws are snugged up tight to begin with.

The nearer to plumb and square the scope reticle is, the better. Among other things, this keeps a horizontal change in zero from affecting the vertical adjustment, and vice versa. It also helps the shooter avoid canting the rifle when firing, which leads to misses at long, unknown ranges. So, that vertical reticle wire should be plumb when the rifle is plumb—not when the shooter *thinks* it's plumb—for almost everyone cants a rifle somewhat when he shoulders it. Even when he gets things square, there's a tendency for the scope to rotate slightly as the ring screws are tightened. Tighten them slowly, working the screws in catty-corner sequence and checking plumbness often. It takes time, but it's worth it. Occasionally, someone recommends holding a screwdriver solidly in each screw slot and tapping the screwdriver with a plastic hammer. Supposedly, the screw can then be tightened a bit

more. That may be true, but it seems to me that all you're doing is bending the contacting surfaces of the threads a trifle. I've gotten along without it for decades.

Even more important than the reticle being absolutely plumb is correct eye relief. Besides being necessary to keep the rear of the tube from bloodying the eyebrow and perhaps making you gun-shy for life, the scope must be precisely positioned so that quick aim comes naturally. You shouldn't have to shift your head back and forth to see through the scope. The scope should "find" your eye when you raise the rifle to your shoulder. When the rifle butt hits your shoulder, your face should be solidly in position on the stock and you should be looking at your target, with the reticle close to where you want it on the target. If this seems impossible, it's because you aren't handling your rifle enough or you're using the wrong scope/mount combination.

Getting the correct eye relief is not simple. It would be if you always shot from the same position and always wore the same clothing. But the eye is closer to the scope when firing prone than when you are standing, and it varies somewhat with every other shooting position. Normally, a shooter adjusts eye relief automatically for offhand shooting because these shots must often be taken quickly. If there's time to assume the prone position, there's time to make sure that the eye is a safe distance from the scope at the moment of firing. The scope should be positioned while you wear the clothes you'll use during hunting season. There can be upward of a 1-inch difference between a summer T-shirt and December's wool shirt and down parka. An inch is a lot when you consider that eye relief (tolerance) in most big-game scopes is only about 3½ inches.

Once the scope is mounted, it has to be zeroed in. That is, the scope's reticle must be brought into proper relationship with a target at a given range so that the rifleman can hit what he's shooting at. If not properly zeroed, the scope only gives you a better view of the game than do iron sights; it's no help in hitting it.

Your First Deer Handgun

By J.B. Wood

Two firearms writers recently described handgun hunting as a "stunt," something that shouldn't be taken seriously. On the other hand, a walk through the Handgun Hunting Hall of Fame at Larry Kelly's MagNa-Port firm in Michigan would quickly prove that handgun hunting is a legitimate part of the shooting sports. Some of the trophies on display there are a lot larger than a deer. A few are even in the category of dangerous game. It's enough to say that there are a lot of hunters who take handgunning very seriously.

For those who are interested in but have never tried handgun hunting, the first step should be deciding which handgun to use. There are three types: single-shot, revolver, and automatic. Before we look at each of these, though, there are other important points to consider. In states that permit handgun hunting, there are regulations regarding not only minimum caliber, but also the power of the ammunition used.

Some states list the .357 Magnum as a minimum. Quite a few deer have been taken with this round; in the hands of an expert, with perfect shot placement, it will do the job. Still, I think that a handgun in this chambering is not the best choice for the beginning handgun hunter.

There is another .357 cartridge that does have some merit in this application—the more powerful .357 Maximum. When it was introduced as a revolver cartridge, the Ruger guns in this chambering immediately had problems with "flame cutting" of the frame topstrap and erosion of the barrel throat.

The guns were quickly withdrawn from the market. The Dan Wesson .357 Maximum revolver, having an adjustable cylinder/barrel gap and an easily replaceable barrel, is still available. The Thompson/Center Contender is also offered in .357 Maximum chambering. Though this cartridge has more power, its bullet weight is a little light for deer-size game. Still, it should be considered.

The best handgun rounds for deer are the .41 Magnum, the .44 Magnum, and the .45 Winchester Magnum, the last being acceptable only when reloaded with some appropriate bullet. In the single-shot pistols, such as the Thompson/Center and the M.O.A. Maximum, it's possible to use rifle-level rounds. With these, of course, the felt recoil can only be described as substantial.

If the shooter is not recoil-sensitive, these could be the ideal deer-hunting handguns. They don't have the advantage of quick follow-up shots, but in many cases one shot is all you get, so this point may have less importance. In addition to the two guns just mentioned there are other fine single-shot handguns—often used in metallic silhouette competition—that could double as hunting pieces. These include the Ljutic, the Wichita, and the Mer-

Right: From top, the Thompson/Center Contender in .30/30 chambering with 4× scope; the .357 Colt Python; and the Ruger Redhawk in .44 Magnum.

This T/C Contender in Armor/Alloy II finish is extremely rust-resistant.

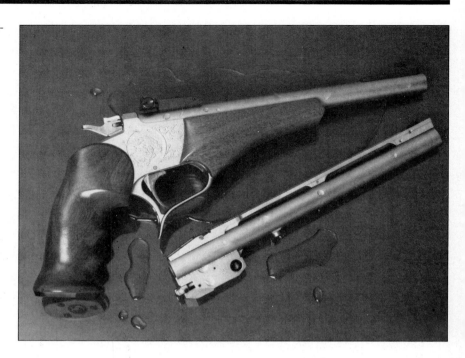

Contender with scope and custom grips adds accuracy and stability when hunting.

Photo by Bill McRae

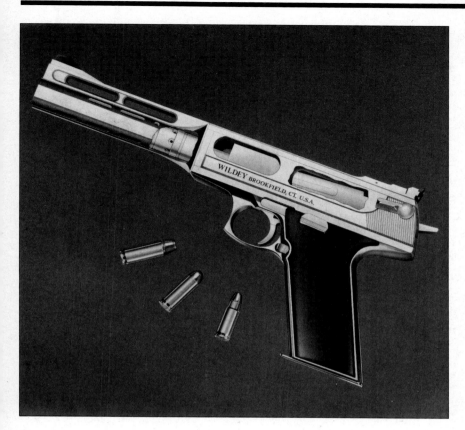

Gas-auto Wildey Ringmaster is chambered for magnum-level rounds.

rill models, the last of which is now made by Rock Pistol Manufacturing.

Single-action revolvers that are suitable for hunting deer-size game include such specialty items as the .454 Casull and the .45/70 Century, but these are not likely to be found at your local gun shop. For the average shooter, the calibers most likely to be chosen are the .41 Magnum and .44 Magnum. There are several good single-actions in these chamberings, but the ones most easily obtained are the Ruger Blackhawk models. In these guns, or any other hunting handgun, the longer barrel length should be chosen. This will give maximum velocity and a longer sight radius.

Among the double-action revolvers in .41 Magnum are the Smith & Wesson Model 57 and Model 657, the Dan Wesson Model 41V, and the Ruger Redhawk. The .44 Magnum is an even better caliber choice, though; it's chambered in the Smith & Wesson Model 29 and Model 629, the Dan Wesson Model 44V, the Ruger Redhawk, and the Llama Super Comanche. For those who prefer optical sights, the Redhawk has provisions for easy scope mounting. The S&W Model 629 and the Redhawk also offer stainless-steel construction. This is more of an advantage in a hunting gun than in a target piece because the weather doesn't always cooperate in the field.

Until recently, no automatic pistols suitable for hunting deer-size game were available. The late la-

mented Auto Mag had a brief time as a hunting piece a few years ago, but shooters soon tired of handloading its special .44 cartridge. Only two small quantities of commercial .44 Auto Mag cartridges were made, and the pistol soon left the market. Then, Wildey Firearms introduced a new gas-operated pistol with a new cartridge, the .45 Winchester Magnum.

For reasons too complex to detail here, the Wildey pistol has been a long time getting into full production. Now, with the company back in the hands of Wildey Moore, there will be a modified version of the original pistol, as well as the Ringmaster, an entirely new gun with a different locking system. The new gun will be available in several chamberings, one of which will be the new .475 Wildey Magnum.

The original round, the .45 Winchester Magnum, is also the principal chambering of the Grizzly Win Mag, made by L.A.R. Manufacturing. An excellent pistol, it has the appearance of a heavier version of the old Government Model. I have fired three of these guns: pre-production No. 001, early production No. 027, and my own Grizzly. All have performed flawlessly with Winchester factory rounds, and the accuracy has been outstanding.

The Grizzly is also available with conversion units for 9mm Winchester Magnum, .357 Magnum, and other rounds, and I have tried it with the two named above. This is the only time I have ever

A couple of decades ago, only a handful of handgunners ventured into the game fields. Today, however, handgun hunting is a legitimate part of the shooting sports—as OUTDOOR LIFE Executive Editor Vin Sparano shows here.
Photo by Stanley Trzoniec

HUNTING HANDGUN MANUFACTURERS

Dan Wesson Arms
293 Main St.
Monson, MA 01057

Colt Ind.
Firearms Div.
25 Talcott Rd.
West Hartford, CT 06110

Thompson/Center Arms
Box 2426
Farmington Rd.
Rochester, NH 03867

M.O.A. Corp.
110 Front St.
Dayton, OH 45402

Sturm, Ruger & Co.
Lacey Place
Southport, CT 06490

Wichita Arms
444 Ellis St.
Wichita, KS 67211

Ljutic Ind., Inc.
Box 2117
918 N. Fifth Ave.
Yakima, WA 98902

Rock Pistol Mfg., Inc.
150 Viking
Brea, CA 92621

Freedom Arms Co. (.454 Casull)
Box 1776
Freedom, WY 83120

Smith & Wesson
2100 Roosevelt Ave.
Springfield, MA 01101

Stoeger Ind. (Llama revolvers)
55 Ruta Court
South Hackensack, NJ 07606

Wildey Firearms
28 Old Rte. 7
Brookfield, CT 06804

L.A.R. Mfg. Co.
4133 West Farm Rd.
West Jordan, UT 84084

Magnum Research, Inc.
7271 Commerce Circle W.
Minneapolis, MN 55432

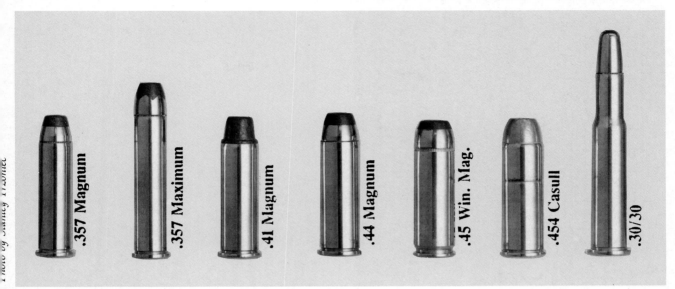

A variety of hunting handguns are chambered for these seven cartridges.

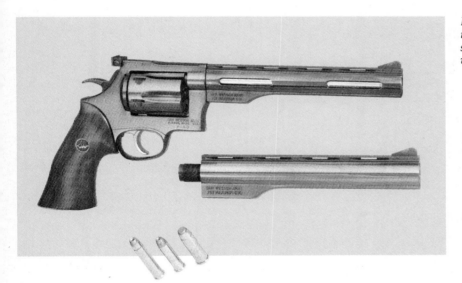

Barrels of various lengths can be easily interchanged on Dan Wesson revolvers, as shown above. This adds greatly to their versatility from a hunter's standpoint.

installed conversion units on a pistol and had them work perfectly, with no adjustments necessary. The quality of materials and workmanship in the Grizzly Win Mag is equal to that of guns that cost considerably more.

The Desert Eagle from Magnum Research, made by IMI in Israel, has been offered for some time in .357 Magnum and will soon be available in a .44 Magnum version. This is another pistol that I have fired quite a lot (in .357), and it, too, is reliable and accurate. Gas-operated with rotating-bolt locking, it is more pleasant to shoot than revolvers of the same chambering. This will likely also be true of the .44 Magnum version. A 14-inch barrel unit is available. Scope mounting is possible, as the barrel does not move in the firing cycle.

Whether the hunting piece is a rifle, shotgun, or handgun, shot placement is always important. For the handgun hunter, this means careful stalking to bring the game within reasonable handgun range. Realistically, there are some shots you shouldn't try with a handgun, even a scoped one, that would be easy with a .30/06 rifle. The best handgun hunters know this, and they don't try to stretch the limits of their equipment.

In choosing a handgun for hunting, first decide which of the three categories best suits your hunting style—single-shot, revolver, or automatic. Then, examine the guns described here, and determine which feels best for you. If possible, borrow the one you've tentatively chosen and try it out at a shooting range. If there's something about it that causes you some difficulty, try another one. When you have settled on the one that feels good in your hand and puts the shots where you aim, you'll be ready for the challenge of handgun hunting.

PART 5

BOWS AND HUNTING

100 Deer With A Bow

By John E. Phillips

For a hunter to bag 100 deer in a lifetime is extraordinary. But to take all of them with a bow makes it a Herculean feat. And when you consider that the majority of those deer were harvested on public lands, it's easy to understand why Clarence Yates of Sterrett, Alabama, is considered one of the country's leading bowhunters.

"I never started out to kill 100 deer with my bow," Yates confided to me modestly. "As a matter of fact, if someone had told me 20 years ago that if I really wanted to be a good bowhunter, I would have to take 100 deer with a bow, I would have thought the task to be impossible."

Actually, during the first five years of Yates' bow-hunting career, taking any deer was an impossible task. But he eventually developed a system of deer hunting that allowed him to take 100 deer in the next 15 years, including an eight-pointer that weighed 178 pounds and a 170-pound nine-pointer. Eighty-eight of Yates' deer were harvested on wildlife management areas open to the hunting public. Yates prefers hunting WMAs because he feels that they don't receive as much hunting pressure in his native state as they do in other regions.

"There are 29 WMAs in Alabama, with almost all holding several weekend gun hunts," Yates said. "However, from October 15 to November 21 this year, there is no gun hunting on these WMAs. So, they are virtually undisturbed and provide plentiful hunting grounds for the bowhunter.

"Then, during the gun season, there will only be three or four weekend gun hunts when gun hunters can come on to most of the WMAs. And even though no bowhunting is allowed on WMAs on days of gun deer hunts, the rest of the time, in most

Illustration by Robert Hunt

areas, the bowhunters have the WMAs to themselves. Therefore, these WMAs make great regions to pattern deer and to hunt from October 15 to January 31. And because the bowhunter can legally bag one deer of either sex per day in Alabama during the hunting season, the state provides ample opportunity."

And Yates takes advantage of this opportunity, spending 30 to 40 days per season hunting whitetails in his native Alabama. But why is Yates so successful, while many sportsmen who hunt public lands do not take nearly as many deer as he does?

"I'm hunting when many other folks aren't," Yates explained. "I go into the woods before daylight, and I don't come out until dark. While in the woods, I'm either in my tree stand, waiting for a deer to show up, or I'm out scouting to find a better place to hunt the next day. If I take a deer at 8 A.M., I'll field-dress the animal, put it in the cooler, and immediately go back into the woods—without my bow, of course—to scout for a better place to hunt the next day."

Yates actually spends more time scouting than he does hunting.

"On one WMA I hunt, I know that I have walked under at least 98 percent of the trees on that management area. If you are going to predict accurately where a deer will show up, you must know as much about the places he lives in as he does. When I go into an area, I begin to investigate one square mile of woodlands. I want to learn the trees, the creeks, the valleys, and everything else I can about that particular part of the woods.

"Then I search for the best spot in that square mile to put up my tree stand. If I am in the very best place within that mile that I can be in and I have confidence in that area, I can stay in my tree stand longer and hunt harder than if I'm in a region in which I don't have any confidence."

Yates becomes so familiar with his hunting territories that he feels he knows many of the individual trees in the places he hunts. "I primarily hunt over the deer's preferred food source, which in my part of the country is acorn trees. If a woodsman scouts a great deal and learns all he can about the trees, he will soon discover that there are some trees that will be the first trees in his hunting area to drop their acorns. So, a sportsman can reason that these trees will be the best ones to hunt around during the early part of the season.

"Then there will be another group of trees that will hold their acorns until the middle of the season before they begin to drop them. Once you know where these trees are, you can begin to hunt them later in the season. And a third group of trees won't drop their acorns until the very end of the season; these will be the trees to hunt around in the late season."

Once Yates knows the location of the preferred food source, he tries to find the very best trees to hunt around.

"I want to find a tree where there are many deer droppings, several trails coming to it, and uneaten acorns left on the ground," Yates explained. "From these signs, I understand that there are deer feeding under this tree, and that enough food is still present so that the animals should return and feed again.

"As a general rule, the deer will most often feed during a two- to four-hour period in the morning and the afternoon. Sometimes, the deer will feed just at daylight. At other times, 10 A.M. or 11 A.M. may arrive before the animals begin to feed. But usually, the deer that feed from daylight until 9 A.M. will continue to feed from daylight until 9 A.M. for a week or two. Then, as the weeks go by, the deer will feed earlier each day. But as you know, there are no absolutes in deer hunting.

"I once found an area that I considered red-hot. The sign showed that the deer were feeding under one particular oak tree. However, I hunted two mornings in a row from daylight until 10 A.M. and never saw a deer. I also hunted the afternoons of those days from 2 P.M. until dark but never spotted a deer. I was frustrated because I didn't see a deer, although I knew that the animals were using the area. So on the third day, I decided to lie with those deer until I took one."

Yates' "lie with the deer" technique is quite simple. He carries his lunch and a rope with him when he climbs into his tree stand before daylight, and he does not come out of it until nightfall.

"On that third day, I had been in the tree all

morning long," Yates remembered. "I ate my lunch at about noon—still not having seen a deer. By then, I was tired, so I took my rope and tied myself into my tree stand. I'm a light sleeper anyway, and even a leaf falling from a tree will wake me up.

"At 1:15 P.M., I woke up and saw a spike buck standing under the tree I had been watching. While I observed the deer, an acorn fell off the tree I was in. Hearing the acorn fall, the spike walked over under my tree to eat the acorn. Because the deer was right under my tree and presented an easy shot, I took him.

"Often, if an outdoorsman locates a real hotspot that he's certain the deer are feeding in, then the best tactic probably is to pack his lunch and determine to stay in that tree until the deer show up or it becomes too dark to see. But most of the time, in a hotspot, you should see a deer within two hours."

In the regions Yates plans to hunt, he will have several hotspots from which to choose.

"You should be able to tell from your scouting from which direction the deer should approach the tree that he will be feeding under," Yates commented. "You should also know which way the wind is blowing and how that will affect your hunting before you go to that tree. If the wind is blowing so that your scent will be carried in the direction that the deer is coming from, you shouldn't hunt that particular hotspot. Instead, go to another hotspot that will afford you a favorable wind."

Another factor that Yates feels determines deer movement through the hotspots is the moon. Depending on how bright the night is, Yates can more accurately predict when the deer will be feeding.

Yates has found that deer will most often begin to feed when darkness falls. "If the moon is bright and the night is clear," Yates said, "deer can see so well to find food that they get filled up quicker than they would on a dark night. Therefore, the animals lie down in the middle of the night to rest. Then, before daylight, these deer will usually get up and feed again when there is a bright moon. Thus, when daylight comes, the deer are full. They will lie back down and may not get up to feed again until 11 A.M. or noon.

"On a dark night, especially if the weather is cloudy, overcast, and/or rainy, the deer can't see as well. Therefore, they may feed all night trying to get enough to eat and still be feeding at first light. These deer won't lie down until about 8 A.M. or 9 A.M. After bright, moonlit nights, I anticipate the deer feeding between 11 A.M. and 2 P.M." Probably the most important key to Yates' success is being in the right place at the right time—and knowing exactly where that right place is.

"I want to hunt the very best place I can locate," Yates said. "That's why I leave my tree stand as soon as I feel that the peak of the deer's feeding time is over. Then, I scout."

Yates is not concerned about leaving his human

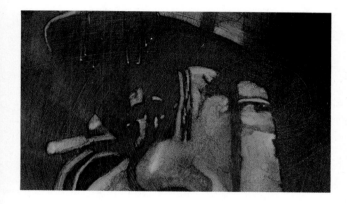

scent while scouting where he plans to hunt, although he is very aware of how much of it a hunter will leave on the ground when he is walking through the woods.

"In fairly dry woods, I don't believe that the scent stays on the ground for more than 1½ hours. And in really dry woods, I have watched deer walk over my trail 30 minutes after I had left it without their noticing my scent. Besides, there is no way to scout without leaving a scent. I would rather leave a little scent on the ground and be in the right place to hunt, than leave no scent on the ground and be hunting in the wrong spot. Besides, if you take care not to walk through the middle of your hunting area or across the path that the deer will be taking to your hunting place, there is a good chance that the deer will not smell you, anyway."

When most of the deer's food is gone in the late season, the right place to hunt is near scrapes.

"When I'm hunting scrapes, I set up my tree stand about 15 yards from the most well-defined scrape I can find in a line of three to four scrapes. I don't necessarily take a stand along the trail leading to and from the scrapes because I've watched bucks approach scrapes from many directions. But I make certain that my tree stand is downwind of the scrapes. Although scrape hunting is effective and I do believe that a woodsman has a better

chance of taking a buck over a scrape, my consistent hunting is in the early part of the season over the best food sources I can locate."

Besides being an excellent woodsman, Yates is an extremely accurate bowman who has won Alabama's state bowhunting championship (a silhouette shooting competition) four times. Recently, while shooting competition archery during the summer to hone his skills, Yates split an arrow at 30 yards.

"All the scouting in the world is not worthwhile if you can't accurately arrow the deer once it is within bow range," Yates said.

And when Yates lets his arrow fly, he is shooting a much bigger broadhead than that used by most bowhunters.

"I started hunting with a bigger broadhead so I could down the deer quicker, make a bigger hole, and leave a better blood trail," Yates pointed out. "One day, I got to thinking about the broadhead I was shooting. I asked myself, why shoot a small broadhead through a deer and stick the arrow 6 or 7 inches into the ground, when I could shoot a wider broadhead through the deer, leave a bigger hole, and only stick the arrow 2 inches into the ground? So, in 1967, I designed a broadhead that was bigger than any broadhead available on the market. Then, a few years later, some friends and I designed another broadhead that we are now using; it's called the Interceptor, and it's also a wide, big broadhead."

Yates' 100th deer, a fat 8-inch spike, dropped in its tracks on October 25, 1985.

"Although I had previously taken three deer from around that same tree, I wasn't really satisfied with the place I was hunting that afternoon," Yates recalled. "The trees were about three weeks late in dropping their acorns, so there wasn't much food on the ground for the deer."

But at 4:45 P.M., the spike walked to within 5 feet of Yates before the bowman let the arrow fly.

"When the broadhead struck, the buck folded," he said. "And I knew I had my 100th deer."

Bowhunting In The South

By Frank Sargeant

Beginning with the southern state of Alabama, bowhunting should be great there this fall. The herd now exceeds 1.2 million animals and is still growing. About 30,000 deer are taken by archers each year.

Either sex may be taken in most of the state throughout the season, and the limit is one per day. The season traditionally runs from mid-October through mid-January—regulations are not available until mid-August.

The better public areas should include Barbour and Butler Wildlife Management Areas (WMAs) in the southeast. T.R. Miller, formerly a good producer, is no longer in the WMA system. Oakmulgee WMA in Talladega National Forest south of Tuscaloosa, and 35,000-acre Skyline WMA in the northeast are also top spots, with perhaps a better chance at a trophy than some of the southeastern locations. The national forests, including Conecuh in the south, Talladega east of Birmingham, and Bankhead in the northwest, are also good. White Oak Plantation, near Tuskeegee, offers outstanding day-lease hunting for trophy sized bucks.

Resident licenses are $10, while nonresidents pay $50 for seven days or $175 for the season. Residents of bordering states pay reciprocal fees of $100 for the season. No special bow permits are required, but a $3 stamp is needed to hunt the WMAs.

For more information, contact the Department of Conservation and Natural Resources, 64 N. Union St., Montgomery, AL 36130.

ARKANSAS

Archers have plenty of time to take their deer in Arkansas, with a season that traditionally begins in early October and extends to the end of February in some parts of the state. About 4,000 deer are usually taken from a herd that has now increased to almost half a million. Leasing of public lands is becoming more of a problem for traveling hunters, but there's still plenty of public hunting on some 300,000 acres of WMAs plus an even greater amount of national forest lands.

Arkansas is one of the few states where the crossbow is legal throughout the archery season, and about 10,000 crossbow users join 25,000 bowmen afield. Archers can take three either-sex deer. The season closing dates vary by zone.

The coastal plain counties have the highest deer densities—Dallas, Drew, Cleveland, Ouachita, and Grant counties should all be excellent for bow hunting this year. White Rock WMA in Ozark National Forest should provide good public hunting. Other good public areas include both Mt. Magazine and Piney Creek.

Some upward adjustment in license fees is expected, but was not finalized at press time. In the past, fees were $17.75 for the resident sportsman's permit, $115 for the nonresident permit.

For more information, contact the Game and Fish Commission, #2 Natural Resources Dr., Little Rock, AR 72205.

FLORIDA

The deer herd has leveled off at around 750,000 in Florida. The herd is still expanding in good habitat, but that is balanced by the loss of other areas to development. Deer of either sex may be taken by archers, and there's no season limit. The *daily* limit is two, three in possession.

The season is October 3 through November 1 in most of the state. In the extreme south, hunting begins September 5 and ends October 4. Bowmen had to wear blaze orange last year through a legislative oversight, but that probably will be corrected this year. (Orange is required during the gun season, however.) A special late-season primitive weapons hunt is slated for February 6–21.

The best bow hunting is by permit on Tosahatchee, Joe Budd, and Citrus WMA's. Also good are two larger WMAs in the game-rich central part of the state: 22,000-acre Bull Creek and 43,000-acre Three Lakes, both in Osceola County. Carey WMA in Levy County should also be very productive, and may be good for a trophy.

Archery permits are $6 in addition to the $12 resident license or $51 nonresident license. WMA stamps are $11.

For more information contact the Game and Fresh Water Fish Commission, 620 S. Meridian St., Tallahassee, FL 32301.

GEORGIA

Georgia cruised right on past the one-million mark in deer population this year, and now has more whitetails than at any time in modern history. More than 4,000 were taken by archers last year, and that number should increase this season. Either sex is legal, and hunters can take up to three deer per season, including two bucks.

The proposed bow season is slated for September 19 through October 23. There should be lots of excellent hunting on WMAs including 12,000-acre Central Georgia Branch in Putnam County, 15,000-acre Clark Hill in Wilkes County, 36,000-acre Ocmulgee in Twiggs County, and 30,000-acre Cedar Creek in Jasper County. For a chance at a trophy, West Point WMA, in Heard and Troup counties on the Alabama border, is one of the best bets.

Some of the coastal islands and military bases in the state are open only to bowmen, but you must be drawn for a quota permit to participate. Check the game commission for specifics.

Archery stamps are $6.50. Additionally, resident bowmen need the resident license for $8.50 and resident big game stamp for $7.50. Nonresidents pay an added $21 for a ten-day license or $50 for a season ticket, plus $100 for the big-game stamp and $21 for an archery stamp. WMA permits are $15.60 for residents, $62 for nonresidents.

For more information, contact the Department of Natural Resources, 270 Washington St. S.W., Atlanta, GA 30334.

KENTUCKY

Bowmen can anticipate another record year in Kentucky, where herd numbers have been rising at least 10 percent per year for the past decade. The herd is now estimated at 240,000, and about 4,800 deer were taken last year by archers including some 3,000 bucks. Either sex can be taken in the better counties, and the limit is two per year by all hunting methods combined.

The season is slated for October 1 through December 31. Crossbows can be used November 24 through December 23. The prime hunting area is in the west central part of the state, with Christian, Hopkins, and Owens counties always among the top producers. The rich farm lands along the major river bottoms produce many trophy deer, including some of the largest taken in the east. The military bases of Fort Campbell and Fort Knox both have good hunting for those with permits, though seasons may vary from those in the rest of the state. There's plenty of hunting on private lands, so the fact that there are few WMAs doesn't cause access problems.

No special bowhunting permit is necessary. Resident licenses are $8.50 while nonresidents pay $75 for the season. The deer permit is an added $11.50, and the military bases charge for permits.

For more information contact the Department of Fish and Wildlife Resources, #1 Game Farm Rd., Frankfort, KY 40601.

LOUISIANA

The herd numbers increased somewhat last year in Louisiana, with the population reaching at least 475,000 due to a strong acorn crop. About 25,000 archers collect some 5,000 deer each year. Both sexes may be taken by bow, except during the gun season when only bucks are legal. Archers must wear hunter orange during the gun season. The limit is one per day, six per year.

Proposed archery season would begin October 1 and extend through the three phases of the regular gun season. Hunting with all sorts of weapons would end January 20 under the proposed rules.

The best public hunting will be found on timber company lands in the counties of DeSoto, Union, Sabine, Grant, Vernon, and Natchitoches counties. Best WMAs include Union, Red River, Three Rivers, West Bay, Sabine, Jackson-Bienville, Thistlethwiaite, and Fort Polk. Saline WMA is a good spot for a trophy, as is Russell Sage and Peason Ridge. There's excellent hunting on the Mississippi River bottomlands, but access here is controlled by lease.

Archery permits are $5.50. Resident licenses are $5.50 plus $5.50 for the big-game tag. Nonresidents pay $20.50 for three days or $40.50 for the season, plus $20.50 for the big-game tag. No WMA stamps are required, but some timber companies charge for permits.

For more information contact the Department of

Wildlife and Fisheries, Division of Game, Box 15570, Baton Rouge, LA 70895.

MISSISSIPPI

Mississippi is second only to Texas in herd size with some 1.5 million animals. Considering the much smaller size of the state, it probably has the densest deer herd in the South. Archers accordingly have excellent hunting—some 15,000 whitetails are taken by bow each season, and success rates exceed 20 percent. Mississippi remains the only state where poisoned arrows are legal, and these undoubtedly contribute to the success rate. Archers can taken one either-sex deer per day to a season limit of three.

The proposed season dates are October 3 through November 20. Crossbows are legal only for the handicapped with a special permit.

All of the land along the riverbottoms are loaded with deer, but most lands are private. Top counties include Holmes, Green, Wayne, and Amite, but all are solidly leased. Of the public lands, the best areas are Copiah in Copiah County, Red Creek in Stone County, Bucatunna in Clarke County, Pascagoula in George County, and Chickasaw in Chickasaw County. Delta and Noxubee national forests are also good.

Archery permits are $7 for residents, $25 for nonresidents. Resident licenses are $13. Nonresidents pay $25 for three days, $30 for seven days or $60 for the season.

For more information contact the Department of Wildlife Conservation, Bureau of Fisheries and Wildlife, Box 451, Jackson, MS 39205.

NORTH CAROLINA

Harvest was up 17 percent in the 1986–87 season, with 75 percent of the counties reporting higher buck kills. Archers took more than 2,500 last year, and should do even better this fall. Total herd is now in excess of 400,000. Either sex is legal and the limit is four, by all hunting methods, in most of the state. However, five may be taken in the east, and only two in the western mountains.

The season is September 7 through October 3 in the east and west, with a second phase October 12 through November 21 in the west only. In the central region the season is September 7 through November 7, while in the northwest it's September 7 through November 14.

The best public lands are Croatan, Gull Rock, Uwharrie, Sandhills, Thurmond Chatham, and Holly Shelter. Counties that turn out the best kills include many of those in the piedmont, with Gates and Edgecomb usually near the top. Alleghany in the west is also very good. So are all the coastal plain counties in the southeast, but all land there is leased. The vast reaches of Nantahala and Pisgah national forests have good hunting where timber opens enough to allow adequate browse.

Fees were not finalized at press time. Last year, bowhunting stamps were $8. The resident license was $11.50, plus $8 for the big-game stamp. Nonresidents paid $25 for six days or $41 for the season, plus $30 for the big-game stamp. WMA stamps were $9.

For more information contact the Wildlife Resources Commission, Archdale Bldg., 512 N. Salisbury St., Raleigh, NC 27611.

OKLAHOMA

Oklahoma had a considerable harvest increase last year, and should produce well this fall. The herd is smaller than that in other southern states at something over 150,000, but the deer are larger. Bowmen harvest around 2,500 annually. Archers can take two deer per season, including a doe.

The proposed first phase is October 1 through November 15. A second phase is proposed for December 1 through 31.

Best public areas are probably Pushmataha WMA and Ouachita National Forest, which extends into Arkansas in the southeast. For those who get permission to hunt private lands, Osage County on the Kansas border is the best bet for a big, grain-fed buck. The western grassland WMAs including Black Kettle, Ellis, Hulah, and Canton don't have large numbers of deer, but they aren't so heavily hunted as other areas and are good for trophy racks.

Resident archer permits are $14.50. The resident license is $10, plus $14.50 for a deer tag. Nonresidents pay $68.75 for a license plus $137.75 for a deer tag, but do not need an archery permit.

For more information contact the Department of Wildlife Conservation, 1801 N. Lincoln, Box 53465, Oklahoma City, OK 73152.

SOUTH CAROLINA

Up some 70 percent since 1980, the herd now stands at over 500,000. About 100,000 deer are taken in the combined hunting seasons—no archery breakout is available, but bowmen get their share. Both bucks and does may be taken by archers, and the limit is three for the season.

The seasons are expected to be about the same as last year, when the first phase ran October 1 through 16 and the second December 1 through 13 in the popular central and western piedmont, where most of the public hunting areas are located. The mountain unit and the coastal counties have different seasons.

The rolling woods and broken farm country of the piedmont provides excellent habitat. Top counties should include Edgefield, Fairfield, Greenwood, Chester, McCormick, Laurens, York, Union, Abbeville, and Cherokee. Francis Marion GMA, near the coast, turned out 672 deer in 1986; it's one of the few areas offering public hunting in the east, where most land is leased.

License fees jumped last year to pay for improved

GMA leases. Current fees are $12 for residents plus $6 for the big-game tag and $30.50 for the GMA stamp. Nonresidents pay $25 for three days, $50 for ten days, or $75 for the season, plus $80 for the big-game tag and $76 for the GMA stamp.

For more information contact the Wildlife and Marine Resources Department, Rembert C. Dennis Bldg., Box 167, Columbia, SC 29202.

TENNESSEE

Tennessee's herd continues to increase rapidly despite ever-liberalized limits. The total population is now near 450,000 and bowmen drop better than 7,000 a year. The archery limit increased to three either-sex deer this past season—and that's on top of one each for the gun, muzzleloader, and WMA limits!

The season, not set at press time, traditionally runs from the end of September through October.

Hickman County remains the top spot to arrow a buck—it turned out more than 4,000 deer in the combined seasons last year. Timber-company lands here provide public access. Other west central counties, particularly Hardeman and Giles, are also top producers. Riverbottom areas near farmlands are among the best terrain. The Land Between the Lakes area and Fort Campbell Military Reservation also provide good hunting, though a fee permit is required.

Resident archers pay $10.50 for a permit, plus $10.50 for a hunting license. Nonresidents pay $70.50, which includes hunting license and archery permit. WMA permits are $10.50, and some special quota hunts charge additional for permits.

For more information contact the Wildlife Resources Agency, Box 40747, Ellington Agricultural Center, Nashville, TN 37204.

TEXAS

With lots of rain resulting in lush pasture, the huge Texas herd made another quantum leap, up some 200,000 to 4.2 million—the nation's largest. More than 445,000 deer were taken last year, including 8,000 by bow. Either sex is legal, and the limit is four per season.

The archery season is October 3 through November 1, with some local variation.

The top archery area remains the Edwards Plateau, where a high percentage of the total herd is located. Best counties are Llano, Mason, Kerr, Kimble, Kendall, Blanco, and Gillespie. Deer continue to do well here despite the dangers of overpopulation and starvation. For trophy deer, the South Texas Brush Country, including Starr, Hidalgo, Duval, Webb, and Zapata counties are all excellent. Here as in the rest of the state, you'll have to pay a day-lease fee to hunt, but the high success rate makes it worthwhile. The eastern Texas Piney-

woods are coming on strong, producing some large deer as well as increasing numbers.

Bowhunting permits are $6. Resident licenses are $10, while nonresidents pay $200 for the season.

For more information contact the Parks and Wildlife Department, 4200 Smith School Rd., Austin, TX 78744.

VIRGINIA

With over 500,000 whitetails, Virginia should offer fine bow hunting this fall. Two deer of either sex can be taken during the bow season.

The archery season is proposed for October 17 through November 16 statewide. A special late hunt is slated for the lands west of the Blue Ridge Mountains. No Sunday hunting is allowed.

For public hunting, the western part of the state is best. Bath, Rockingham, Grayson, and Augusta are all good producers. The eastern counties have very little public land, and trespass laws are strictly enforced. However, those who are invited to hunt the leases do very well in coastal plain lands of Sussex, Surrey, and Isle of Wight. Southampton, in the piedmont, is also very good, though leases are a requirement here as well. There's lots of public land in the west. Among the best WMAs are Amelia, Hardware River, Horsepen Lake, Goshen-Little North Mountain, Jame River, and White Oak Mountain.

The archery permit is $10 for residents, $20 for nonresidents. The resident license is $7.50, plus $7.50 for the big-game permit. Nonresidents pay $30 for the license plus $30 for the big-game tag. No WMA stamps are required, but a $2 permit is needed to hunt national forest lands.

For more information contact the Commission of Game and Inland Fisheries, Education Division, Box 11104, Richmond, VA 23230.

The Cold, The Silence, And The Deer

By James E. Churchill

After three days of shooting, I found a feeding area in a clearing located on the western side of a large wilderness pond. It was ideal for my purpose because I could hunt from the eastern edge of the feeding area. The prevailing westerly winds would not blow my scent to incoming deer, and they weren't likely to circle around and come in upwind because they would have to cross the open ice of the pond.

In a substantial blind that would break the wind, I could wait through the frigid hours until the deer came to feed. Building a ground blind of evergreen boughs and sticks kept me busy for most of an hour because I tried to be as quiet as possible.

I finally finished, hung my Jennings Split-T compound bow on a handy limb, and rested by sitting on a pail that I carry with me during late-season bowhunting. I had barely relaxed when a fawn suddenly appeared from the fringe of the woods and walked purposefully toward the area where the deer had been feeding on tall grass that they had pawed free of snow.

That was predictable. The rest of the deer used the fawn as their bellwether. If no harm came to it, they would cautiously feel their way out of the maple fringe and join in the feast. Therefore, I wasn't surprised when a group of does suddenly came forward. And behind them, a spectacular eight-point buck's antlers showed above a brush pile. He did not come out far enough so that I could get a shot.

Several attempts had probably been made on his

life during the regular deer gun season that had just closed, and he would not completely leave the security of the forest again that year. Although I could have shot at one of the does, I thought that if I waited long enough, the buck would make a mistake. It was a long, futile wait. In subsequent hunts, I tried every trick I could think of to get a shot at that buck, but except for one opportunity at long range that I passed up, I struck out.

After a few days, during which he apparently sensed danger, the buck decided to stay away during the daylight hours. I finally arrowed a big doe during a snowstorm and was satisfied with the good meat she provided.

Even a doe can be considered a trophy during a late bowhunting season. Many people think that this is the most challenging and interesting time to hunt. In most states, the gun season has closed, and the orange-clad army has gone back to their jobs and their families.

Shortly after the gun season closes, a snowfall covers the well-scarred logging roads and the tracks of hunters. A restful hush settles over the forest. Then the deer steal out of the swamps and brush-choked creek beds where they have been hiding. Food is foremost in their minds because the cold weather and the stress of the hunting season have depleted their energy.

Whether you're after bucks or does, you'll find late-season deer think more about their stomachs than their surroundings.

Photo by Richard P. Smith

The animals will probably group into small herds and move into their yarding areas. The late-season hunter can walk miles of snow-covered forest without seeing a deer track, but once he finds a yarding herd, it usually gets bigger every day as scattered animals join the herd.

At the onset of the late bow season, the deer are wary enough to bed in dense cover and range out from it to a food source. This daily activity creates easily found trails in the snow that offer a fine opportunity to set up an ambush.

I hunt such locations from a ground blind or semi-permanent tree blind. Noisy climbing tree stands can make enough noise to panic deer that have been hunted hard. The deer may leave for distant parts and never come back.

The weather usually has stabilized to some extent by the late season, and the prevailing wind comes from the west. The wind direction has a considerable effect on how successful you are in getting into the blind without being scented by the deer, and how closely the deer will approach your stand after you are in it.

Set up the blind east of the trail and approach it from downwind. Try to avoid walking over the deer trail to get to the blind. A whiff of human scent can alter a deer's usual route considerably, and if the animal catches your scent too many times, it may head for unknown parts.

Late-season deer congregate around whatever food sources are available. In forested areas, this may include the tops and limbs of trees that loggers have recently cut. The wise hunter knows about logging operations in his area and listens for the sound of chain saws. Most deer have learned that whenever they hear the sound of chain saws in one place for several days, there are tender buds and twigs lying on the ground within easy reach. Many deer have been saved from starvation by utilizing this food source. In agricultural areas, the deer may stay around hay piles, unpicked cornfields, or other sources of agricultural produce.

If they can't find such rich sources of food, the deer often yard up in cedar swamps and live on the green cedar foliage and twigs, or they find a cutover area where new hardwood growth offers a good supply of twigs within their reach. Wherever they congregate, the deer usually stay all winter, unless the food supply runs out or man or predators chase them out.

As the winter progresses, the deer become more and more concerned about food and less alert. Finally, they start bedding down very near the food supply, and you can't ambush them between the food supply and the bedding grounds.

There are at least two good ways to hunt deer that act in this manner. The first is to stillhunt very slowly upwind. The snow usually muffles the sounds of your approach. Stay alert and keep an arrow on the string because a deer can appear at any time.

I usually carry a large plastic pail to use as a shooting stool. Once I reach the feeding grounds, I use any brush pile or clump of evergreens as the basis for a blind that is located in the proper place. Being able to sit down makes the hunter less visible.

The second method is to walk quietly into the feeding area and build a blind. Wait two or three days and return with two companions if this can be arranged. All three walk into the area, the hunter drops off at the blind, and the two decoys walk out, making plenty of noise so that the deer will hear them leave. In about an hour, the deer will decide that the coast is clear and will filter back to resume their feeding.

The later the season gets, the more deer move about in the middle of the day. They almost always seem to move in the middle of the day on warm days. The increased light and warmth apparently stimulate their metabolism, and they want to feed. There's no need to rise early to hunt. You would probably freeze and go home anyway before the deer started moving. There also is no need to hunt during the traditional evening hours. The deer probably have fed and lain down again and won't move until the next day. Probably the best time to go out is about 10 A.M. Try to stay on stand until about 2 P.M.

In northern states, the late-season hunter is going to encounter feet-chilling, hand-numbing, face-searing cold. He must be prepared to stay warm during long hours in an immobile position.

I load up on carbohydrates. I literally stuff myself with heat-generating foods such as nuts and dried fruits if I expect extremely low temperatures. Foods that accelerate digestive functions are avoided, however.

Yet, the most important thing is dressing for the cold. I wear cotton long underwear under a set of insulated underwear. My outer clothing consists of a pair of wool logger pants and two shirts, one cotton and one wool, under snowmobile coveralls. When camouflage is important, I wear a white parka and a white face mask as the outer layer.

I keep my feet fairly warm by wearing a pair of cotton socks, a pair of wool socks, and Sorrel boots with the thickest felt liners I can find. It takes a pair of jersey gloves worn inside leather chopper mittens with liners to keep my hands warm. When I expect a shot, I take off the chopper mittens and they dangle from an elastic cord around my neck. The cord keeps them from falling into the snow if they must be shed in a hurry.

When it is below 0°F, the bow should be flexed by pulling it two or three times every half-hour. If you don't keep it warmed up, it may not shoot accurately because the cold can cause uneven stress in the limbs.

There is another reason for pulling the bow from time to time during cold weather. Your muscles can become chilled and stiff, and you may not realize it. When the time comes to shoot, you may not be able to get off a well-aimed shot. This is true of bowhunting much more than gun hunting, including muzzleloading.

Be alert for any changes in the weather. Deer almost always move a lot when the weather suddenly gets colder or warmer or when a storm first hits.

Some people do not like to standhunt for deer, and falling snow offers about the best opportunity for stillhunting late-season deer. The fresh layer of snow muffles the sound of footsteps, and twigs don't snap so loudly when you step on them. It also reduces visibility and "knocks down" human scent so that the deer don't wind you very readily.

But hunting during a heavy snowstorm creates some problems for hunters, too. Arrow fletching gets wet and can cause the arrows to fly erratically, especially if you shoot at more than 25 yards. Prevent this by spraying the feathers with silicon spray or by covering them with a plastic bag. The bag has to be removed before the arrow is used, however. Plastic vanes are not affected as much by wet conditions, but the bow must be tuned for plastic vanes before shooting.

Late-season hunters who shoot muzzleloaders may have misfires caused by moisture getting into the barrel or lock. This can frequently happen if you they don't take some precautions.

The charge can be kept dry by placing a light plastic bag or toy balloon over the end of the barrel. The bag must be tied or held in place with a rubber band, but the bag or balloon can be left in place when the gun is fired. Neither will cause any inaccuracy whatsoever.

Flintlock shooters can protect the powder in the pan by covering the lock with a plastic bag. A commercially made powder shield that snaps over the lock is also available, but purists use a piece of greased deerskin tied in place with a leather thong. All lock covers must be removed before the gun is fired.

Percussion caps are less sensitive to moisture, but they can also become inoperative very quickly in snow or rain. Cures include covering the lock or using a plastic cap guard, which is available from most blackpowder suppliers.

Some experienced hunters do not place the cap on the nipple until they are ready to shoot. This ensures that the cap is dry, and it also prevents accidental discharge. The lock still has to be covered to protect the charge from moisture. The lock can be left ready for a quick shot if you change the cap every time it comes in contact with a wet tree trunk or limb or other moisture-laden object.

If you hunt with a muzzleloader, your effective shooting range is considerably longer than a bowman's, and you have a better chance to get a deer by tracking.

Get out early in the morning after a fresh snowfall, find the biggest track in the woods, and follow it. Usually, these efforts follow a pattern. If the hunter is careful, he may see the deer when it jumps out of its day bed. If you miss him, just follow. The deer probably will run 300 yards to one-quarter mile and then stop and watch his backtrack. When you catch up, he will take off again and stop again in about the same distance. He probably will repeat this procedure several times before he decides that you are trailing him.

Within three or four hours of when you began to follow him, you should start to get a glimpse of him now and then. If you move slowly and deliberately and don't shoot until you get a decent shot, you have a good chance to take the deer within a half-day.

Don't worry about the wind. He already knows that you are following. Gradually, he will get used to having you on his track and will partially disregard the danger. He may even stop and feed awhile. I've seen them do that several times.

The main reason why this kind of stalk is usually unsuccessful is that the deer often does everything he can to throw you off his track. He may join other deer crossing a river and go into nearly impenetrable swamps and thickets. If you can manage to keep tracking the same deer for a half-day or more, though, you have an excellent chance of bagging him.

After you track a deer for most of the day and then stop following, he sometimes will circle back to see where you are. Some good bucks have been bagged by hunters who were worn out from walking and stopped to take a long rest. In these cases, you sometimes are startled when you see the buck staring at you from a nearby patch of brush. Tracking deer is often more successful if a pair of hunters follows the deer.

Late-season deer can be successfully driven. Usually it only takes one or two drivers to chase all of the deer out of a yard. Their escape paths are easy to find because the trails are easy to see in the snow. Post a stander on each heavily used escape trail.

All but a handful of states offer a special late-season hunt. Deer populations currently are so high in many areas that even an army of hunters during the regular season cannot reduce the herd to the carrying capacity of the range. Late-season bow or muzzleloader hunters often do a service by trimming the surplus animals.

In some mountainous states, heavy snow drives the deer herd down from the mountains to places where they are accessible from the road system. It's a good time for low-budget hunting for trophy bucks. Instead of having to hire a guide or outfitter, the hunter can stay in his camper on a road and walk to excellent hunting.

In many southern states, the very best time to be afield is during the late season. Insects, snakes, and uncomfortably warm weather are no longer troublesome, and your kill can be cooled in the field without worrying about spoilage.

Try late-season deer hunting this year. It is a second opportunity to score. Hunters are few, and if you are like me, you'll go every year.

PART 6

HUNTING GEAR ROUNDUP

How To Choose A Tree Stand

By Richard C. McGee

T he hunter is threading his way carefully through the heavily timbered swamp. He is working toward an island he located the previous weekend while scouting the swamp. The "island" is simply a two-acre area maybe 6 inches above the water level in the surrounding swamp, but the canopy of hardwood and pine make it a magnet for deer and feral hogs that range the swamp's perimeter. Pine and cypress trees as thick as a man's leg have been shredded at the base by heavy antlers powered by massive neck muscles.

It is Saturday morning about an hour before daylight. Hip-waders are needed to negotiate this kind of flooded swamp and, as he wades forward, the hunter tests the bottom under foot with each step to avoid creek channels and ancient stump holes that could send a less careful hunter plunging into neck-deep water. The hunter's small flashlight beam dances off the water surface and tree trunks, picking up the reflective thumb tacks placed the previous weekend to blaze the trail back into this hunter-forsaken treasure island.

The hunter knows that a sudden lurch to maintain footing will slam the packpacked tree stand against a tree, alerting the deer on and around the island that is still another 150 yards ahead in the

pre-dawn darkness. Suddenly the black silence of the swamp is shattered by the alarm squawk of some winged denizen as it is spooked from its roost. Then the flashlight beam strikes the white exposed base of a 4-inch-thick cypress, its bark and cambium hanging in tatters. It is the unmistakable calling card of a trophy buck. The water is shallow now. The island is just ahead.

The surrounding woods and swamp are turning gray but are still devoid of color as the hunter mounts his portable climbing stand. Sounds of the new day permeate the area, making the faint *splash, splash* sound almost imperceptible. From years of hunting swamps, this hunter knows a deer is approaching through the water. The splashing footsteps turn to light crunching as the deer leaves the water and walks onto the island. The buck is completely gray against the still-unilluminated forest floor as the crosshairs find him emerging from behind a honeysuckle clump. His modest eight-point rack attests to the fact that he is not the buck that made the huge rub, though he certainly will be good venison.

My reason for relating the preceding sequence as it occurred this past season is to suggest that hunters can backpack portable stands into hidden-away, hard-to-get-to whitetail havens. After the season opener, it's no secret that trophy animals seem to vanish. Those big bucks can often be found and harvested by the hunter who slips into the backpack straps of a portable tree stand and, with a good hunting partner, heads back into the remote re-

cesses of a swamp or other forbidding boondocks.

This kind of mobile, maneuverable tree-stand deer hunting has been an option for only the past 20 years of so. You might say the space age has removed a few handicap points for us hunters so that we might compete with the super nose of the whitetail. Lightweight extruded aluminum and other materials used in the production of stands were not available when our fathers were young hunters, and certainly our grandfathers never even dreamed of such a contraption as a portable tree stand.

Let's take a look at what I consider the four basic types of portable tree stands.

ONE-PIECE CLIMBING STANDS

There are some definite advantages to using this one-piece climbing stand over its two-piece counterpart. Usually (but not always) the one-piece is lighter in weight. One-piece stands are also inherently quicker to attach and detach from a tree—especially important when daylight is rapidly approaching and you're trying to get up in the tree by shooting light. Such an advantage is equally important when darkness is setting in and you're a long way from camp or car without a flashlight.

Another key advantage is the one-piece stand's simple construction. The attached seat folds back against the trunk of the tree and out of the way when not in use—making it much easier to maneuver gun and especially bow at all angles. On the minus side, climbing with the one-piece is more physically demanding since the hunter's weight must be suspended on the tree trunk while raising the platform attached to the feet. Even more exer-

tion is required to climb quietly with this equipment, because the weight must be suspended that much longer so that the blades can be carefully engaged against the tree without creating loud scraping noises.

Two-piece climbing stands. One at left is made by Autumn Woods Manufacturing Company, 8716 Lem Turner Road, Jacksonville, FL 32208. Right: API Outdoors Inc., PO Box 1432, Tallulah, LA 71282.

Hang-on stands. At left is one made by the Loc-On Company, PO Box 11, Summerfield, NC 27358. Right: C & F Products Company, Rt. 2, Box 251, Creal Springs, IL 62922.

Ladder stands. One at left is made by East Enterprises, 2208 Mallory Place, Monroe, LA 71201. Right: API Outdoors, PO Box 1432, Tullulah, LA 71282.

TWO-PIECE CLIMBING STANDS

This is the one that truly deserves to be referred to as a *climbing* stand. It consists of a platform section and seat section, and requires almost no physical effort to climb to any height. I jokingly chide one of my hunting friends that he climbs so high with his two-piece stand that the ground is out of rifle range. The stand-sit sequence used to ascend and descend the tree is in no way comparable with the one-piece that requires at least some exertion for each foot of height gained.

With a two-piece stand a hunter can climb with ease in almost complete silence. You might say this stand has a built-in patience factor. The comfort offered by the two-piece enables the hunter to be content and remain aloft for longer periods—often the crucial factor in putting antlers on the wall and venison in the freezer. Another plus feature is the added measure of safety provided by the two-piece

tree stand. While standing or seated in the stand, the hunter is surrounded by the structural components of the seat section. In the unlikely event that either section should fail or break, the unaffected section should still support you.

A disadvantage of the two-piece stand (as well as the one-piece mentioned earlier) is the fact that you can't proceed in your climb above limbs that are too big to be removed with a hunting knife or pack saw. Be sure to visually check the tree for this problem before climbing. A word of caution: when climbing with this stand, always attach a cord or rope joining the two sections together. Should the feet become disengaged from the platform, that section will not fall beyond reach.

HANG-ON STANDS

As the name implies, this stand is secured to the tree trunk at the desired height and then reached by means of steps installed into or onto the trunk. All manufactured models consist of some type of platform and a means of securing the stand to the tree. Beyond that, hang-on stands as well as climbing stands may have accessories such as a seat (usually folding), underbracing, carpeting on platform, backpack straps, or storage pouch.

Hang-on stands are attached to the tree with a chain, strap, or rope. These stands are secured to the trunk while the hunter stands on steps placed at convenient climbing intervals. Once the stand is installed, you can climb or descend with relative ease using the tree steps. And by removing the steps while leaving the stand in place, it becomes almost impossible for someone else to occupy your stand or pilfer it.

The hunter equipped with a hang-on stand has a much broader selection of trees to hunt from than he would with a climbing stand. Hang-on stands can be installed on virtually any tree that isn't too large in diameter to accommodate the attaching chain, strap, or rope. Regardless of the size or number of limbs protruding from the trunk below the desired hunting height, the simple design makes it easy to find a suitable section of tree. As with the one-piece climbing stand, hang-on stands are free of encumbering structural members, allowing the hunter to turn around with rifle or bow and shoot at almost any angle or direction.

Tree steps used with the hang-on stands are commercially available in two types: screw-on and tie-on. Screw-in steps are threaded like a large wood screw and are simply "cranked" into the tree trunk with little or no damage to the tree. Tie-on models, as the name implies, are secured with rope, chain, or webbing and are usually rigged with a protrusion that serves as the step. I recommend using the screw-in type where permissible.

LADDER STANDS

If you travel many back roads during the course of a deer season as I do, you probably pass other hunting vehicles. I suppose I've developed the habit of checking to see what kind of tree stands they are transporting. Much as I extol the virtues of backpacked compact stands, I must admit that I see as many or more ladder stands protruding from pickups than any of the others discussed.

Though not as portable as the climbing and hang-on types, most ladder stands are manufactured in several sections for at least a measure of compactness and portability. They are then assembled, erected, and secured to the tree trunk on reaching the hunting area. Once in place, the ladder stand is a comfortable place from which to hunt. The ease with which you can climb up and down is perhaps its greatest appeal. Most commercial models consist of three sections, each approximately 3 to 4 feet long, forming a ladder stand 9 to 12 feet high.

Many ladder stands are also designed to be backpacked with the sections strung together with straps

or bungee cord. This is an acceptable way to transport the stand, though the unit is often quite heavy and either protrudes above the shoulders to catch on branches, or extends so far down it interferes with walking, especially through rough cover. For that reason, ladder stands are often left in position for the duration of a several-day hunt, and in many cases, the entire season.

Allow me to pass along this tip concerning ladder stands. As secure and comfortable as these stands may be, there is nevertheless an inherent (albeit limited) danger associated with their installation. At the point where the stand has been positioned with the platform resting against the tree trunk, the ladder is not secured to anything; the hunter must climb up and fasten stand to tree with a chain, rope, or strap. The same problem exists when removing the ladder stand from the tree. Often the stand tends to slip sideways, with the hunter left to do a balancing act or leap to the ground to avoid going down with the ladder. I've found that by attaching a length of rope to each back corner of the platform, winding the rope around the tree in opposite directions, and tying the ends together, the ladder stand will be stable enough to let you go up or down without the primary lashing system in place.

In general, tree-stand hunting can be hazardous for hunters not strong or agile enough to be perched precipitously many feet above the ground on a small platform, as well as for those without the willpower to resist becoming preoccupied with visions of a huge buck approaching. Tree-stand hunting can also be risky for hunters impaired by age (old or young) or poor health, drugs that cause drowsiness, or other physical problems. Another category of individuals even more likely to become tree-stand casualties are outdoor "circus performers" who think they can defy gravity.

All things considered, I feel ladder stands are generally safer than the others mentioned here. My prime reasons are that these stands provide a solid structure between you and the ground and are easy to climb and descend. However, the arboreal hunter should try to sample different types until he finds one that works best for him. I cannot overemphasize the importance of checking out a new stand regardless of type. Your backyard, local park, or woodlot—*not* the deer woods on opening morning—is the place to familiarize yourself with a stand and learn its idiosyncracies. Numerous amenities can be added to a new stand to make it safer, quieter, and more comfortable. Take the time *before* hunting season to add any refinements that will make your stand a more effective piece of hunting equipment. And always hunt with a safety belt attached around your waist and to the tree trunk.

Regardless of the terrain found in your area, backpacking portable stands in remote areas is an effective deer-hunting tactic that can open up many new hunting opportunities. Get yourself a portable tree stand, topo maps, and a good hunting partner—and put some adventure in your hunts.

Clothes For The Hunter

By Kathy Etling

The pursuit of big game requires a special breed of hunter. Hunts may be planned for a year or more before they take place. Deposits reserve the services of outfitters and guides far in advance. License lotteries and drawings are entered with high hopes and higher fees just for the *chance* to hunt in a coveted area. High-priced equipment is selected carefully and paid for readily. It even costs big money to travel to hunt sites. No matter; serious big-game hunters don't even blink when tallying up the total.

When it comes to clothing, though, that's when hunters get budget-conscious. "Whoa," they say. "How much is that jacket? Forget it. I'll wear the old Army surplus."

Their reasoning is usually faulty and along the lines of: "I'll only be gone two weeks," "How cold can it get in September?" and "It's never snowed before." These can all be surefire blueprints for a miserable hunt.

Why is it that when hunters plan for so long and spend so much for their hunts, they scrimp on the one item that can make or break them? Indeed, the right clothing can make the difference between success and failure; it can even make the difference between life and death.

Never before have there been so many clothing choices for the big-game hunter. Emerging technologies offer fieldwear that is reasonably priced and works throughout the season.

Big game is hunted in the United States and Canada from mid-August until mid-February. Weather, especially in the mountain states, can be totally unpredictable. Wise hunters prepare for any eventuality—hot or bitter cold—by layering.

Layers trap air that's been warmed by your body. This trapped, dead air is an excellent insulator. The more air you trap, the warmer you'll feel. So, several thin layers of clothing work better than one thick layer because more air can be trapped and warmed between the layers themselves. Conversely, if it's too warm, you can shed one or more layers to cool off.

Remington's choice for underwear is a material called Thermax ($24 per item). Constructed of a fine, hollow-core polyester fiber, Thermax wicks moisture away from the skin while trapping air. It's soft, easy to care for, and won't shrink. Remington designed the top with extra-long tails that stay tucked into parts .

Thinsulate radiates warmth the minute you put it on and is an excellent choice for hunters who spend long, cold hours on stand. Thinsulate long johns ($45 for the top, $40 for the bottom) are available from Columbia Sportswear and 10X Products Group.

Duofold has developed another type of transmission-layer garment called Prolon 2000 (about $24 for top or bottom), which is available from Eddie Bauer. Marketed as a self-contained layering system, its inner layer is spun polypropylene; the outer layer is a blend of 70 percent acrylic and 30 percent wool. This other layer traps body heat yet facilitates moisture-wicking to keep you dry. It can be machine-washed, too.

The insulation layer's job is to keep warmth in and cold out. One, two, or even three separate layers can join forces to make the insulation group work the way it should.

Remington offers a new concept in hunting shirts.

Hunter at left has Remington's Big Game parka, overpant, and Polarfleece jacket, Gates-Mills blaze orange gloves, Dunham Duraflex boots; hunter at right is wearing Browning Woodland Blaze camouflage coveralls, Meldisco Texas steer boots, and Bob Allen cap.

Photo by John Hamel

The Worsterlon shirt ($39.95), woven from Du Pont Dacron polyester, is an excellent substitute for wool. These shirts are soft, nonallergenic, and washable.

Also from Remington, and another good mid-layer choice, is the Polarfleece Jacket ($59.95). Polarfleece weighs less than wool but insulates at the same rate.

The reversible Polarfleece Jacket is a product of Browning Arms. The Polarfleece side is noiseless (take heed, stalkers), nonabsorbent, and abrasion-resistant. This jacket is available in two color combinations: blaze camouflage 50/50 (polyester/cotton blend) cloth reversing to red buffalo plaid Polarfleece ($99.95), and woodland-green camouflage 50/50 cloth reversing to charcoal-gray Polarfleece ($89.95).

Some people, however, will wear nothing but wool. Some of the best woolens come from Woolrich. The Woolrich Alaskan Shirt ($41) has an extra-long tail. Quality is apparent in its double-needle lap-fold seams. Buy it a little large and wear it over a sweater.

Cabela's sells ragg wool sweaters ($20). I have

several and they're rugged, good-looking, and warm. They layer and compress well, and after the hunt easily make the transition to the home front.

Woolrich has heavy Malone hunting trousers ($52) that are a blend of 85 percent wool and 15 percent nylon. Malones are also offered in a bib-overall style ($66.50).

C.C. Filson's Wool Whipcord Trail Pants (about $100) are a superb product and cost more for the extra luxury. Made here in the United States of fine 100 percent virgin wool, the pants have lots of deep, snap-closing pockets.

When deciding on clothing for the insulation layer, be sure to choose at least one high-bulk layer (down or synthetic substitute) to trap large masses of air. One good option would be a vest.

A vest's armless design keeps you warm while freeing your arms for climbing. When the day begins to heat up, cram the vest into your daypack or fannypack. No bulky arm material means that you can compress the vest into a tiny package—especially if it's made of down or Quallofil.

One example is Eddie Bauer's Downlight Canadian Vest ($39). Insulated with prime goose down, the Downlight comes in both regular and king sizes.

L.L. Bean sells down and Quallofil vests, too. The Trail Model ($47) is insulated with goose down and has an extra-high neck, kidney-warmer tail, and snap closures.

Bean also offers the Quallofil Northwoods Vest ($44). This vest looks like the Trail Model but is insulated with Quallofil. Quallofil packs and warms like down but with one big difference: get it wet, and it stays warmer and dries much faster than down does.

One area where real ingenuity has been displayed is in rugged outerwear for the big-game hunter. Manufacturers have jumped into the clothing fray with every weapon at their disposal. New fabrics, insulations, and designs are rampant in the industry today.

Columbia Sportswear is a case in point. The company offers so many choices that it's tough to pick just one or two. The designs are extremely functional from a hunter's standpoint.

Columbia's Radial Sleeve, for instance, has been submitted for a patent. This sleeve is a clever way to make arm movement easier in traditionally confining outerwear. A diamond-shaped insert has been sewn under each sleeve. This insert allows much more freedom of movement when the arms are raised.

Columbia's Quad Parka ($300) features radial sleeve construction. The Quad also provides the ultimate in hunting-garment versatility with a Gore-Tex/Stealth Cloth outer shell that's been certified waterproof by W.I. Gore, the manufacturer of Gore-Tex. The reversible liner jacket can be zipped into

Hunter in foreground is wearing Red Head's reversible NorthWester vest and L.L. Bean's Canada Gray trousers, Maine guide shirt, and Maine eight-inch hunting shoe; hunter in background is wearing a Woolrich Richie 4-in-1 coat, L.L. Bean Woodsman's pants and cotton turtleneck, and Kaufman's Sorel stag boots.

Photo by John Hamel

the shell and is insulated with 200 grams of Thinsulate.

There are four ways to wear the Quad: shell and liner worn zipped together; liner worn alone—one side out; liner worn alone but reversed so that the other side shows; and shell worn alone as raingear or windbreaker. The Quad is proof that layering works, and manufacturers are eager to jump on the bandwagon. Look for this parka in tan camouflage, woodland camouflage, Blaze Orange, or Treebark camouflage.

Browning's variation of the Quad is called the Four-In-One Big Game parka ($249.95). This parka also has matching pants ($158.50). Browning has chosen Ten-Mile Cloth—100 percent acrylic duck—laminated to Gore-Tex for the outer shell, and an insulation of Thermolite. Color selection is limited to Blaze Orange for the outer shell and blaze camouflage/solid brown for the reversible liner.

The Four For One Parka ($250) has been designed by Duxbak. The fabric used for the shell is truly revolutionary. Whisper-Soft Gore-Tex took W.L. Gore months to develop but was well worth the wait. Gore-Tex laminated to moleskin chamois cloth creates a waterproof/breathable fabric that is definitely the softest and quietest Gore-Tex I've ever seen. Duxbak's Four For One Parka has a removable Thinsulate jacket lining and is available in brown and green camouflage.

Not all jackets are Quad or Four-In-One types. Remington has a traditional overpant/parka combination that's designed for the big-game hunter's comfort. This ensemble is made of tough 330-denier Cordura nylon that's been laminated to Gore-Tex. This new shell fabric has been dubbed ".30/06" by Remington. The Remington Big Game Parka ($234.95) is insulated with Thermolite, Du Pont's answer to 3M's Thinsulate.

One feature that big-game hunters will appreciate is the windskirt. By tightening both the windskirt and the drawstring bottom, it's possible to thwart cold air by creating two additional, large dead-air spaces.

Remington's Big Game Overpants are available either with ($134.95) or without ($114.95) Thermolite insulation. Double-facing makes them tough, and ankle-to-knee side-seam zippers make them easy to put on over boots. Belt loops and suspender buttons eliminate some traditional laments of hunters who own pants with elastic waists. Both parka and pants are available in your choice of Blaze Orange and brown camouflage.

Plain shell-type Gore-Tex parkas are available from many sources for less than $150. When combined with a wool jacket and insulated vest beneath, they perform extremely well—especially as "protection" from severe weather.

Bowhunters may want to check out Columbia's Bow-Duck Parka ($210). The parka is a reversible jacket and hood with a waterproof Gore-Tex side that's been laminated to Stalker Cloth. The other side is Ninja Cloth—one of the quietest hunting

Some Sources Of Hunting Clothes

Browning
Route 1
Morgan, UT 84050

Campmor
810 Route 17 N.
PO Box 999
Paramus, NJ 07653-0999

Cabela's
812-13th Avenue
Sidney, NE 69160

Columbia Sportswear Company
6600 N. Baltimore
Portland, OR 97203

Duxbak
Utica Duxbak Corp.
815 Noyes St.
Utica, NY 13502

Eddie Bauer
15010 N.E. 36th St.
Redmond, WA 98052

L.L. Bean
Freeport, Maine 04033

Refrigiwear, Inc.
71 Inip Drive
Inwood, NY 11696

Remington Arms Company, Inc.
1007 Market Street
Wilmington, DE 19898

Peter Storm
PO Box 451
52 Bradford St.
Concord, MA 01742

10X Products Group
2828 Forest lane
Suite 1107
Dallas, TX 75234

fabrics on the market. With its radial sleeve design, the jacket is ideal for bowhunters who want silent, all-purpose clothing.

Columbia's Ninja Cloth pants ($56) and jacket ($73.50) are made of this same 100 percent polyester fabric but without the Gore-Tex. Named for the 14th-century Japanese assassin teams, Ninja Cloth is tough yet easily cared for.

Browning's Polarfleece Archer's Suit is also quiet. A two-piece style of 100 percent Dacron polyester Polarfleece, the suit's sleeves are designed to be close-fitting so that they don't catch on the bowstring. Suggested retail price for the top is $74.95; the bottom costs $56.95.

I've worn coveralls while stand hunting for white-tails for the past ten years. My last one saw many good times, and I took a lot of bucks while wearing it. The difference between that suit and the one I got last Christmas, however, is the difference between night and day.

My new overall is by 10X Products Group. The Gore-Tex fabric exterior comes in handy when it rains or snows. It's also quiet, and the Thinsulate lining keeps me warm even when the weather turns bitter cold. I can now be comfortable on stand at temperatures that used to make me miserable.

10X doesn't only offer the Gore-Tex version ($250). There's also the Big Horn Coverall ($150) with a shell of water-repellent Burlington Ten-Mile Cloth. Though the Gore-Tex coverall is available only in brown camouflage, the Big Horn comes in brown, green, and blaze camouflage plus solid Blaze Orange.

Refrigiwear has several one-piece suits on the market right now. The Minus 50 Suit ($173) features super-tough nylon duck outer fabric and 10 ounces of polyester fiberfill.

Finally, the dedicated big-game hunter must consider his head, toes, and hands. Luckily, with the wide selection of caps, socks, boots, and gloves to choose from, this isn't too difficult.

Socks will always be socks, but your feet will be genuinely grateful if you purchase some socks of a wool/polypropylene blend. They'll wick moisture and keep your feet warm. If you buy heavyweight socks, they'll cushion your feet, too. Just be sure that your hunting boots are large enough to accommodate the extra thickness. Cabela's and Campmor sell a fine variety of hunting socks, including the heavy wool/polypropylene blends ($5 to $7).

Gaiters should always be in your daypack or backpack. I don't know how many times I've grumbled about the slight extra weight gaiters add and then felt like kissing them eight hours later when I'm in snow up to my knees. I even wear them while hunting at home in Missouri. You can purchase gaiters from L.L. Bean ($15) or Recreational Equipment, Inc. ($12.95).

Caps and gloves also take advantage of the latest fabrics and fills. Cabela's Balaclava ($8.95) has an inner polypropylene lining that wicks away moisture while its wool outer shell insulates. This hat also doubles as a face mask.

Cabela's Gore-Tex/Thinsulate field cap ($8.95 to $10.95) is made of non-glare material that helps keep big game from spotting you. The bill shields your eyes from the sun. Foam/knit earflaps can be pulled down from the inside when the temperature nosedives.

Thinsulate gloves ($9.95) cost about the same as a pair of ragg wool gloves. Gore-Tex/Thinsulate gloves ($24.95) are bulky but keep your hands warm. Don't wear them if you might have to shoot quickly, however.

Wool shooting gloves ($7.99) or mittens ($9.95) are still an excellent choice for big-game hunters. For quick shots, they can't be beat. Leather palms help you grip your rifle. All of these gloves and mittens are available from Cabela's.

Big-game hunting is rewarding, but it can also be tough. Weather, altitude, terrain, and unfamiliar conditions all join forces, challenging you at every turn. When the going gets tough, you need tough clothing. You can't be without it.

Choosing A Hunting Boot

By Kathy Etling

Did you ever stop to realize that whenever you go deer hunting, two good friends go with you? These friends offer support, provide transportation, even help you stalk your quarry, and ask little in return.

And little is what we often give them. We force them to carry more weight than they should. We let them get soaking wet and stay that way for hours. When they're cold, we ignore them. And then we make them stand for long hours without letting them move. What kind of friends would take this abuse? Our feet would. And until they ache or blister, many of us take them for granted.

The human body is a physiological marvel whose very foundation is made up of the feet. Each foot consists of 26 separate bones—tarsals, metatarsals, and phalanges that are connected to each other by tough bands of tissue called *ligaments*.

The tarsal and metatarsal bones form the two arches of the foot, and a thick layer of fatty tissue right under the sole helps these arches absorb pressure and shock.

And do we ever shock them. Especially in some of the more serious phases of deer hunting, which can run the gamut from easy to brutal. Good deer hunting footwear is important, though it's not always possible to be prepared for every eventuality you might encounter. I'm reminded especially of my roughest deer hunt.

I was hunting trophy mule deer above timberline along Grey's River in Wyoming. My outfitter,

Maury Jones of Bedford, Wyoming, was determined to help me find one of the huge 30-inch bucks he'd seen during pre-season scouting.

We arose at 3:00 A.M. every morning, trucked our horses for 45 minutes, and then rode in the dark up narrow switchbacking trails for two hours. The stirrups held my feet in their vise-like grip and the cold Wyoming air quickly turned them numb.

Then I sat for several hours in a snowstorm covering what I could of a stark, barren basin. By the time we decided to stalk and glass, my feet were so cold I could hardly feel the ground beneath them. Noise became a factor as I tried to silently negotiate a steep rocky slope in my hiking boots in an attempt to get closer to a buck.

Later, I followed Jonesy straight down an icy rock face for several hundred feet and then stumbled along a treacherous rock slide. Afterwards, we made our way along faint deer trails that dropped off into sheer space. During my five days I hunted in sleet, ice, snow, rain, and mud. I stalked, rode, and just sat glassing.

I could have used at least *four* different pairs of boots in terrain and weather conditions like those. But when space and weight and money are at a premium you make compromises. The problem is deciding on the best all around boot for the deer hunt you want to do.

When looking for that ideal deer-hunting boot, there are three main factors to consider: support, comfort, and warmth.

162

Wearing the right boots for the right hunting conditions can make all the difference between success and failure your next time out. Shown here are Rocky Boots Stalkers.

SUPPORT

According to Dr. Glenn Gastwirth, D.P.M., of the American Podiatric Medical Association, "Without proper foot support, pressure is created and foot problems may result." Boots should be as supportive as possible. One way to increase support is to choose deer-hunting boots with laces.

American Footwear, Danner Boots, and Cabela's all offer boots with to-the-toe lacing for even *more* support. To-the-toe lacing also helps hunters avoid bruised toes by restraining the foot from sliding within the boot.

Chippewa Boot, a division of Justin, markets their Sidewinder with side laces, which give needed support to hunters who can't stand laces cutting into high insteps and ankles. The Sidewinder is lined with sheepskin and insulated with Thinsulate ($140).

For even more support look for boots with such features as steel-shank arch supports, Fiberglass shanks for support without weight, orthotic insoles, and EVA (ethylene vinyl acetate) midsoles to act as shock absorbers.

Kenko International's Trail II-S features the Asoflex midsole—the only midsole on the market with a patent. It's anatomically contoured to cradle and support the entire foot. The Trail II-S also has a high-friction Pirelli sole to absorb heel-strike shock and reduce stress on ankles, knees, hips, and backs ($160).

Cabella's Mountain Hunters.

Kenko Trail II-S boots.

Danner's new Rainier boot.

A well-constructed hiking boot like this is ideal for the high-country trophy mule-deer hunter, especially if backpacking is involved. Other good hiking boot choices are made by Fabiano, Wolverine, and Red Wing in their Vasque line.

Danner Boot's new Rainier is a good *light* hiking boot. The Rainier weighs just 40 ounces and features a Vibram Infinity outsole, a cushioned poron insole, steel shank, and EVA foam midsole ($110).

Because a good hiking boot is so supportive, use it to kick right into the side of the soft slope to gain a foothold when chasing that trophy muley. Ankles that would ordinarily turn or twist are held firm and steady.

"Don't expect new boots to take care of existing foot problems," Dr. Gastwirth added. "If your feet are chronically sore and painful you may need professional help. Foot pain isn't normal. And sometimes it's due to a simple lack of support. See a specialist if pain continues after your boots have been broken in."

COMFORT

"Breaking in boots is important," continued Dr. Gastwirth, "but first choose the right boot for the job. Pick a boot that's flexible and feels good. If it's a heavy hiking boot, allow yourself extra breaking-in time. Aches, pains, and cramping from improperly fitted or broken-in footwear can ruin your hunt.

"Nail discoloration and even painful separation from the nail bed may result if your toes hit the front of your boot. And blisters because of friction on toes and soles are typical of poor-fitting footwear.

"Try on boots with the same kind and number of socks that you'll be wearing when hunting," Dr. Gastwirth concluded. "And always try on boots

later in the day, because as the day progresses your feet will swell and give a more accurate determination of fit."

WARMTH

Closely allied with comfort is warmth. The human body is set to such delicate balance that feet feel comfortable when body temperature is about 99°F. But if body core temperature drops *just one degree*—to 98°—your feet will get cold. And at 97°, your feet are no longer just cold; they're numb.

When body temperature drops to less than 99°F, nerves pick up the message "cold" from the skin's surface. The brain constricts surface blood vessels and slows the heartbeat. These two involuntary responses chill toes, hands, and fingers as the body redirects heat to the brain and internal organs.

Insulated boots won't keep your feet warm all by themselves, no matter how well they are constructed. Hunters who complain about cold feet are probably the ones who won't wear caps or scarves even in the coldest weather. An unprotected head and neck may lose 50 percent of the body's total heat production at 40°F, and *75 percent* at 5°.

Sweat also contributes to cold feet because the purpose of sweating is to *lose* body heat. As moisture evaporates from the body's surface, cooling takes place and body heat is lost through evaporation. Breathable fabrics and fibers that also wick minimize such heat loss, particularly if you must walk any distance to your tree stand.

To do their part in keeping your feet warm, boots have to keep water out, heat in, and move perspiration away from the skin. Since the skin gives off at least 20 ounces of water per day in the form of perspiration, boot liners and insulators have their work cut out for them.

Materials such as polypropylene and wool actually suck up moisture and wick it away. But it is possible to overload even these fibers and get chilled because of sweat. Whenever you head for your deer stand, carry an extra pair of socks as well as a plastic bag for your old ones (no self-respecting deer will come near the smell of dirty socks).

Insulation is the material placed between the skin and the atmosphere to prevent or reduce heat loss. But no material insulates by itself. Insulation is the result of the warmed dead air that the insulation entraps.

Insulation's basic principle is to store the warm air that comes off your skin in air spaces or pockets in fibers. This works best if 1.) the air spaces between the fibers are very small; and 2.) if the material won't compress. If the fibers compress too tightly, *conductive heat loss* occurs. Some boot soles are excellent conductors of heat—and cold feet are the result.

New technology has provided thin insulations that combine microscopic polyester and polyolefin fibers. Thinsulate, for example, has up to 20 times the surface area of other fibers in the same amount of space. The result is more warmth with less weight.

Many good deer-hunting boots combine wicking action, breathability, and insulation for warmth under a variety of temperature conditions. These boots may or may not be guaranteed waterproof. Before buying, determine what is most important for your style of deer hunting and choose accordingly. You may really need *more* than one pair of boots for the kind of deer hunting that you do most, or for that special Western hunt you're planning this fall. Here are some choices and a few features of each:

William Brooks Shoe Co./Rocky Boots Stalker 8-inch boots ($115) come in Brown Camo combination Cordura/leather styling with a new brown camo Vibram sole for the hunter who's looking for total camouflage. Stalkers combine Thinsulate and Gore-Tex for warmth and water resistance.

Northlake's Safari collection also have camo soles. Camouflage uppers are of leather and 1,000-denier Cordura—the heaviest and toughest used on hunting boots. Safaris also feature a cushioned insole and Cambrelle liners. They *aren't* guaranteed waterproof and are warm-weather hunting boots. Safaris are available in both boys' and women's sizes ($39–$59).

Mountain Stalkers are Rocky's deluxe 9-inch versions of the Stalker. In addition to the other features, Mountain Stalkers offer a polyurtehane midsole, Goodyear welt construction (machine-sewn sole to boot), and special Vibram slip-resistant outsoles ($125).

Browning's Nomad combines leather with tough 1000-denier Cordura to complete the outer boot. The interior includes a four-layer insulated bootie. The sole is a lug-style cleat design made of shock-absorbing urethane. And it is guaranteed waterproof ($130). Browning's economy version of the Nomad is called the Ranger ($100) and is also guaranteed waterproof. Very similar to the Nomad, the Ranger has a self-cleaning lug design that delivers traction and reduces cleat clogging.

Other Browning boots include the Kangaroo Waterproof—a light kangaroo leather boot that's waterproof and advertised as 62 percent stronger than leather ($110).

Cabela's Big-Game Expedition has a full sock lining of Gore-Tex and 200 grams of Thinsulate insu-

Browning's Ranger.

Browning's Nomad.

Herman Survivors Calgary model.

Red Wing's Irish Setter.

lation. The midsole is EVA, and the liner is 3-Bar-Knit—woven polypropylene that wicks moisture away and quickly dries. Cabela's provides a 60-day wear guarantee to buyers of the boot ($150).

Danner's Yukon, weighing 74 ounces, is the ultimate heavy-duty hunting boot. The Yukon comes with Thinsulate/Gore-Tex full sock lining and is guaranteed waterproof ($149). Danner also offers Men's and Women's Winter Lights, which weigh 62 ounces complete with poron cushioned insole, steel shank, and dual neoprene/EVA midsole. Vibram Kletterlift outsoles provide traction ($125).

Herman Survivors from the Joseph M. Herman Shoe Co. feature dual-density guaranteed-waterproof boots. This line includes the Klondike ($100) and Calgary ($130) and are guaranteed waterproof for as long as you own them provided they're properly cared for. Hermans are also sold with a two-week, 14-day comfort trial. If during that time the boots are uncomfortable, you will be given a full refund with no questions asked.

Red Wing introduces two new Gore-Tex waterproof insulated boots to the Irish Setter line—style numbers 806 ($139) and 808 ($145). They're insulated with Thinsulate and liners of 3-Bar-Knit. Barcleat SuperSoles—molded polyurethane with a self-cleaning tread—work as you walk because the tread expands when it flexes.

10X's all-camouflage leather boot, the Camohide Hunter, comes with a Gore-Tex liner, Thinsulate insulation, Cambrelle lining, and Vibram soles stitched to the boot with a Goodyear welt ($115).

Weinbrenner Shoes offers their medium-priced Wood 'n Stream leather boots. These boots are advertised as completely waterproof and feature injec-

tion-molded polyurethane soles for light weight and durability ($85).

Wolverine's Thermalites apply ski-boot technology to hunting boots. Waterproof polyurethane shells encase the entire foot while all-leather uppers finish the package. Thermalites are lined and insulated with pigskin that's backed with thermal foam ($40). Note, however, that because the soles on Thermalites—as well as on Weinbrenner Wood 'N Streams—are injection-molded and not sewn, they are not repairable when they finally do wear out.

If you pursue muleys or whitetails in snake country, consider Chippewa Boot's Camouflage Viperlites. These boots are designed primarily for protection from snakes and come with 17-inch snakeproof camouflage Cordura nylon uppers and Vibram cushion soles. The Viperlite will help keep you camouflaged and snake-proofed at the same time ($125).

RUBBER BOOTS

Serious trophy-whitetail hunters wouldn't think of heading into the woods without rubber boots. Pants legs can be tucked into high rubber boots to reduce scent. Another benefit: rubber won't retain odor like leather. And if you hunt swampland whitetails, rubber boots are an indispensable part of your deer-hunting wardrobe.

Nelson Recreation Products/Weather-Rite, Inc., introduces their Camouflage Rubber Boot. This boot is insulated with foam and has a steel shank for support. Unlike many rubber boots, this one has a cleated sole and heel for traction in mud, snow, or rain ($24.95).

Red Ball has two all-rubber insulated boots with

Nelson Recreation/Weather-Rite Camouflage Rubber Boot

thick felt midsoles and steel shanks. Removable foot-contoured polytherm insoles are also included ($31).

Lacrosse offers the noninsulated all-rubber Hudson for warm-weather trophy buck hunters ($25).

PACS OR PACKS

Rubber-bottomed, leather-topped boots terms *pacs* or *packs* have been around for many years. These boots are especially suited for boggy terrain. With many of the new liners available, however, some packs are the warmest boots that are currently on the market.

Browning has three different packs: the McKinley ($84), Yukon ($75), and Alaskan ($68).

Cabela's Professional Thinsulate Camo Guide Boots are reasonably priced rubber-bottom/nylon-top boots that really perform. I bought mine for only $35 and they really keep my feet warm and dry during the hunt.

Kaufman/Sorel's Superior pack may be the warmest boot they've ever made. It's comfort-rated to −85°F ($75).

HUNTING-BOOT MANUFACTURERS:

American Footwear Corp.
One Oak Hill Road
Fitchburg, MA 01420

L.L. Bean
Casco Street
Freeport, ME 04033

Browning
Route 1
Morgan, UT 84050

Cabela's
812 13th Ave.
Sidney, NE 69160

Chippewa Shoe Company
PO Box 2521
Fort Worth, TX 76113–2521

Danner Shoe Manufacturing
PO Box 22204
Portland, OR 97222

Dunham Boots
Cottonmill Hill
Brattleboro, VT 05301

Georgia Boot Co.
1810 Columbia Ave.
Franklin, TN 37064

Joseph M. Herman Shoe Co.
5 Cambridge Center
Cambridge, MA 02142

Kaufman/Sorel Footwear
410 King St.
W. Kitchener, Ontario, Canada N2G 4J8

Kenko International/Asolo Boots
8141 West I70
Frontage Road North
Arvada, CO 80002

LaCrosse Footwear
1407 St. Andrew St.
LaCrosse, WI 54603

Nelson Recreation Products, Inc./
Weather-Rite, Inc.
PO Box 14488
Lenexa, KS 66215–0488

Red Ball/Oneida
PO Box 3200
Manchester, NH 03105

Red Wing, Inc.
419 Bush St.
Red Wing, MN 55066

Rocky Boots Division
William Brooks Shoe Co.
Nelsonville, OH 45764

10X Products Group
2828 Forest Lane
Suite 1107
Dallas, TX 75234

Weinbrenner Shoe Co.
108 South Polk St.
Merrill, WI 54452

Wolverine Boots
9341 Courtland Dr.
Rockford, MI 49351

Browning Yukon packs.

Browning Alaskan packs.

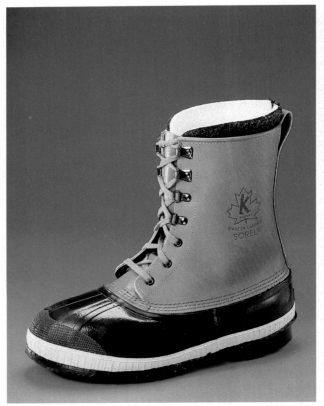

Kaufman/Sorel Superior.

Lacrosse Iceman packs.

L. L. Bean's Maine Hunting Boot.

Red Ball/Oneida leather-top packs.

Oneida insulated bootee.

Lacrosse's Iceman ($70–$80) was trail-tested on the 1986 Iditarod Sled Dog Race from Anchorage to Nome, Alaska. The Iceman is good to temperatures of −80°—far colder than any temperature a deer hunter should have to endure, but mighty comforting to a Saskatchewan or Montana stand hunter in December. Lacrosse also features the Whitetail for women deer hunters. This insulated pack is an ultra-light 10-inch boot designed to fit a woman's foot. The Whitetail has removable Thinsulate liner with Velcro fasteners that hold it in place ($65).

Bean's Maine Hunting Shoes ($45–$65) one of the first packs on the market, are still available at reasonable prices. When a pair of Bean's Maine Hunting Shoes wears out you can return them to Bean to be repaired and reconditioned for a fee.

Red Ball/Oneida has two leather-top packs ($60), which come with the Oneida insulated bootee. This bootee is made of a nylon tricot shell lined with cellular foam, and can also be bought separately for $14. Thinsulate is provided underfoot.

Deer are unpredictable. We never really know what to expect from them. They can be found in any kind of habitat thriving in all kinds of weather conditions. To succeed we must be able to meet them on their own terms, in their own environment, and be prepared to stick it out. That's when good gear can mean the difference between success and failure. And choosing the right deer-hunting footwear is a step in the right direction.

PART 7

OUTDOOR COOKING

Deer-Camp Cooking

By John Weiss

Long after they've forgotten the exact measurements of their deer racks collected over the years, still firm in the memories of most hunters are their camp cooking experiences—whether they're worth remembering or not.

Just a few of my fondest recollections of deer-camp cooking include memories of venison tenderloin steaks broiling over aspen coals in the high country of Colorado's White River National Forest; the sumptuous rashers of crisp bacon and tall stacks of buckwheat cakes drooling with maple syrup that make us eagerly look forward to 4 o'clock wakenings in our southern Ohio deer camp; the freshly picked papaws we once transformed into a toothsome pie backed in a reflector oven in a bowhunting camp in western Kentucky. And, at numerous outposts, the special technique of preparing savory camp coffee, which, strangely, no one ever seems to try to duplicate on the home front during other months of the year.

There also are camp-cooking memories that I'd just as soon forget but will probably haunt me forever. There was the Wyoming camp many years ago when we scrimped on the grocery list, later found ourselves unexpectedly snowed in, and for three grueling days had to subsist on nothing but whiskey and cornflakes. The South Carolina hunting club where "Cookie" believed in frying absolutely everything, even the bread for our noontime sandwiches, and the greaseball feeling we all had by the end of the week. The New York deer camp where an unknowledgeable young hunter in charge of the evening meal broiled our meat over spruce wood and then served us what looked like T-bones but tasted like turpentine. And the Minnesota camp

Photo by Bob Hirsch/Professional Images

where the supposedly authentic camp coffee, I still insist, actually tasted more like printer's ink.

As a result of these and more than 25 years of other deer camp cooking adventures, I've learned there are several axioms about deer hunters and their regimen that hold so consistently true that they might as well be set in concrete. Foremost, at the end of a long day afield, any hunter who has invested himself body and soul into the effort is as tired as a cross-country runner and as hungry as a bear first emerging from its den in the spring. Another is that hunters dote upon meals that are ready to eat at a moment's notice. And, of course, with the advance knowledge of having to rise again at some ungodly hour the following morning, few hunters have much enthusiasm for staying up late and scrubbing an endless array of encrusted pots and pans.

It follows, then, there also are several rules of thumb about deer-camp cooking and what it should—and should not—entail.

At the outset, when planning a shopping list, it's always better to err on the side of buying too much food rather than too little. Like the national deficit, the appetites of active deer hunters seem to have no bounds. Of equal importance, make sure that your food choices are packed with "go-power" because now is no time to count calories, as it is when pursuing a more sedentary lifestyle at home.

Simplicity of preparation is also crucial when you want to spend as much time as possible in the field. Contrary to many of the meal suggestions listed in "outdoor" cookbooks, any recipe that requires more than seven ingredients or 45 minutes of cooking time is wholly unsuitable for most deer camp menus. By the same token, if after-meal cleanup time exceeds 15 minutes, whoever has been in charge of culinary duties should be immediately relieved of his post and placed on woodchopping detail.

The climate should play a premier role in the choice of foods selected for deer-camp cooking. Altitude, weather, and air temperature have telling influences on the body's fuel requirements and metabolic processes (the efficiency with which foods are digested and converted into energy). Unfortunately, most hunters tend to rely upon the same favorite food choices, no matter when or where they're hunting. The usual result is at least a slight reduction in both their comfort and in their level of energy reserves that they periodically need to call upon during the hunt.

All foods are comprised of various percentages of proteins, fats, and carbohydrates. Each of these elements has entirely different effects upon bodily processes. However, it is not necessary to consult with a professional dietitian in the planning of a deer-camp menu. Just keep the following basics in mind when you plan your hunt.

Proteins do not afford high levels of energy, so don't count on them too heavily when you know in advance that a particular hunt is going to require plenty of physical exertion. Proteins have many responsibilities, such as the building of cells and maintenance of skin tissues and muscle. But one of the most important roles played by proteins is the production of body heat. It stands to reason, then, that on cold-weather hunts you'll want your grub list to be weighted heavily with diary products, legumes such as peas and beans, peanuts, eggs, and especially meat and fish. In hot weather, just the opposite applies. Then, you'll want to turn down your internal thermostat by slightly reducing the protein content of each meal.

Fats provide the body with modest amounts of energy. But of the three basic food elements, fats take the longest to digest and are therefore prone to accumulate in the body rather than be quickly utilized. Examples of foods high in fat content are cheese, butter, nuts, saturated cooking oils, highly marbled cuts of red meat, and most cuts of pork (particularly bacon, sausage, and ham). Fats also aid in the production of body heat, but to a far lesser extent than protein. Therefore, though fats are a necessary component of any balanced menu, overdoing them, especially in warm weather, is almost guaranteed to see them stored as excess body weight, giving everyone in camp a logy feeling.

Even in bitterly cold weather, proteins and fats together should never comprise more than half of one's total caloric intake. The remaining 50 percent of the deer-camp menu should be in the form of carbohydrates.

There are two types of carbohydrates: sugars and starches. High-starch carbohydrates include bread products, potatoes, beans, fruits, vegetables, and cereals (especially wheat, rice, and oats). High-sugar carbohydrates include not only common sweets such as chocolate, hard candy, and pastries, but also the natural sugars found in dried fruits such as raisins and dates.

Carbohydrates are essential components of deer-camp menus in all types of weather because they are metabolized far more quickly than proteins and fats to liberate almost instant energy during strenuous physical exertion. And, of particular importance to high-county hunters, carbohydrates are quite easy for the body to digest at elevations above 5,000 feet, where oxygen levels begin to diminish and rapidly rob the body of its ability to operate efficiently.

The evening before serious sports competition, many athletes—particularly marathon runners—engage in an eating ritual known as "carbo-loading" in which they literally stuff themselves with pasta and beer. These two exceptionally high-carbohydrate foods, accentuated by several chocolate bars the following morning, produce an enormous energy reserve that supposedly allows them to push themselves to the limit of their physical capabilities.

During a typical cold-weather outing, deer hunters can subscribe to much the same philosophy by tailoring their meals along these examples: Evening meals should be high in carbohydrates (pasta, potatoes, vegetables) so that everyone will have plenty of go-power during the following day's activities. The next morning, breakfast should again include carbohydrates (pastries, pancakes) but also protein (meat, eggs, milk) for day-long production of body heat. Lunch should focus on high-protein intake (such as bean soup and ham sandwiches), which will be digested in plenty of time to generate body warmth when snuggled in sleeping bags later that night. Between meals, while in the field, everyone should liberally snack on candy bars and other sweets for sustained energy levels. In this latter regard, "gorp" is ideal: a mix of peanuts, dried fruits, and candies such as M & Ms that can be placed in plastic bags and stowed in coat pockets.

It's worth repeating that deer hunters need not worry about the calorie content of their menus during brief outings, say, less than three weeks. In fact, though an average person at home may get along just fine on only 2,500 calories per day, it's quite common for that same person hunting deer in mountain terrain to consume as much as 5,000 calories per day—and arrive home later to discover that he has actually lost weight!

Because most hunters are not familiar with the fat, protein, and carbohydrate contents of the foods they eat, or their caloric values, I suggest obtaining a copy of the *Agricultural Handbook, No. 8: Composition of Goods,* available for $7 postpaid from the Superintendent of Documents, U.S. Government Printing Office, Washington, DC 20402. By consulting this publication, any hunter will easily be able to consider the nature of an upcoming outing and instantly know which food items to emphasize in his menu planning.

Curiously, in a society that is becoming more conscious about reducing salt intake, briefly increasing the level of salt in the diet actually is beneficial during the course of cold-weather deer hunts. Paul Petzold, the world-famous mountain climber and expedition leader, explains that a lack of salt in daily menus has the effect of drawing blood away from the extremities and toward the body core, which greatly contributes to cold hands, feet, and ears. Additional salt intake keeps blood vigorously flowing to the extremities. You'll want to increase your salt intake during warm weather as well, but not to such an extent as during cold weather; in the former case, the goal is merely to replace those salts lost through perspiration to maintain a desirable electrolyte balance.

As for some specific foods that seem to find the greatest favor among deer hunters, we've learned through trial and error to rely heavily upon one-pot meals. The variety of such dishes is limited only by the ingenuity of the hunters in the party. We especially like spaghetti, hearty soups, stews, chili, macaroni and cheese, chicken and dumplings, meat-and-noodle casseroles, meat/vegetable/rice medleys—the list is almost endless. Yet the unique composition of each one-pot meal should always be geared toward the climatic conditions of the outing.

For example, during a warm-weather deer hunt, a one-pot spaghetti dinner may be comprised mainly of pasta and tomato sauce, because we're concerned mainly with a high-carbohydrate intake that will provide sustained levels of energy. But if we know that we'll be camping in cold weather, we'll add a liberal quantity of meatballs to the spaghetti to achieve our protein requirement for maintaining body warmth. Similarly, our soups and stews during hot weather typically are laced with large quantities of vegetables, compared with hunts taking place in frigid climates, when we slightly reduce the vegetable content in favor of adding beans and large chunks of stew beef.

Our standard procedure for preparing one-pot meals is for each hunter in the group to prepare two meals of his choice in advance at home and freeze them in one-gallon cardboard milk cartons. These are then labeled and stowed in camping coolers, acting in place of ice to keep other foods cool during the travel time required to reach our destination. Even in warm weather, such meals will stay frozen for at least two days before thawing slowly. After they are completely thawed, you've got at least an additional four days of safe storage time before they must be eaten. If the temperature is below freezing, all of these storage times can be extended almost indefinitely.

But it's the convenience of one-pot meals that makes them especially popular because all that's required is opening a given milk carton, dumping the contents into a deep pan, and heating them over a camp stove or open fire. This greatly simplifies not only menu planning but also satisfies the unpredictable eating times so common to deer hunts.

We also find aluminum foil to be indispensable in our deer-camp cooking, primarily in concocting one-pot meals on the spur of the moment without the bother of later having to wash dishes. First, lay out a large square of heavy-duty foil for each hunter and place a meat cut of your choice in the center (chicken, thick slab of ham or beef). Now add sliced potatoes, onions, or other vegetables. Top the works with cheese, if you like. Cup the foil slightly, add several tablespoons of water, then crimp the edges of the foil tightly so that steam cannot escape. Lay each foil pouch on the coals of your campfire for 20 minutes, then flip it over onto its opposite side for another 20 minutes. Not only are these one-pot meals delicious, but each hunter needs only a knife and fork because he can turn back the edges of the foil and eat right from the makeshift plate.

Other food choices that can be considered for deer-camp cooking generally depend on the logistics of the hunt itself and the type of transportation that is being used to arrive on location. Naturally, if you can drive your vehicle right to the door of your cabin, the choice of menu items is far less limited than during four-wheel-drive, backpacking, or packhorse excursions into remote regions.

For example, take the transportation of fragile items such as eggs. In many instances, you can leave them right in their conventional paper or foam cartons with no problems, or you can transfer them to protective plastic egg boxes, available at any camping-supply store. But if it's necessary to endure a bouncy ride over rough terrain, try one of these tricks. Place each egg in a plastic sandwich bag secured with a twist-tie and then bury it in your flour bag. The eggs shouldn't break, but if they do, they're still within their individually sealed pouches and can be scrambled. Or, at home, break the eggs into a wide-mouth plastic bottle with a screw-cap lid. The yolks will not break, and you can later pour them out one by one into your frying pan.

We also transfer liquids such as cooking oil and maple syrup from their glass bottles to plastic jars to avoid the possibility of breakage. Margarine, peanut butter, jam, and similar soft foods can be transferred to plastic tubes, available at any backpacking shop. All that's necessary is to remove the metal retaining clip at the wide end of the tube, insert the food, replace the clip, and then squeeze the food out the small screw-cap opening at the other end.

Although deer-camp menus should be tailored to the individual circumstances of each hunt, there are nevertheless certain favorite foods most hunters always want to eat. For example, I can't recall a single camp where we haven't enjoyed a skillet containing heaping mounds of fried potatoes.

But after a while, spuds prepared the traditional way become tiring fare. So, we vary the routine by cooking them a different way each time. Instead of using lard or cooking oil each time, try bacon drippings, or a mixture of one-half cooking oil and one-half butter. You can add a liberal quantity of chopped onions, green peppers, canned whole mushrooms, or chunks of ham. As always, the secret to fried potatoes that will have everyone asking for seconds is to begin with low heat until the taters are almost cooked through; then add the vegetables and turn the heat up high to brown and crisp everything around the edges.

Deer liver is another universal favorite, generally served the very evening that the first buck is brought back to camp. The key to this delicious meal is to first cut the liver into several large chunks and allow it to soak in a saltwater bath for several hours to draw our any remaining blood; change the salt water as many times as necessary until it no longer turns red. Then slice the liver into slabs no more than one-quarter-inch thick, dust them with flour, and place them into a frying pan containing a modest amount of cooking oil over medium-high heat. Deer liver should never be cooked until it is well-done; when it is crispy-brown around the edges but still pink in the center, it's ready to be served.

Despite the popularity of deer liver in thousands of camps every year, there are many hunters who simply do not care for liver, yet nevertheless would like to share in the first-night celebration of eating venison with their partners. Our remedy is simple. In addition to cooking the liver, we remove the mini-tenderloins from the animal and serve them as well. We're not referring here to the large backstraps found along both sides of the exterior of the spinal column but rather the smaller "true" tenderloins located *inside* the body cavity along the backbone. They are easily removed without having to skin the deer or do any major butchering. Merely reach inside the field-dressing incision and pluck them out with a small knife in less than two minutes' time. When sliced diagonally into small steaks, then either broiled or fried, they are the tenderest cuts a deer possesses and will be duly appreciated.

Then there is the venerable, often fire-blackened coffeepot that is a familiar sight in every deer camp. Ours has undoubtedly traveled more miles than Marco Polo, yet to some hunters the brewing of authentic camp coffee still remains a mystery.

Begin by filling the pot with *cold* water and adding one heaping teaspoon of coffee grounds for each cup. Next, add one teaspoon of salt and a whole, fresh egg (including the broken shell). Bring the potion to a rolling boil, then just before serving add one-half cup of cold water, which will cause all of the grounds in suspension to settle instantly to the bottom of the pot.

Then there's the necessary evil associated with nearly all types of deer-camp cooking—washing the dishes later. Although it's an unavoidable task, we've at least managed to expedite the procedure to such an extent that only the pots and frying pans themselves have to be scrubbed by hand. As for glasses, coffee cups, dishes, silverware, and other utensils, each hunter washes his own in just two minutes by using the old military dunk-bag routine.

Each hunter should acquire his own 14-inch-square nylon mesh bag with a drawstring closure, available in the housewares section of most department stores. After scraping food remnants from his plate, all eating gear is placed in the bag. Then, as the hunter holds the drawstring to prevent burned fingers, the bag is sloshed around in a deep pot of boiling, soapy water. The bag is then extracted and sloshed around in a second pot of boiling rinse water. No drying of the eating ware is necessary; just hang the works by the drawstring from a handy tree branch, and everything will soon drip-dry.

Keep the basics in mind—plenty of good grub, quick preparation time, and easy cleanup—and your crew of hunters will have nothing but contented smiles on their faces. Moreover, nutritious and efficient deer-camp cooking will give them a distinct edge when it comes to the most important part of the hunt: trying to collect their bucks.

For your copy of John Weiss' *VENISON: FROM FIELD TO TABLE*, please send $24.95 plus $2.64 for postage and handling to Outdoor Life Books, Dept. DHY8, Box 2018, Latham, NY 12111.

Four Opening-Day Delicacies

By Fred Bouwman

Picture it. Six men and a boy perched on sawed-off stumps around an open fire that flickers, shimmers, and snaps at the darkness. The shadowy glow of deer hanging at the edge of the pale light. The evening is chilly without being cold, with a promise of snow in the air. Smoke and steam rise and mix over the fire and the blackened, dented pots and pans of supper on the grate. From the first

Photo by Carl Doney

deer came a heart, liver, and tenderloins sliced from the backbone—real meat, deer hunter's food. Laughter, a boast or two, and promises. Opening day supper.

Among those things that make deer hunting more than a sport or recreation—it's an obsession—are the customs and traditions that accompany the season. From opening day "first blood" rituals to something as simple as dividing the game after the hunt, you can bet that any hunting party devoid of some type of autumn rite will soon invent one.

One noteworthy tradition fast becoming an endangered species is taking the heart, liver, and tenderloins of that first camp deer to prepare the best meal of all the great meals of the season, the opening day evening feast. Dr. Robert Jackson of the University of Wisconsin, author of several deer-hunter studies, noted the importance of food to a deer camp when a veteran hunter told him that deer camp was 60 percent of the hunt, and good food the most important item.

Camp kitchens and camp cooks come in as many varieties as there are camps, from travel trailers so ornate they carry a mortgage to tarpaper shacks to tents; and kitchen facilities range from all the amenities and conveniences of home to an open fire. The cooking we're going to do consists of simple, time-tested, traditional deer-camp techniques that don't require a hunter to spend long hours over a hot stove or firepit and can be easily adapted from fireside to the electric stove at home. The point here is not only to introduce some hunters to a tradition that deserves to be perpetuated, but to fulfill your ethical obligation to the resource by utilizing every part of the deer possible.

Proper field care is taken a step further looking forward to a traditional deer-camp feast. The tenderloins, of course, aren't going anywhere until you remove them, but the liver and heart demand some extra attention. Your field-dressing technique may need some improvement. While many deer hunters easily roll out the entrails in a neat package, some of the piles I come across appear as if the hunter went to work with an ax instead of a knife. Once you remove the entrails, detach the heart and liver immediately and set them aside to cool before placing them in a plastic bag.

Of the three meats that compose our opening-day feast, the tenderloins are the most familiar. For hunters accustomed to taking the whole animal to a processor, look inside the cavity after hanging the deer. The tenderloins will be the two fat "snakes" on either side of the backbone. You can feel them as separate muscles, and they are easily removed with a sharp knife and some careful probing.

Probably the most common way of preparing tenderloins is to cut them into 3- or 4-inch long segments, make a slit crossways almost all the way through each section, fold in half, and broil. The only potential problem here is that tenderloin, a very lean meat even on domestic cattle, is even leaner when it's called venison. Broiling often as

not produces dried out, stringy results—not the desired outcome for what should be the best meal you eat this year.

Using a mildly-flavored marinade that enhances, not overpowers, the natural flavor of venison and gently frying in butter overcomes the dryness and offers an easy, no-hassle alternative to the broiler grate. Hunters turned off at the mention of a marinade are probably the victims of one of the many vinegar-based concoctions, found in many outdoor cookbooks, that hide the flavor of the game. If you like venison, mix two parts olive oil to one part wine, add a bay leaf or two, a few onion slices, a shake of pepper and granulated garlic, and let this sit for a few hours at room temperature to let the flavors blend.

Slice your tenderloins about a half-inch thick, let soak in the marinade while you get the rest of the meal ready, and fry slowly and gently in butter or a mixture of butter and oil. I've converted more than one broiled-deer-tenderloin-lover with this recipe, and you will too.

Feelings about liver seem to run to either love or hate—with no middle ground allowed. Like you, my mother force-fed me liver because "It's good for you," and perhaps, like me, you never overcame that experience and grew up regarding liver as a great cat-food ingredient but definitely not suitable for human consumption.

For you liver-haters out there, just take my word for it. Deer is different. Those evil, brown slices accompanied by a baleful motherly glare have as much relation to fresh, pan-fried venison liver and onions bubbling in butter as the previously mentioned cat food does to a steak dinner.

Getting a liver back to camp doesn't guarantee good eating, however. It needs to be sliced thin—the thinner the better—dipped in flour, seasoned with salt and pepper, and cooked slowly and carefully. This one you can't put on the heat and forget while you get the rest of the meal going; too much heat and you're back to square one, gnawing on a shoe sole and reliving those childhood memories. When done, your liver slices will be firm to the touch, like pressing your finger lightly against the underside of your forearm. Get them out of the pan without delay and you'll have no complaints and a lot of talk about how they just can't believe this is liver. My deer camp includes four others who have also cooked professionally at one time or another and one 14-year-old, and the consensus is that livers will no longer be left in the woods.

We find food prejudices in every culture. The deer hunter chuckling at a Hindu for not eating beef will likely turn up his nose at the thought of eating heart, this while eating a plate of over-easy chicken embryos and washing it down with an excretion from a cow.

Ancient hunters believed that eating the heart of your quarry endowed you with some of the attributes of that animal. While there isn't much in the way of scientific evidence for that, it's like tradi-

Braised heart is quick and easy to prepare—no matter how primitive your kitchen.   *Photo by Fred Bouwman*

tional cold remedies—while it might not help, it certainly can't hurt. I don't know about you, but my woodsmanship can use all the help it can get.

One way of introducing different foods to the leery is by camouflaging it the first time. I've seen crayfish served as shrimp and Rocky Mountain oysters passed off as fried clams. Cold, sliced heart served in a sandwich is one way of getting your foot in the finicky eater's door.

Most outdoor cookbooks contain a recipe for stuffed heart on the last page next to the porcupine chowder and armadillo stew. The recipes require an oven and time, items often found singly in deer camps but seldom together.

Braised deer heart takes no longer than an hour from start to finish, is made on a stove top or over an open fire in one skillet, is simple to prepare and guaranteed to be the high point of the season if the cook does his part. Here's a simple recipe:

One heart
Red wine
One onion
Several bouillon cubes or beef gravy mix
Oil
One small can of mushrooms
The seasoned flour from the liver
A couple of vegetables—carrots, green peppers, celery, etc.
Garlic powder
Black pepper

The heart will be contained in a membrane when you remove it from the animal. Leave this on while transporting it to keep it clean. To prepare for cooking, remove the membrane and any fat, cut off the top which contains most of the blood vessels and valves, cut down one side, and unfold like opening a book. Trim any membranes and blood vessels from the meat, and cut into strips.

The rest is easy. Dip the heart meat in the seasoned flour you made up for the liver, brown in oil, and when half-done add the onions, carrots, or whatever vegetables are handy, the can of mushrooms with its liquid, a bouillon cube, and a shot or two of red wine and cover tightly. If the heart is from your deer, have a shot yourself.

The whole business will thicken up a bit and can be set aside in a warm place while you prepare the liver or tenderloins. Some noodles are nice with this dish.

For the camouflaged heart sandwiches mentioned earlier, clean the heart as above, boil with a little garlic, onion, Worcestershire sauce, and a bay leaf until done. Cool overnight, slice, and eat for lunch. If this trick doesn't do it, at least save your heart to grind with your burger or sausage meat.

Whether you try one or all three of these foods this season, you're going to find that you've added to the quality of the hunt for yourself and the rest of your party. Long after the memories of the stalk and the echoes of the shot have dimmed, a scene similar to the one I showed you at the beginning of this chapter will remain. And that's what it's really all about.

Jim Zumbo's Favorite Outdoor Recipes

By Jim and Lois Zumbo

DEER CAMP VENISON

1 barked green willow branch
2 to 3 pounds venison roast
½ cup parsley
4 cloves garlic, minced
½ teaspoon leaf oregano
½ cup olive oil
½ teaspoon salt
⅛ teaspoon pepper

Thread venison onto willow branch or onto a back-yard rotisserie. Combine remaining ingredients and baste roast with mixture. Turn and baste frequently as meat cooks. Cook about 1½ to 2½ hours, or until meat loses pink color. Cooking time will vary due to variation in heat of open fires and other factors. Serves 4 to 6.

CAMPFIRE VENISON

3 tablespoons butter or margarine
1½ to 2 pounds venison steak
1 envelope onion soup mix (1⅜ ounce)
1 envelope tomato soup mix (1⅜ ounce)
½ teaspoon garlic salt
¼ teaspoon seasoned salt

Dot butter on pieces of aluminum foil large enough to wrap meat completely. Mix soup mixes and salts together in a small bowl. Sprinkle half of mixture on meat. Turn meat over and sprinkle remaining soup mixture on the other side. Dot with remaining butter and wrap securely in foil. Cook over open campfire or bake in 350°F oven for 1 hour. (Time would vary somewhat over campfire, depending on the temperature of fire and how close to the coals the meat is placed.) Serves 6.

VENISON KABOBS

1 to 2 pounds venison steaks (any cut), cubed
Bottled French dressing
Mushrooms
Pineapple chunks
Green peppers, sliced
Water chestnuts
Small onion chunks

Place cubed venison in a bowl. Pour enough French dressing over meat to coat well. Marinate for 1 hour or more. Skewer meat, mushrooms, pineapple, peppers, water chestnuts, and onions on skewers according to individual taste. Grill over charcoal, basting lightly with dressing.

ROMAN DEERBURGERS

1½ pounds ground venison
¼ cup chopped parsley
1 clove garlic, minced
1 teaspoon leaf oregano, crumbled
¾ teaspoon salt
⅛ teaspoon pepper
2 tablespoons grated onion
2 tablespoons grated Parmesan cheese
4 thin slices mozzarella cheese
4 wedges Italian bread, toasted and buttered

Mix meat with parsley, garlic, oregano, salt, pepper, onion, and Parmesan cheese. Shape into 4 patties. Grill over coals. Top each burger with mozzarella cheese when meat is cooked through. Remove

Photo by Tom Yates

Excerpted from the book THE VENISON COOKBOOK by Jim Zumbo. Copyright © 1983 by Jim Zumbo. An Arco book published by Prentice-Hall Press, a division of Simon & Schuster, Inc.

when cheese is just melted and place on buttered toasted Italian bread. Serves 4.

COUNTRY-FRIED VENISON

2 pounds venison steak
¼ cup flour
1 teaspoon salt
⅛ teaspoon pepper
3 tablespoons bacon drippings
¼ cup chopped celery
3 medium onions, sliced
1 tablespoon Worcestershire sauce
2 cups canned whole tomatoes

Cut venison into serving-size pieces. Combine flour, salt, and pepper in a small bowl. Dredge each piece of meat in flour mixture. In a large heavy skillet, brown the meat on both sides in bacon drippings. Add celery, onions, and Worcestershire sauce; cook until vegetables are tender. Add undrained tomatoes and simmer, covered 1½ to 2 hours or until meat is tender. Serves 6.

DOWN-HOME VENISON

6 thick slices of leftover cooked venison roast, cut 1 inch thick
2 tablespoons olive oil
¼ to ½ teaspoon garlic salt
18 ounces canned baked beans
1 cup mild barbecue sauce
4 strips bacon, fried crisp and crumbled

Brush oil on both sides of venison, then sprinkle with garlic salt. Grill over coals 8 to 10 minutes or until well browned on each side. Meanwhile, heat beans until hot. Turn meat and spread beans carefully on one side of the meat. Spoon barbecue sauce over beans. Cook until second side is well-browned. Then carefully lift each piece onto warmed plates. Serves 6.

VENISON RAGOUT

3 pounds venison, cubed
3 tablespoons olive oil
3 large onions, chopped
3 to 4 garlic cloves, minced
½ pound bacon, diced
1 teaspoon curry powder
1½ quarts water
2 teaspoons bourbon whiskey
¼ cup beer
1 teaspoon salt
½ pound fresh mushrooms, sliced

Brown meat in olive oil in a Dutch oven. Add onions, garlic, and bacon. Cook until onions are soft and shiny, stirring frequently. Add remaining ingredients except for mushrooms; then cover and simmer for 1½ hours or until meat is tender. Add mushrooms and simmer 20 minutes more. Serve over rice. Serves 8 to 10.

CURRANT VENISON

1½ pounds venison, cut into 1-inch cubes
Salt
Pepper
3 tablespoons butter or margarine
1 teaspoon chili powder
4 tablespoons sweet red wine
2 tablespoons red currant jelly
½ cup water

Sprinkle meat with salt and pepper. Brown meat in butter in a Dutch oven. Sprinkle chili powder on meat. Stir in wine, jelly, and water. Cover and simmer 1½ hours or until meat is tender, adding more water if necessary. Serves 4 to 5.

BOLD CHARCOAL STEAK

12 ounces beer
½ cup chili sauce (recipe given on page 19)
¼ cup cooking oil
2 tablespoons soy sauce
1 tablespoon prepared mustard
½ teaspoon Tabasco sauce
¼ teaspoon liquid smoke
½ cup chopped onion
2 cloves garlic, minced
3 pounds venison steak
1 teaspoon salt
½ teaspoon pepper

In saucepan mix all ingredients together except steak, salt, and pepper and simmer 30 minutes. Brush meat well with sauce. Cook over charcoal briquets, 20 to 30 minutes per side or until well done, basting frequently with sauce. Season both sides of steaks with salt and pepper during the last few minutes of cooking and serve. Serves 6.

BUTTERFLY STEAKS

1 pound butterfly or backstrap steaks
½ cup flour
Salt
Pepper
Unseasoned meat tenderizer
Cooking oil

Flatten steaks and cut almost completely through horizontally to resemble a butterfly shape when opened. Pound lightly with a meat mallet on both sides. Sprinkle salt, pepper, and meat tenderizer on both sides of meat. Heat the oil in a large heavy skillet. Dredge meat in flour and fry in a half-inch of oil 2 to 3 minutes on each side. Serves 3.

STEAKS WITH VERMOUTH

Salt, Pepper
4 venison steaks, about 1½ inches thick (2-3 pounds)
Butter
4 tablespoons dry vermouth or dry white wine
4 tablespoons water

Salt and pepper steaks to taste. Brown steaks in butter in heavy skillet, approximately 5 minutes on each side. Add vermouth and cover. Simmer 20 to

25 minutes or until completely done. Add more water if necessary. Serves 4.

GRILLED PEPPER STEAK

2 pounds venison round steak (cut 2 inches thick)
1 small onion, chopped
2 teaspoons thyme
1 teaspoon melted margarine
1 bay leaf
1 cup wine vinegar
½ cup cooking oil
3 teaspoons lemon juice
2 teaspoons unseasoned meat tenderizer
½ cup whole peppercorns, coarsely ground

Place meat in a plastic container. Combine the rest of the ingredients, except tenderizer and peppercorns, in a bowl. Mix well and pour over meat. Cover and marinate for 8 hours or overnight. Drain off marinade and reserve. Pound pepper and tenderizer into meat, then grill over hot coals, basting periodically with marinade until meat is well-done. Cut meat into ¼- to ½-inch strips and serve immediately. Serves 6 to 8.

STRIP STEAK

1 pound venison steak
½ teaspoon meat tenderizer
½ teaspoon leaf oregano
2 tablespoons cornstarch
½ teaspoon parsley flakes
3 tablespoons sherry
½ teaspoon salt
4 to 6 large onions, sliced
2 tablespoons cooking oil

Cut meat into strips ¼ inch wide and 3 to 5 inches long. Place strips in a bowl. Add meat tenderizer, oregano, cornstarch, parsley, and sherry. Sprinkle with salt. Mix and let stand at least 15 minutes. Separate onion slices into rings and fry in oil in a heavy skillet for 2 to 4 minutes, stirring constantly. They should still be somewhat crisp. Remove to a heated platter. Place steak strips into a skillet, stirring constantly for 2 to 4 minutes longer. Add more oil if needed. Put onions back into the skillet and heat through with meat. Serve at once. Serves 4.

BARBECUED VENISON CHOPS

¼ teaspoon onion salt
½ teaspoon salt
¼ teaspoon pepper
3 tablespoons flour
4 venison chops or steaks (1½ to 2 pounds)
4 tablespoons oil
½ cup ketchup
¼ cup vinegar
½ teaspoon garlic salt
1 teaspoon liquid smoke
1 tablespoon Worcestershire sauce
Dash Tabasco sauce

In a small shallow bowl, mix together onion, salt, pepper, and flour. Dip chops or steaks in the mixture and coat on all sides. Fry meat in oil until brown. Mix remaining ingredients in a small bowl.

Pour over browned meat and simmer for 1 to 1½ hours until meat is tender. Serves 4.

SMOKY RIBS

4 pounds venison ribs
1 to 2 teaspoons salt (or to taste)

Sprinkle 2 teaspoons salt evenly over ribs. Start charcoal in a barbecue/smoker. When coals are burning well, cover them completely with hickory chips that have been soaked in water for a half hour. Place ribs, bone-side down, on grill of smoker away from coals. Close hood on smoker and cook slowly for 3½ to 4 hours, basting with Cowboy Sauce frequently. Serves 4 to 5.

COWBOY SAUCE

1 tablespoon Worcestershire sauce
⅛ teaspoon Tabasco sauce
1 cup ketchup
1 cup water
¼ cup vinegar
1 tablespoon sugar
1 teaspoon salt
1 teaspoon sesame seed
1 teaspoon celery seed

Combine all ingredients and brush on ribs.

FAST MACARONI-AND-CHEESE CASSEROLE

1½ to 2 pounds ground venison
1 tablespoon cooking oil
1 teaspoon dried minced onion
½ teaspoon garlic powder
¼ teaspoon salt
¼ cup tomato sauce
2 cups hot water
7¼-ounce package macaroni-and-cheese dinner

In a skillet, brown meat in oil. Add dry seasonings, tomato sauce, water, packet of powdered cheese from macaroni-and-cheese dinner, and macaroni to skillet. Cover and simmer over low heat for 30 to 35 minutes, or until macaroni is cooked. Serves 4.

MEXICAN-STYLE LIVER

6 slices bacon
⅔ cup chopped onion
2 cloves garlic, minced
¼ cup flour
1¼ teaspoons chili powder
¾ teaspoon salt
2 ounces canned chopped green chilies
1½ pound venison liver
16 ounces or 2 cups canned whole tomatoes, cut up
12 ounces or 1½ cups canned whole kernel corn, drained
12 flour tortillas

In skillet, cook bacon until crisp. Remove bacon; crumble and set aside. Cook onion and garlic in bacon fat until onion is tender but not brown—about 5 minutes. Combine flour, chili powder, and salt. Cut liver into thin strips and dredge in flour mixture. Add liver to onion in skillet and brown quickly on all sides. Stir in crumbled bacon, undrained tomatoes, chilies, and corn. Simmer covered for 15 minutes. Serve with tortillas. Serves 6.

Index